DATE DUE

MAY 0 4 2006 7/17	
GAYLORD	PRINTED IN U.S.A.

CLIMBING
PARNASSUS

CLIMBING PARNASSUS

A New Apologia for Greek and Latin

TRACY LEE SIMMONS

ISI BOOKS
WILMINGTON, DELAWARE
2002

Library of Congress Cataloging-in-Publication Data:

Simmons, Tracy Lee
    Climbing Parnassus : a new apologia for Greek and Latin /
Tracy Lee Simmons. — 1st ed. — Wilmington, Del.: ISI Books, 2002.

    p. ; cm.

    ISBN 1-882926-62-5
    1. Classical education. 2. Classical languages. 3. Classical literature--
Appreciation. I. Title.

LC1011 .S56 2002   2001097019
373.24/2--dc21   CIP

Published in the United States by:

ISI Books
P.O. Box 4431
Wilmington, DE 19807-0431
www.isibooks.org

To Scot Hicks

Il miglior umanista

οὐ πόλλ᾽ ἀλλὰ πολύ

PARNASSUS (mod. *Liákoura* or *Likeri*), a mountain of Greece, 8070 ft., in the south of Phocis, rising over the town of Delphi. It had several prominent peaks, the chief known as Tithorea and Lycoreia (whence the modern name). Parnassus was one of the most holy mountains in Greece, hallowed by the worship of Apollo, of the Muses, and of the Corycian nymphs, and by the orgies of the Bacchantes. Two projecting cliffs, named the Phaedriadae, frame the gorge in which the Castalian spring flows out, and just to the west of this, on a shelf above the ravine of the Pleistus, is the site of the Pythian shrine of Apollo and the Delphic oracle. The Corycian cave is on the plateau between Delphi and the summit.

Encyclopedia Britannica, 11th edition

Acknowledgments

While very little research of the original kind went into this essay, it is nonetheless the fruit of many years' reading, thinking and, most of all, hundreds of beer-, sherry-, or whisky-soaked conversations with teachers, mentors, friends, and colleagues, not all of whom work professionally in the harvest fields of classics. I must render special thanks to my friend and former supervising don Michael Winterbottom, lately Corpus Christi Professor of Latin at Oxford, as well as Stephen Harrison, Donald Russell, the late Don Fowler, and Jasper Griffin, also of Oxford. Harold C. Gotoff and A. J. Christopherson have also inspired this small work in ways they can't even know. My brazen exaggerations and missteps have arisen in spite of, not because of, their teaching, advising, and erstwhile companionship. Yet just as much I must thank the friends and comrades who acted as first sounding boards for this fanciful *opusculum*: Scot Hicks, Wolfgang Grassl, Andrew Oliver II, Richard Brookhiser, Joseph Epstein, Robert Royal, James Taylor, Jack Taylor, Richard Seymann and, ever and always, the late Sheldon Vanauken.

I must also thank Jeffrey O. Nelson and Jeremy Beer of ISI Books, who, from its inception, saw through the outlandish idea for this book courageously and with expert editorial advice and direction.

Contents

FOREWORD

I first came across the name of this book's author when I read his review of one of my sailing adventures. I was attracted immediately by the lucidity of his writing style and by the generosity of his mind. Subsequently I encouraged a professional association that brought him, as an associate editor, to *National Review*, which I then served as editor-in-chief. A friendship evolved, and as it did I became privy to his deep, and almost secret, devotion to the classical world. He has reveled in the literatures he here celebrates, in the languages — Greek and Latin — he loves, and pleads now, as fervently as someone recovered from deafness and exposed to music might do, that we understand the joy he has found, and labor to unplug our own ears.

Relax. Tracy Lee Simmons is not telling us to get off the bus and hire a Latin teacher. We aren't going to do this, most of us, but that doesn't matter, any more than a written description of music would gall the deaf man. He wants us to know what is there, accumulated over millennia, and ponder its historic achievements and unique tones of voice. ("Not to know Greek is to be ignorant of the most flexible and subtle instrument of expression which the human mind has devised," he quotes one old author, "and not to know Latin is to have missed an admirable training in precise and logical thought.") Simmons does not play the pedant in this graceful testimonial to the classical languages. He is the eager and eloquent reporter giving us some idea of what lies in those great repositories, so inexplicably neglected in modern schooling, and what pleasures await those whose curiosity he succeeds in awakening and how gratefully the mind repays itself when flexed on languages which are not dead because, as he quotes another author, they are no longer mortal.

Our author is greatly learned, but he rebuffs any suggestion that he is a scholar or an academic. Only in this exercise in self-abasement is he unconvincing — whatever it is that he chooses to call himself, we (I, certainly) might wish we could qualify to call ourselves. He is of course the teacher, but also the journalist, and he sets out in this book to write about the classical heritage informatively and unpretentiously. And, I should stress, readably; which he succeeds in doing, probably without even noticing the odes he brings to our attention by sharp-eyed scholars who have acclaimed, for instance, the mastery of Latin because, in part, it engenders a verbal sensitivity and dexterity that lead to good writing and, prospectively, fine writing.

Mr. Simmons manages something else, difficult to do. At once he unequivocally rejects the proposition that all practitioners are equal, that just as we assert our equality at the voting booth, we cannot assume equality in achievement or in the capacity to enjoy. I welcome his ample reminder of Albert Jay Nock's stern lectures at the University of Virginia in 1931, in which Nock ate alive the preposterous idea that all who check in at school are educable, let alone equally educable. But Mr. Simmons is more genial, really, than Mr. Nock ever was, and his effort in pointing out the glory and the joys resulting from any attempt to climb Parnassus — that ancient peak symbolizing the source of inspiration and eloquence — never gives way to the exclusionist appetite of Nock. In this matter he is in the good company of Mortimer Adler, who never suggested that even his own students could rise as high as he wished, but adamantly insisted that efforts to learn were rewarding, however modest one's achievement, while Parnassus itself must always stand undiminished and hallowed. Nock's elitism can be read as a fatalistic consignment of the great body of students to the assembly-line life of the kind Charlie Chaplin memorialized. Not Simmons. No, he is here the bard of the classical legacy, and ends not by rejecting suitors, but by seducing them.

I reproduce from this book the autobiographical passage from Evelyn Waugh, because it is supremely informative, and because it achieves so masterfully the sweetness of the perfect prose Simmons envisions and encourages:

> My knowledge of English literature derived chiefly from my home. Most of my hours in the form room for ten years had been spent on Latin and Greek, History and Mathematics. Today I remember no Greek. I have never read Latin for pleasure and should now be hard put to compose a simple epitaph. But I do not regret my superficial classical studies. I believe that the conventional defence of them is valid; that only by them can a boy fully understand that a sentence is a logical construction and that words have basic inalienable meanings, departure from which is either conscious metaphor or inexcusable vulgarity. Those who have not been so taught — most Americans and most women — unless they are guided by some rare genius, betray their

deprivation. The old-fashioned test of an English sentence — will it translate? — still stands after we have lost the trick of translation.

Severe, yes, even cranky, as Mr. Waugh always sought to be. But his declaration acknowledges the high call to seek and climb Parnassus, and Mr. Simmons is himself an eloquent votary in this sacramental calling.

— WILLIAM F. BUCKLEY JR.

PREFACE

"I never touched a trained mind yet which had not been disciplined by grammar and mathematics — grammar both Greek and Latin; nor have I ever discovered mental elegance except in those familiar with Greek and Latin classics." William Milligan Sloane, a professor of history at Columbia, uttered this monolithic ruling from on high in 1917. Here blows the confidence of a bygone era, a sentiment that went out with hansom cabs and iceboxes. Imagine these words emanating from any professor of history, or professor of anything else, in our day. This isn't a thought likely to win friends and influence colleagues. But I cannot say that Sloane's experience has been mine. I have known quite a few people blessed with "mental elegance" who haven't so much as touched the hem of Greek and Latin. They got it quite on their own. One shouldn't promise too much. It may be that the buoyant, complacent faith of statements like this one helped to sink for good the dominion of classics in American education.

Yet on the whole I believe that Sloane was ambling up the

right road. Greek and Latin can certainly discipline and form the mind. But they can do far more. Taught with an aim to cultivate and humanize, they can render something more and greater to the intelligent, talented, and patient. "Mental elegance" may not be the right term — of all places, words may fail us here — but this phrase rings with truth. There's a fresh breeze passing through it. It's also one that hasn't blown through public conversation in a long time. While I do not believe a classical education to be the only one worth having — far from it — I do believe that its passing from schools and colleges has impoverished our culture and, incidentally, degraded our politics. The classical languages can change and enhance one's intellectual and aesthetic nature, shaping both the mind and the heart. And I am not the first to say so.

I seek to do at least two things within the pages of this essay. First, I hope to elucidate the centuries-long corner Greek and Latin held on school and university curricula, limiting myself, mostly for the sake of convenience, to English and American experience. Readers of English novels or American biography, for instance, have often noticed the peculiar spectacle of young innocents getting carted off to school only to be cast into the thorny thicket of these two ancient and difficult tongues. By the threat of the stinging rod, they were made to memorize the words and rules of two languages they would never speak. It was a curious affair. What was the point of it all? We stand sufficiently remote from those times to have forgotten utterly the *raison d'être* for this grueling, seemingly senseless drudgery. Here is doubtless a criminally brief account of whence classical education arose and what it set out to achieve. This book ought to be and, with sufficient leisure could have been, a multi-volume work. The theme deserves much more than I have given it. For this I can but beg the reader's pardon.

But I try not only to explain; I try to exhort. I wish to defend, by witness and running commentary, this long path to the formed, cultivated mind even as I recount the long journey the classical languages have walked along the thoroughfares of Western history. Greek and Latin are still valuable, even today — and perhaps especially today.

I write as a layman. I am a writer, not a scholar. Although I have drunk strong draughts of classical learning in my life from a fairly young age, and owe incalculably to classical teachers and scholars both known and unknown to me, I am not myself a classical scholar, nor anything close to one. And apart from one splendid year teaching Greek and Latin in a private school, I have never made my living by them. I have no professional bed to feather. Classics have stood more in the background of my life than in the foreground. But while this book is not a work of scholarship, it's deeply indebted to the thought and scholarship of my betters. I hasten to add that this is one man's defense of an august inheritance and practice. The case here is by no means complete; brighter devotees to classics would brew their own case quite differently and just as legitimately. There's nothing definitive about mine. I have written this book for the simple, pedestrian reason that no one else more qualified has stepped forward to write it. Little original research of my own has gone into its making. Indeed this may be the most impudently un-original work to be published in many years. If I have brought anything *original* to the task — a tricky when not ridiculous word — other than my own limited experience, it's probably just a bit of retrograde thinking feared and eschewed by others saddled with that side-glancing reticence often awarded with academic tenure. I say here a few forbidden things.

A Few Notes at Base Camp

A nyone setting out to defend what Albert Jay Nock once called "the grand old fortifying classical curriculum" — essentially Greek and Latin — does so knowing that he flies the tattered flag of a lost cause. Surrender to the victors has already been signed, the army dispersed. The guns are silent. That day is done. Why, in the age of the Internet and the global economy, dwell upon the words and deeds of people long dead who spoke and wrote in tongues equally dead? Surely education should help us to enjoy our fair share of bread and circuses. Education should help us to get things. It's about the future. A recent American president, after all, made much ado about "building bridges to the twenty-first century." We had best be crossing. But the happy bands of those who fend for classical education, along with other tilters at windmills, are not so easily daunted. They would make a last stand for the barricades. They have wandered as exiles in occupied territory. But the land is worth fighting for, even if the battle should yield but a few paces.

Ralph Waldo Emerson once chided the brashness of a lost cause like this one. I proffer to him my apologies. "It is ominous," he wrote, "that this word Education has so cold, so hopeless a sound. A treatise on education, a convention on education, affects us with slight paralysis and a certain yawning of the jaws." Ominous indeed, for ponderous books on education proliferate and provide what one historian has called a "dismal consolation to the misanthrope." We ought to cast a caustic eye on such trickery, for the utopian promises what he cannot deliver. Beware the man with a new truth to preach. He bids to do our thinking for us. Better, in the words of Auden, to "read *The New Yorker*, trust in God, and take short views."

The American soil is not naturally fertile for classics. The seed falls on hard clay. As another man of letters told us nearly eighty years ago, we as a nation possess "a weakness for new gospels," a vital but hazardous trait, as we stand in danger of discarding both the good and useful in a quest for the dubious and untried. We reconfigure our lives daily. We pride ourselves on our capacity to reach far and entertain the fantastic idea. And we think of ourselves more as doers than as thinkers. While others waxed about going to the moon, we went. We are forever on the move. But this restless drive, which we Americans are wont to think unique to us, also fuels the rest of the frenetic modern world, particularly in the West where — despite some multiculturalists' claims — our civilization supplies the model most peoples around the globe wish to emulate. We spell Progress with a capital. Here the new is always better, the old worse; the new is always rich and relevant, the old threadbare and obsolete. Ours is the "shining city on a hill," in John Winthrop's memorable coinage, a city that could begin afresh because it had no past. We could start from scratch and travel lightly.

Yet having crossed the threshold of a millennium, we feel a

few spiritual tremors. Impetuosity does not reflect. The super-annuated, ever-changing mind cannot speak to the whole of life. It cannot contemplate; it cannot assign value. It can drive us to build new roads and bridges, but it cannot explain where we want to go. It can build rockets to Mars and beyond, but it cannot tell us whether it's wise to go there. It cannot answer questions it long ago lost the wisdom to ask. The life of the mind and soul it leaves bereft of standards, those talking points of judgment, which are acquired only with time and patient effort. We appeal to the freakish in witless arts and entertainment — to serve the boring or the bored is not always clear — leading inexorably to the shocking that melts into a monotonous vulgarity in the public square. (Even shock cannot shock indefinitely.) Intellectuals are not immune. Scratch a believer in bold new ideas and find a slave to fashion, proving the adage that the newest is always the most quickly dated, whether it come from Madison Avenue or the Modern Language Association. Nor is our political life unaffected. We call for candidates with "new ideas," votaries to a perpetually malleable Future. Here is the spirit of El Dorado, the hope that riches and salvation wait around the next bend in the road. Old gospels lack the beckoning allure of the road not taken. But like explorers in the desert ever prone to mirage, we have had, along with remarkable discoveries, a few false sightings. And we are beginning to sense a certain lack of point and permanence in modern life. The new gospels have certainly delivered, but they have not saved.

Education, that vague and official word for what goes on in our schools, has also been a trinket on the shelves of snake oil salesmen and a plaything for social planners in America for well over a century. They too have been driven by the spirit of ceaseless innovation. And we have paid a high price. The peddlers have shrouded the higher and subtler goals of learning which

former generations accepted and promoted. These bringers of
the New have traded in the ancient ideal of wisdom for a spuri-
ous "adjustment" of mind, settling for fitting us with the most
menial of skills needful for the world of the interchangeable
part. They have decided we are less, not more, than wiser people have hoped humanity might become. We are masses to be
housed and fed, not minds and souls seeking something beyond
ourselves. Ask anyone today, for instance, to identify the aims of
a "liberal education" and expect a long pause. Everett Dean
Martin — he who informed us of our predilection for "new
gospels" — wrote a book in 1926 titled *The Meaning of a Liberal
Education*, and in 1973 another scholar produced *The Uses of a
Liberal Education*. We might detect in the latter title a falling
away from an older ideal. Instead of seeking to discern what a
liberal education can bring to us, we now ask what we can get
out of it; there's a difference. And the benefits accrued do not
exist, apparently, if they cannot be measured — and measured
by tools calibrated by craftsmen out to replicate themselves.
Standards require standard-makers.

Nonetheless, on the face of it at least, the question of *use* is
a fair one. Philosopher Alfred North Whitehead reminded us
that any education not useful is wasted. An education, he said,
must be "useful, because understanding is useful." But what
must we understand? If education must be useful, what uses are
to be served? And, more importantly, are there differing kinds
of use we should acknowledge?

The modern mind, schooled to be practical, stands ill prepared to wrestle with these questions because they are at bottom
philosophical ones; our practicality has, ironically, rendered us
incapable of answering them. So while thinking ourselves a
knowing and enlightened lot, we stand deaf to our own ignorance, which has become a white noise. Gilded degrees hanging

on our walls bear witness to our certified smarts. But we have stood Socrates on his head: Whereas the only thing that sage Athenian knew was that he knew nothing, the only thing we *don't* know — and with far thinner credentials, it would seem — is that we know so very little. ("He knows nothing, and he thinks he knows everything," George Bernard Shaw put it. "That points clearly to a political career.") We do not know, in other words, what more reflective ages have deemed the important things. And we don't know them because they have not been taught us, or gentle prods to our self-esteem have spurred us to consult only our own druthers in deciding what is worth knowing. We have adopted the leveling assumptions we've inherited — *whatever works for you* — and fed off intellectual capital earned by others who, we presume, have already done the hard thinking for us. We pride ourselves on self-reliance while following uncritically the roadmaps of others. For an independently skeptical people, we ask few questions.

Milton once wrote that the reform of education is "one of the greatest and noblest designs that can be thought on," and many have been drawn to the drafting table as willing architects of the future. Within this workshop we have hammered out our highest aspirations and ideals. Yet few pursuits, however noble, promise so little. The wares are cheap, their shiny surfaces a veneer hiding shoddy work. "As with most gospels," Martin observed, "we are in such a hurry to save souls that we would begin proclaiming the new salvation to the nation before pausing to find out what education is." Unable to explain what education is or is for, we have created state departments of education out of a desperate hope that what we have not had the wisdom and intellectual fortitude to determine in the light of day might emerge miraculously from a flurry of committee reports, public opinion polls, and bureaucratic fiat.

So to pen — and read — still another tract such as this runs counter to that hope and makes for dreary work. We should shrink from more gospels, further means of deliverance from a predicament we do not fully understand, especially when the search is likely to prove less than edifying and close on unresolved chords. I do not intend to offer a new gospel. Instead, I hope to direct our gaze behind us, so that we may more securely find our footing on the road ahead. If in fact "the past is prologue," it is only the past that can instruct and guide us. The present is too close. And the future is but a haze of possibilities and dreams. The future does not yet belong to us.

■   ■   ■

We do not lack defenses of traditional education. Disquisitions abound. They offer comfort and guidance to the seeking few. Allan Bloom's *The Closing of the American Mind* set off a radioactive buzz in the late 1980s with sales no doubt astounding author and publisher alike. It was an unlikely bestseller, at once a philosophical excursion and a gripe against a noisy, tawdry world. But we don't know who read the book. It was enough, for many, simply to buy it and add their voices to the swelling chorus of those suspecting a decline in the intellectual quality not only of educated people, but also of the world they plan and steer. Its presence on the coffee table advertised one's disquiet, becoming for a moment a badge of intellectual chic. E. D. Hirsch's *Cultural Literacy* described the paucity of hard information today's high school graduates are likely to know — and to be taught — about history, science, and literature. "Illiterate and semiliterate Americans are condemned not only to poverty," Hirsch wrote, "but also to the powerlessness of incomprehension. Knowing that they do not understand the issues, and feeling prey to manipulative oversimplifications, they do not trust the system of which they are supposed to be the masters. They do not feel themselves to be active participants in our republic, and they often do not turn out to vote." And of course, for better or worse, many *do* turn out to vote.

What we don't know can hurt us. With the blitzing of these two books, we began to talk openly not only about fifteen-year-olds who cannot identify the order of American presidents since Franklin Roosevelt or the century in which the American Civil War was fought, but also about eighteen-year-olds who cannot read even with ground-level competence. Granting that the world has yet to see a Golden Age in education, we began to ask: What exactly are they doing in those schools? And why do our schools' and colleges' graduates, so smart and promising in so many ways, not seem to know, really *know*, anything of substance? They're heavy on proudly held opinions — opinions are always in abundant supply — but light on knowledge. Is this, we wondered, the best we can do?

This we can say: Publicly funded ignorance began to seem a positive liability. It became the family lunatic we finally consented to bring up in mixed company. But these books did another salutary thing: they directed us to question the uses of the tools at our disposal. On the one hand, there is the skill needed to use the proverbial wrench properly and efficiently, on the other the judgment required to use it for right and good purposes. Bloom and Hirsch drew us back to fundamentals, throwing light not only on what ought to be taught in our schools and universities, but on goals, on the kind of citizens we wish to create and the kind of polity we wish to engender. For education is never neutral. Embedded within any course of study lie assumptions about what people ought to know, and about human nature itself: Are we Man or Machine? Education is, in the end, an auxiliary of philosophy — an embodiment of aims and ideals. It was therefore fruitless for President Clinton to demand that politics "stop at the school house door." Perhaps politics cannot stop there because philosophy and idealism cannot stop there.

And the anxiety spreads. With each new bit of bad news issued from think tanks and blue-ribbon commissions, the same *dramatis personae* pound out newspaper and magazine commentaries, taking to cable talk programs to spout their views and entertain rejoinders from viewers across the country, usually with no one understanding the essential matters at stake. (Watching cable call-in programs is like listening to the desperate yawping of thousands mesmerized by the sounds of their own voices.) Back in the mid-1980s, a National Commission on Excellence in Education — an instance of grandiloquent dubbing — released a study called *A Nation at Risk*, which contended that "If an unfriendly foreign power had attempted to impose on America the mediocre educational performance that exists today, we might have viewed it as an act of war. As it stands, we have allowed this to happen to ourselves...we have, in effect, been committing an act of unthinking, unilateral educational disarmament." Whatever the nature of our troubles may be, they are deeply rooted. But a backward glance at history reveals that we have been here before.

Nor are our troubles confined to our shores. Sir Richard Livingstone, once president of Corpus Christi College, Oxford, wrote in 1944 on the ferment in England for reform in education. The worries were many, he wrote, including the "obvious and increasing importance of knowledge to life; a sense of the great possibilities of modern civilization and of its disorders and dangers; the perception that our democracy is very ill-educated; a realization that in foreign politics between 1919 and 1939 we [threw] away a great victory with a rapidity and completeness perhaps unexampled in history and that this has been partly due to political ignorance; [and] the need of extending education if equality of opportunity is to be more than a phrase." The parallels to our own day suggest themselves. But they go further. Livingstone added that the interest given to education in his time was "political and social rather than educational." Such interest was, in other words, not intellectual. It was not about the mind.

Much the same may be said of contemporary schemes to reform our schools, whether inspired by the Left or Right. Politics has come with a vengeance. But the modern political impulse — the outraged mania for incessant, stupid interference — has little to do with intellectual formation and higher aims. Those dealing the thrusts and jabs today do not seem fit with the calm, disinterested intelligence distinguishing those of true philosophical temperament. Battles rage out there. Partisans angle provocatively to "empower" hitherto neglected groups, but the struggle has become a play for power, not a sober philosophical or cultural inquiry. Whatever be the relative merits of these labors, we must not fail to note that markedly less light is now thrown on matters of actual learning: how students' minds will be altered, formed, and filled, and their abilities to think enhanced. This is modern shortsightedness at its most vexatious. The intoxication of politics has poisoned the debate, making it narrow, strained, and fraught with hazards to disputants' reputations. Dissent carries a high price, especially in the Age of the Open Mind.

■   ■   ■

But we are still dogged by a practical question: Why do our schools and universities seem to accomplish so little for individual minds? One answer is that instead of doing a few things well, we have tried to do many things and have done them badly. We have striven, historian Jacques Barzun has written, "to make ideal citizens, supertolerant neighbors, agents of world peace, and happy family folk, at once sexually adept and flawless drivers of cars." Our schools have been a place where high hopes have gone to die. Education is the *tabula rasa* on which we inscribe all our social desires and expectations. But Isocrates, a Greek rhetorician of the fourth century B.C., got it right. "If all who are engaged in the profession of education," he wrote, "were willing to state the facts instead of making greater promises than they can possibly fulfill, they would not be in such bad repute with the lay public." Many centuries later — a tale that ought to serve as an object lesson for today's evangelists for the New Age in education — a German reformer out to emend the crusty old classical curriculum was eventually thrown into prison and released only after confessing that he could not deliver what he had promised, for he had promised too much. The Latin stayed.

"Forget Education," Barzun has written, clearing the board. "Education is a result, a slow growth, and hard to judge. Let us talk rather about Teaching and Learning, a joint activity that can be provided for, though as a nation we have lost the knack of it." We have lost the knack of it as a culture, too. We must limit our promises and rein in our expectations. But first we must define our ideals. We need to describe the ideal type of human being we wish to see around us. Do we wish merely to produce better skilled, smoothly cut cogs in the elaborate machine we now call the "global economy"? Have we finally determined that supertolerant neighbors and sexually adept, flawless drivers are all we can hope to be? Is this the juncture to which 3,000 years of civilized life have brought us?

Somehow we think not. And we sense that the ideals adopted from the previous couple of generations stand pale when compared to those of other ages. History and literature rebuke our self-sufficiency; that's one reason why we ought to study them. It's not so much that people of olden times were the finest exemplars of higher humanity, for they too fell short of their ideals, as must all who aspire to higher things — that's what ideals are for. It's that we have abandoned those ideals once animating our civilization, refusing to learn them anew with each generation. We have assumed their transfer to be automatic. We have not indeed jettisoned the hope and drive that keep us working for a better world (that's the good news), but we have forgotten to cultivate ourselves as *individuals*. We drive by autopilot. We measure our Gross National Product, but we are left with a hunch that getting and spending don't quite make for the fuller life we read about and fear exists somewhere beyond our avarice and ennui.

So we live in an era propitious for a re-ignited conversation not only about pedagogical methods — those quotidian details of teaching and learning — but also about the aims those methods serve. We need to ask first questions. And we need to answer them without political posturing, perhaps a Herculean task in a politically charged age. We need to freshen our vision and, at least momentarily, put our modernity aside and try to see the world as others have seen it. We must try to transcend ourselves. We are not compelled in doing so to reject modern concerns, but simply to view them with new eyes. G. K. Chesterton once said that there are two ways of getting home, and one of them is never to have left. That last path is shut to us; we have strayed too far. We must circumnavigate the entire world until we arrive where we started and, as T. S. Eliot wrote, "know the place for the first time." We need to shore up our foundations. *Il faut cultiver notre jardin.*

But I have gone further than I am fit to go. For this is not a case for educational reform of the garden variety. We need sway no public officials. I have happily abandoned hope for change in that sphere. Yet we can lengthen our prospect, broaden our view, and clear a path back home. We need simply to recommit ourselves individually to a rich and humane heritage long neglected, the effects of which neglect appear in a diminished, where not impoverished, intellectual and cultural life. This is not to be another tiresome case for "educational standards" merely confirming assumptions of the intelligentsia about what must be known. Let them crunch numbers as they may. We must ask not only what ought to be known by educated people, but — given what *can* be known — what should be taught in our schools and what left to acquire outside school doors. (It's of paramount importance, for example, whether vocational courses like computer training, or "lifestyle" courses like driver's ed. and home economics, should be placed on par with the purer — because cultural or theoretical — subjects like French and physics.)

Given the world's fixation on technology and all things financially gainful, that "grand old fortifying classical curriculum" requires not an uncritical re-adoption (of which there's no chance anyway) but a sympathetic reappraisal, if for no other reason than that so many men and women of centuries past who established and refined the standards by which we live today held that gem in such high esteem. Thus can we regain some sense of history and our place along its timeline. Gratitude, according to Chesterton, is the truest sign of happiness in individuals. A safe corollary seems then to be that a happier society would feel a debt to the past and its treasures, and this debt would be paid gladly by those taught in the ways of respect and humility. For those without respect and humility stand to these riches as those without a knowledge of geometry once stood before the gates of Plato's Academy: they are forever excluded. Such respect (if not always such humility) classical education fostered for centuries. It lent an anchoring to intellectual life and provided all educated people, as we now say, with a common set of references. Or, to switch metaphors, it placed a true north on our cultural compass. It maintained a horizon. We could see where we were.

But before we trudge forward, let's clarify a few key words and terms.

■   ■   ■

Just what is *classical education* nowadays? We find that, in an uninstructed age, the old regimen needs not only defending but also defining. Once classical education pointed to an elite course of instruction based upon Greek and Latin, the two great languages of the classical world. But it also delved into the history, philosophy, literature, and art of the Greek and Roman worlds, affording over time to the more perspicacious devotees a remarkably high degree of cultural understanding, an understanding that endured and marked the learner for life. Classical education was classical immersion. Students in the great and exclusive Public Schools of England were once made to learn far more about the archons of Greek city-states and emperors of Rome, and commit to memory far more lines of Greek and Roman poetry and drama, than they ever had to learn about Tudors and Stuarts, about Chaucer and Shakespeare. But the languages never took second seat: mastering them came first, and doing so became the crowning achievement of a classical education. Why? Because knowledge and information were not quite enough.

Classical education did not set itself to instilling knowledge alone; it also sought to polish and refine. And neither rigor nor beauty in one's use of language obtained firmly without Greek and Latin. Together they provided both a mental gymnastic and a training in taste.

Today we use the term licentiously. We apply "classic" or "classical" to anything we believe to be excellent and universal. Once I was asked my field of study. "Classics," I replied. To which my interlocutor responded, "Oh, you mean Dickens, Melville, and all that?" — a response common and understandable now. *Sic semper verbis*. Also, the field of classics, while still signifying the old meaning (Greek and Latin) to most of the intellectually inclined, has been extended to embrace a study of the classical world innocent of the languages, a sense we readily recognize in university course catalogues as "Classical Civ." and "Classical Literature," both customarily indicating (often fine) courses of readings in translation. The chains have loosened.

Thus nowadays may classical education refer to something not linked to the classical world at all — never mind the languages — and get equated with what might once have been called simply traditional or orthodox education. This is schooling based on "classics," on books of the Great Tradition, an education that serves to inform us of the best works of our civilization and to provide us with models for spotting ethical and aesthetic norms. These two functions the valuable "Great Books" programs try to perform. Used in this way, classical education describes the quest for what has also been called a "liberal education" or, more particularly, an education in the "humanities." And now legions of well-intending home schoolers rush to put dibs on the term and bask in the light of the glory they believe it to exude. To many home schoolers, "classical education" simply means the opposite of whatever is going on in those dreaded public schools. We can sympathize with them. I will only say to all these good people that extending "classical" to mark an approach or course of study without reference to Greek and Latin seems an unnecessarily promiscuous usage. But I am afraid we're stuck with it.

Here I trust that the reader will allow me the archaism of reverting to the older definition of classical education as a curriculum grounded upon — if not strictly limited to — Greek, Latin, and the study of the civilization from which they arose. For though my allies have appropriated the term for good purposes, I can find no other that carries the weight of classical study as does "classics," the pursuit of which results, if we're lucky, in a "classical education." To use any other term would also break my rule of respecting the past, not to mention causing a semantic severance with generations of men and women who used the term quite differently and, I think, more accurately. I'll stick to the antique ways.

■   ■   ■

Mount Parnassus, a limestone mass hovering over the ancient shrine of Delphi, has stood as a prime symbol of poetic inspiration and perfection since the dawn of the West. It fixed anxious eyes on the heavens. The Castalian spring, being a sacred source of life-sustaining water, trickled far below. The hushed tones of ritual echoed from its slopes. But over time it came to embody those things which man, at his best, wishes — and ought to wish — to achieve. It became a sign of his better, divinely inspired self. To "climb Parnassus" was to strive after the favor of Apollo and the nine muses — Calliope, Erato, Clio, Euterpe, Melpomene, Polymnia, Thalia, Terpsichore, Urania — ensconced up there, forever unseen. While representing the unattainable for most pilgrims, Parnassus also pointed to those treasures bestowed by the muses upon the faithful and diligent ones who wait and work. And among those gifts most sought was the civilizing, cultivating boon of eloquence, of right and beautiful expression. Throughout the centuries to come, this forbidding image got lifted from its geographical and mythological settings to be transposed, in the wake of Renaissance Humanism, as an emblem of linguistic flair. "Climbing Parnassus" eventually became a code for the painfully glorious exertions of Greek and Latin.

The hard, precipitous path of classical education ideally led not to knowledge alone, but to the cultivation of mind and spirit. Knowledge did not, in and of itself, justify the sweat. The climb was meant to transform one's intellectual and aesthetic nature as well. The classical course held sway over the Western mind for centuries, right up until three or four generations ago. Much of our intellectual history from the Dark Ages, through the Renaissance, and on to the modern world witnessed the assiduous spadework of clerics and lay scholars alike reaching back to the ancient world to retrieve, preserve, and propagate the wealth of learning and experience it held. And the classical languages enshrining that wealth had to be taught. Thus a classical education was the queen of all scholastic endeavors; it constituted the original humanities curriculum. Whatever hodgepodge of diverse and disconnected topics humanistic studies have become — their emaciated children now simply called "the humanities" — they were once, first and last, a prolonged inquiry into Greek and Roman achievements in literature, history, thought, and art. That path, as I hope to show, is still a valid one to tread.

Yet this too we must admit all these centuries later. Classical claims, while bolstered by tradition and intellectual coherence alike, cannot be advanced with proof. They are not the stuff of Venn diagrams. We cannot cash them at a bank. A classical education is different in kind to the training of a technician, where the trained man demonstrates his training with a testable skill. This, we may say, is *training* in the narrow sense, not an education — and many people today, without admitting it, prefer training to education, and they must have their heart's desire. Much of the value of classics we must take on the witness of mellowed experience. Arguing this case now is partly an impressionistic exercise; it always has been. A firm knowledge of the classical languages, history, and culture will not of itself create virtue. It cannot shine a light into corners we have elected to keep dark, nor into those that cannot be illumined. But this knowledge can form the mind and light a path to understanding. For it is noble to rediscover and attend to the voices of the past. We ignore them to our peril and to the peril of all those whom we would presume to teach. Without a finely tuned and oft-nourished sense of the past, both near and distant, we have no culture.

■   ■   ■

And immediately we are thrown into another thicket. What do we mean by these mushy words *culture* and *cultural*? This ubiquitous idea too requires clarifying, and maybe a little fumigating. I do not use these words exclusively as we hear them bandied about by many who rant from the ranks of the politically concerned when discussing ethnicity and "multiculturalism," that is, merely to describe group identities. Everyone has a "culture" now: we have African-American culture, Hispanic culture, corporate culture, youth culture. This use of the word hails from the halls of anthropology. If only there it had stayed. But it slithered forth from the laboratory to infect us all. "From the anthropologists," Barzun has explained, "the public picked up the word *culture* in [this] overarching meaning, and then proceeded to reapply it for various purposes. For example, the artist is 'conditioned by his culture' (meaning social circumstances); he also fights against his culture (meaning certain beliefs and mores)." Here was a word hot for serving up on a steaming platter to the over-degreed and half-educated. It not only exfoliates before our eyes; it excuses ignorance and inoculates the ignorant from any responsibility to know anything beyond their kith and kin. Culture now "makes neurotics — they are the ones who can't fight back. Not long after such twists and turns the term *culture* began to split like an atom, and we have had to cope with the two cultures, the counterculture, ethnic culture, and any number of subcultures. Culture now is any chunk of social reality you like or dislike." Occasionally I use it in this its sociological sense, though I trust rarely enough and judiciously.

While I do not eschew this newer sense of the word entirely, I wish to restore the older parlance to a place in our social lexicon. Therefore, my use of *culture* is often unapologetically evaluative. It refers to lower and higher, better and best. A "cultural" achievement elevates. It improves. Once we could talk unselfconsciously of symphony concerts, opera performances, museum exhibitions, and poetry readings as cultural events. They did not merely entertain; they exposed us to something better than we could find elsewhere. And we hoped that such exposure would make us better as well — healthier intellectually and emotionally. Now, of course, this older idea is not quite safe, or at least not safely expressed, because it attributes higher qualities to some people and things and not to others. ("Who are *you* to tell me what's good?") Mozart's music is not better than rap, just different, we say today. It's the great democratic hedge. Here the anthropological invades a realm properly guided by the aesthetic, perverting both thought and senti-ment. But some judgments cannot be made by a show of hands. The majority doesn't always rule. Nor in some matters — and here's the rub—should it. Classical education was thought to *improve* the learner, not simply to make him more knowledge-able or tolerant or mentally skillful, but better and stronger, just as there survives today a residual belief that one who has, say, read and digested all of Shakespeare is better, more insight-ful, than one who has not.

Perhaps this very attribution of quality to those equipped with classical learning poses the most formidable barrier to its return. We talk no more about "better people." No one wishes — and I certainly do not — to revert to rigid class lines, to a time when only the well-to-do learned Greek and Latin and all they have to offer, leaving the lower classes to learn the trades and mop the floors. (Again, no chance of that.) But neither should we confuse contingency with necessity. That which may cater to the privileged in one period might prime the aspira-tions of democracy in another. Nonetheless, we ought not to shy away from confronting views of former ages simply because they don't conform to current notions, for doing so exposes us to the most blinding of parochialisms: the glaring assumption that one's own time, particularly our own with all its hypersensitiv-ities, is always right.

So here *culture* often refers to *high culture*. It's about cultiva-tion and refinement, about what makes one thought or act or expression better than another. This kind of culture embodies, as I shall repeat later in the words of fairer lights, "the conscious ideal of human perfection" and "the habitual vision of greatness." I once heard a tweedy, bespectacled professor of archaeology pause during a lecture on primitive peoples to remind his class that when he spoke of culture, he did not refer — holding to his eye an imaginary monocle — "to Beethoven's Fifth Symphony." Sometimes I do mean it that way. Culture is that which climbs high on the scale of human achievement, is not easily apprehensible to all, and requires patient thought and sympathy. We are not born into culture; we acquire it. And we can lose it.

Climbing Parnassus once helped to form the unformed mind. The arduous ascent fostered intellectual and aesthetic culture within those who had endured the strain. It helped to bring mental and even emotional order out of chaos. And a classical training still provides the surest footing for the educated mind and a high perch from which to view other periods and nations. The foundations of the modern world are viewed more competently from this height. Poetry, drama, democracy, idealism, scientific curiosity, and so much else furnishing our minds are better grasped, and better judged. We drift without classics, floating on our own deracinated, exiguous islands. And we become fodder for demagogues. We need not a revolution, but a restoration.

The classical pursuit fosters gratitude for the fruits of the past and feeds the sense that we stand on the shoulders of giants. The student of history gains a means of judging other times seriously and fairly. He learns to see that a civilized culture is a delicately poised edifice, a fragile creation, erected with monumental exertion, yet easily destroyed. The historian Christopher Dawson once wrote that culture — in the older sense here — is "an artificial product. It is like a city that has been built up laboriously by the work of successive generations, not a jungle which has grown up spontaneously by the blind pressure of natural forces. It is the essence of culture that it is communicated and acquired, and although it is inherited by one generation from another, it is a social not a biological inheritance, a tradition of learning, an accumulated capital of knowledge." And one, we may add, always in danger of perishing. The Greeks dreamed, in the words of Werner Jaeger, of "building a state so skillfully that it might keep strength and spirit in perpetual equipoise," while recognizing that "even the most solid of earthly powers must vanish into the air, and that only the seemingly brittle splendor of the spirit can long endure." The classical world is a richly instructive model of civilized life. We are bound as heirs to ask anew what made it great, with all its faults, and why it expired, with all its strengths. Who knows? We may find ourselves on the decks of our own listing ship someday.

This journey takes us high into the uplands of thought. Whitehead claimed all modern philosophy to be mere footnotes to Plato. An expedition into the classical world will lead us to philosophy, that highest of human quests after the spiritual, and a pursuit Plutarch once called "the head and font of all education." We see philosophy wooed in those days when she still held a link, and perhaps a key, to wisdom. Matters of ethics, morality, and politics jostle as the *vita beata*, the good or happy life, is delineated, as it so supremely was during the fifth and fourth centuries B.C. in Greece, an age that, according to Livingstone, "had to face the questions which — now veiled now visible, now remote now insistent — constitute the eternal human problem: what should men believe about life, how should they live it, in what state of society can the good life be best lived, [and] how can we create such a state?"

B. L. Gildersleeve, an American classicist who flourished a century ago, once said that while, for the ancients, the actual conduct of life took precedence over its contemplation — that is, to deep thinking about it — still the wisdom informing the good and fruitful life came of contemplation and humble learning. This is why we should sup at their table. "It seems to be impossible," Gildersleeve said, "to live in constant communion with the first minds of antiquity and not imbibe something of the spirit of moderation, of self-control, of cautious wisdom, that breathes through their counsels," for "there is no department of human thought or endeavor in which the counsel of antiquity is not directly or indirectly valuable." Even if all one has gained from a classical education were to be forgotten in later life, anyone trained, at least for a time, to view the world as the Greeks and Romans saw it may learn to ask pregnant questions. And even if the ancient answers be rejected, the student — of whatever age — will know what they are, and approach his own world with freshened vision, one no longer blinkered by ideology and the reigning fashion. He would have a liberal, because liberating, education indeed. No longer would he be imprisoned exclusively within the velvet walls of his own world's preoccupations and fetishes. No longer would he be just and only a child of his own time. He might even partake of the divine.

■   ■   ■

Classical education again needs defending. We labor, after all, under the modern and, for this reason, rarely challenged belief that the classical world and its works have little to teach anyone but specialists, scholars, and teachers of classics. Let there be no mistake. For well over a century, classicists themselves have helped to create this fix. They have encouraged classical teaching emulating the (necessarily) precisian methods of technicians. They have tried to habituate classics to the halls of science and, in doing so, have ignored or obscured those humanizing balms many of us believe classics to apply. If indeed classical study is to consist merely, and for everyone, in nothing but memorizing grammar or toting up the number of slaves lugging amphorae in the Athens of Pericles, then truly classics has become a domain of specialists only, warranting no more — though no less — reverence and respect than any other worthwhile scholarly pursuit. This is the way many professional classicists would have it be, to which we can say only that they have their reward.

Here I should draw a distinction between classical *scholarship* and classical *education*. They are not the same thing. Classical scholarship inhabits a province in which few of us are equipped to travel, either by training or temperament, as scholarship requires not only devotion to a subject, but also entails years of painstaking preparation and the fine tuning of precise judgment. Fine classical scholars, like fine nuclear physicists, are rare birds. Would that they were a little rarer. As with nuclear physicists, few are needed in a healthy, intelligent society. Classical *education*, on the other hand, comes as the result of a classical course of study, usually lasting several years, often, though not necessarily, through one's undergraduate days. Perhaps classical education isn't as profound or as exacting as classical scholarship — though one may suspect that many tenured classics professors today would be hard pressed to compose Greek iambics the way classically trained adolescents once could. Classical education aims at larger numbers; it's fit to serve more people. Some of those blessed with the benefits of an early classical training may be well suited to the scholarly life, even if they do not opt for it. Nonetheless they will have been transformed by that training. I don't dismiss the importance of high scholarship; I owe too much to too many scholars, and there can be no classical education without classical scholarship. Indeed I would hope that a select few of the talented would be attracted to the academy to teach the languages, edit texts, elucidate ideas, dig shards, and think great thoughts. But it is primarily classical education — Parnassus — not scholarship, I argue for in this essay. The world could do with fewer scholars and more cultivated people.

If classical study is to survive to guide our intellectual life, we must reassert its cultural significance and value. Classics must make a difference not just in the way we think, but in the way we live. Its humanistic roots cut in an era hounded by utilitarian demands, classics has found itself in recent decades jockeying to justify its place in the cluttered academic catalogues to a technologically driven age. Ours is a time and place where many have decided, through ignorance or neglect, that culture, whatever it is, will somehow take care of itself.

Yet the Greeks and Romans taught us, by edict and example, the dangers of cultural complacency. Culture does not breathe on its own; it is preserved by those convinced of its value. This is not a new gospel. It is simply true. The classical vision has been renewed time and again down the long centuries after being threatened with extinction by prophets touting their New Jerusalems. But for students of history, the burden of proof must lie on the shoulders of those who would deny that vision's value. The case for classical education is not airtight, nor can it be; it contains too many provisos. But it deserves another hearing. Homage has been paid to it before our time, and by finer minds.

■ ■ ■

Lastly for a delicate matter. And here I part company with many apologists for classical education, especially in modern America. Greek and Latin, this unique and rarefied base of education, revered so long by the best and brightest, is not for everyone. The tireless study of classics has always been — to put it bluntly — an elite pursuit, a privilege of a comparative few. We should not skirt this fact. Classical education must not be patronizingly defended, must not be sold, for its "democratizing" traits the way some of our allies spearheading the "Great Books" have done. These traits exist — knowledge and understanding and taste all serve splendidly the interests of a democratic people — but they are accidental, not essential. Classics serves no class. Tyrants and oligarchs can quote Cicero too. Critics of classical education have, in one sense, been right for centuries: classics is, in at least one inescapable sense, *elitist*. But so what? We may admit this, while also saying that this does not tell the whole story. Anyone with a modicum of talent and energy can take on large dollops that classics offers; it is a mansion with many rooms and corridors. But the indisputable fact is that those of higher culture have perennially constituted those few at the top who, through their gifts and privileges, have influenced disproportionately the larger society of which they are members.

Still, I believe that the size of this minority as a proportion of the larger literate populace need not be infinitesimal. While initiates into classical learning have always been small in number, that number was always too small. Talent is no respecter of social status. No one with the requisite ability need be left out. Parnassus can be scaled by anyone with intelligence and curiosity who is also possessed of a doggedness for detail. With so much of the climbing gear available now to the disciplined autodidact in the forms of books, films, and computer software, the vistas have never been accessible to so many. Despite other disadvantages of a world unfriendly to the rigors and elevations of classical learning, we can in this day bypass the oversights and soft ignorance of the educational "experts" who have maintained a stranglehold on our schools for generations. We have the liberty of free agents. We should use it.

Finally, a concession. Many wonder whether the classical languages themselves make for an absolutely essential ingredient in a classical education. Can someone be "classically educated" without a reading knowledge of Greek and Latin? This sticky question, despite dogmatic claims on both sides, should not be answered glibly. One must probe a little to discover precisely what kind of knowledge the questioner wishes to gain. The judgment of history is No. And certainly I argue for the full package, the deluxe deal — declensions, conjugations, syntax, lexicons, verse exercises, and all. Nonetheless, it is safe to say that we can procure, with enterprise, certain intellectual and cultural benefits of classics by means other than a formal classical schooling. Not all knowledge worth having need be worn with scholastic exactitude. Acute intelligence matched to an active imagination can do wonders. Many paths can lead us home. If we can say anything with hopeful certainty about the future of classical education, it is that there will be many steep and dusty roads back to Rome.

Bent Twigs and
Trees Inclined

C lassical education, that odd and antiquated custom setting generations of bewildered youth to suffering the inky travails of learning Greek and Latin, two lan-guages they would never speak, can hardly be defended or even explained without a long look at the nature of liberal education. Nor can we neglect to tap the roots of that distant descendent of humanistic learning, the modern "humanities," where we now find classics nestling obscurely in college catalogues. For at the pinnacle of both sat the classical curriculum. But while granting that, once upon a time, classical learning might have borne some relation to professional skills, surely, we think, it has failed to remain useful in an age no longer requiring the services of scholastic monks, courtiers, and imperial civil ser-vants. So does this curriculum remain at all relevant in a world that measures success in stock averages and megabytes? For as classical scholar Gilbert Murray once conceded, "Even if we neglect merely material things and take as our standard the actual achievements of [the Greeks] in conduct and knowledge, the average clerk who goes to town daily, idly glancing at his morning newspaper, is probably a better behaved and infinitely better informed person than the average Athenian who sat spellbound at the tragedies of Aeschylus."

That clerk cannot be too badly off; he gets along. And if education is not to promote material success, what should it do? Must we lend any legitimacy to an older idea that education exists primarily to form the inner man as well as to impart those all-important skills for making a living? Have we in fact grown out of that ideal? Or have we fallen so far short of it that we cannot even spy its majestic peaks?

We praise liberal education zealously. It's a term of marble grandeur. But few of us know what it means. It has become grist for commencement addresses and high-flown commentary expounding the true mission of our schools and universities, best used by people removed from the rough and tumble of life. As with pornography, we cannot define it, but we think we know it when we see it. Liberal education rests comfortably in a haze where it no longer calls us to commit to anything exemplary, hard, or heroic. For some, liberal education has become synonymous with the "humanities," that free-for-all of open curricula where the dazed and confused spend irreplaceable years browsing among survey courses, taking ant bites out of whatever nuggets randomly lie among the crumbs, learning little or nothing in particular. The humanities provide a direction for the directionless, a path for the pathless, certifying ignorance in the guise of a "knowledge" too easily acquired. This wandering listlessness can envelop teachers of the liberal arts as well, the average figure being, according to Mark Van Doren, too often "neither lay nor learned, but a bored fellow who mixes prescriptions wherein all tastes are flat or bad. So much knowledge 'about' one thing and another, and never the tincture of wisdom." To others liberal education has become wedded to the propounding of social grievances — "freedom studies," we might call them. To others still it marks an expenditure of time and effort largely wasted when a technological world wants technologists. Liberal education, in short, means today whatever we wish it to mean in all our idealistic or disputatious moods. It is like a loose constitution, open to any fanciful interpretation of the moment. But some contemporary thinkers have tried to spy its essence.

Philosopher Leo Strauss once defined a liberal education, nebulously, as one "in culture or toward culture," in doing so drawing on the ancient metaphor of agricultural husbandry. "'Culture' means...chiefly the cultivation of the mind, the taking care and improving of the native faculties of the mind in accordance with the nature of the mind. Just as the soil needs cultivators of the soil, [so] the mind needs teachers." Further, liberal education "consists in reminding oneself of human excellence, of human greatness," and in "listening to the conversation among the greatest minds" as heard through the channel of great books, an idea owing more than a little to Matthew Arnold's ideal of culture as trumpeting forth the "best that has been thought and said." A. Bartlett Giamatti, a staunch defender of the principles of liberal education as he saw them, described it — again, not too clearly — as an "attitude of the mind toward knowledge the mind explores and creates. Such education occurs when you pursue knowledge because you are motivated to experience and absorb what comes of thinking — thinking about the traditions of our common heritage in all its forms, thinking about new patterns or designs...whether in philosophic texts or financial markets or chemical combinations — thinking in order to create new knowledge that others will then explore." Here the *new* presides; knowledge is not to be learned so much as created. Indeed, it exists almost for what it produces.

Broad claims like these typify the rhetoric of liberal education, and such definitions can be both revealing and helpful. But somehow they smell of formaldehyde; they seem just a bit sterile. We are still daunted and challenged, though, by Everett Dean Martin's spirited declaration many decades ago that the best education is "the organization of knowledge into human excellence." An education, he said, is not "the mere possession of knowledge, but the ability to reflect upon it and grow in wisdom." Liberal education ought to aim not just at furnishing the mind with serviceable knowledge and information, nor even at habituating the mind to rational methods, but at leading it to wisdom, to a quality of knowledge tempered by experience and imbued with understanding. It should, in a word, humanize. Unguided by such an aim, education loses its true character and finds itself degraded to servile training for the world's daily drudgeries. Liberal education civilizes. It transforms us. We are better for having run its course.

Nonetheless, these flourishes of eloquence glow with the light of dying embers. The case must be made, but hope for the cause has long since waned.

We lose an opportunity if we accept defeat too quickly. Not in decades perhaps — at a time when our schools have lost the capacity either to kindle a passion for history, or even to teach it intelligently — has there been a better time to search out our roots and recover our identity as citizens of the West by reasserting an intellectual training that reminds us who we are, where we came from, and the heights to which we have aspired, and to which we might aspire again. We have a large and many-branched family tree to trace. So before we explore the history of a *classical* education, let's examine further the meaning and growth of *liberal* education and the subsidiary curriculum known as the *humanities*, winging a few theoretical flights along the way.

■   ■   ■

Take a classroom example. Imagine we are teachers trying to define liberal education for students. We may do so by shaving off its political barnacles and drilling down to its etymological source. We say that "liberal" derives from a Latin word for freedom. "So what makes an education liberal?" we plead, our target in the scope. "It's an education that makes us free, an education that liberates us." Then we roll in the big guns. Robert Hutchins once explained that the "liberal arts are the arts of freedom. To be free a man must understand the arts of freedom." Much along these lines, Martin contended that "education is a spiritual revaluation of human life. Its task is to *reorient* the individual, to enable him to take a rich and more significant view of his experiences." Yes, education must be "liberalizing," but "not in the political sense, as if it meant half measures, but in its original sense," meaning "the kind of education which sets the mind free from the servitude of the crowd and from vulgar self-interests…. Education is simply philosophy at work. It is the search for the 'good life.' Education is itself a way of living." Giamatti addressed the freshman class at Yale in 1983 with much the same spirit. "I believe a liberal education is…the liberty of the free mind to explore itself," he said, "to draw itself out, to connect with other minds and spirits in the quest for truth. Its main goal is to train the whole person to be at once intellectually discerning and humanly flexible, tough-minded and openhearted; to be responsive to the new and responsible for values that make us civilized." Although later proclamations may lack the older definitions' strident vigor, they agree. Liberal education, we tell our class, fosters a mind that struggles against insularity. It aims to make us better than our untutored natures lead us to be.

But usually at this point the discussion, so usefully begun, breaks down. What do we need liberating from? *Ignorance* is the hackneyed answer. But of what exactly are we ignorant? Here the teacher confronts the often willful confusions of the immature, easily suggestible mind. We might strategically avoid Strauss's idea that education should act as a "counterpoison to the corroding effects of mass culture." One thing at a time. But we have raised questions, questions we hope will set patterns of inquiry and steer the students' energies away from slavery to intellectual fashion and sense impressions to careful self-examination. For whatever else it seeks to do, a liberal education seeks not only to instill essential knowledge, but also to prompt the asking of questions; it both provides a content and confers a method. And ideally the search will be for hard and hard-won answers, which those students, pupils of life, can *use*. For such an education is eminently practical.

So far we sail the stratosphere; the air is thin and rarefied. We have yet to utter those great names of the Western tradition: Homer, Plato, Aristotle, Cicero, Virgil, Dante, Shakespeare, Milton, Dr. Johnson, which shine as distant lights. But something is happening. Students learn that maybe answers are possible, and that there may be ways of getting at them, keys available to all who find within themselves the humility to learn and are determined to search beyond sentiment and circumstance to a common base of truth about human life and history. In this one crucial way will they "adjust": they will become responsible agents. They will tap intellectual depths.

They will also learn to use words more responsibly. They

will learn how to paw an abstraction. The concept of *freedom*, for example, is a stick of dynamite. Books and life both teach them that a freedom without discipline may not only be useless, but a hindrance to grasping something true beyond the veil of illusion. They may come to see, with Milton, that "liberty hath a double edge, fit only to be handled by just and virtuous men; to bad and dissolute, it becomes a mischief unwieldy in their own hands." Further, the idea of *equality*, held with catechetical reverence in a democratic society, they begin to view as yet another social and political ideal that, however good, has nonetheless been created by minds that came before theirs, minds formed by ethical and intellectual ideals themselves handed down from still other minds. And they will begin to spot complications: not everything is "democratic" in the modern sense of being equally accessible to or achievable by all. They will begin to see what C. S. Lewis meant when he said that equality "has no place in the world of the mind."

> Beauty is not democratic; she reveals herself more to the few than to the many, more to the persistent and disciplined seekers than to the careless. Virtue is not democratic; she is achieved by those who pursue her more hotly than most men. Truth is not democratic; she demands special talents and special industry in those to whom she gives her favours. Political democracy is doomed if it tries to extend its demands for equality into these higher spheres. Ethical, intellectual, or aesthetic democracy is death.

These words, merely "elitist" at first sight to the unseeing or electively blind, point us to a difference between those who view education as a matter of equal attainment and those who regard it as a result of highly individual and strenuous labor guided by logic, experience, and wisdom of former ages, a search for the objective and knowable over the subjective and unknowable, an assertion of the common over the eclectic. The first, more leveling view would seem the mandatory one today among those who teach — and among those who teach the teachers.

"'Tis education forms the common mind," wrote Alexander Pope. "Just as the twig is bent, the tree's inclined." At the heart of liberal education stands the conviction that the well-touted freedom of mind comes only by submission to standards external to oneself, that the discipline precedes the freedom, and that this kind of freedom can only be earned as a reward, not conferred as a right. "Openness to new experiences" — the experiential heresy — is not sufficient. One needs to know how to respond to experience, not simply with an enlightened intellect, but with an enlightened heart. Understanding like this must be achieved; it does not come without effort. And it certainly cannot be assumed. If only it were otherwise.

The struggle shown here in simple terms is not new. It points up age-old divergences in the theory of education, and indeed radically differing notions of human nature. These lead us into robust philosophical hair-splitting. Philosophy stands on the doorstep, bidding us to enter and make choices, to make distinctions, to discriminate. Generations of students have been taught that the very word education means the "bringing out" of children their native genius. The word can just as easily sustain the opposite idea of "building up," and even "putting in." Of course any education worthy of the name will do all. But at least the claims serve to place these ideas on their proper philosophical playing field, where we can begin to carve out a clear and defensible idea of what education, liberal or not, is supposed to do. For the true liberal ideal, despite fulsome praise, has found few buyers in the modern marketplace of ideas.

John Henry Newman, a nineteenth-century cleric and fount of crystalline clarity, bestowed the seminal statement of the aims of liberal education in his *Idea of a University*. He trusted a religious upbringing to inculcate virtue. Formal education, though, is a different thing. Perfection of the intellect, he wrote, is "an object as intelligible as a cultivation of virtue, while, at the same time, it is absolutely distinct from it." And he described, with axiomatic sagacity, what the liberally educated mind looks like. Instruction is one thing: it has "little or no effect upon the mind itself.... But education is a higher word; it implies an action upon our mental nature, and the formation of a character; it is something individual and permanent, and is commonly spoken of in connection with religion and virtue." For Newman a proper education forms "a habit of mind" that "lasts through life, of which the attributes are freedom, equitableness, calmness, moderation, and wisdom," all of which add up to what he called "the philosophical habit."

Knowledge is to be sought for its own sake, irrespective of immediate and material gain. Any other attitude to knowledge betrays the servile mind. All inquiry springs from the curious and rationally formed sensibility. "The principle of real dignity in knowledge, its worth...is this germ within it of a scientific or a philosophical process. This is how it comes to be an end in itself; this is why it admits of being called liberal." By this kind of knowledge we come to know "the relative disposition of things." "Such is the constitution of the human mind that any kind of knowledge, if it be really such, is its own reward." For only "liberal knowledge...stands on its own pretensions, is independent of sequel, expects no complement, refuses to be informed...by any end, or absorbed into any art, in order duly to present itself to our contemplation." Liberal education is "simply the cultivation of the intellect, as such, and its object is nothing more or less than intellectual excellence."

The bar is high, but we can reach it — with straining effort. Here is a definition as fine as we are likely to find, in this or in any other life.

■   ■   ■

Forming intellectual virtue is not the only task that liberal education has sought to perform. Along with imparting knowledge and inculcating the ways of sound thinking, it has also tried to transmit culture — in both senses of the word. This task often gets neglected now, unless its object be to raise the self-esteem of a particular minority, and then of course the emphasis lies no longer on a common culture, but on discrete, separate ones. Furthermore, we have over time quietly adopted a truncated, utilitarian notion of education as serving solely to help students get ahead, so inured have we become to public demands to teach "Skills for Tomorrow," as though education has never done anything else.

Yet it was largely to transmit culture that the brands of education we dub *liberal* and *humanistic* evolved. Prior generations believed that citizens should know the meaning of *justice*, for instance, not only so they might practice it in the streets, but so they might raise their children to practice it as well, thus perpetuating one more social ideal, one both felt and enacted. They also judged human instinct — appetite unchecked by reason — to be a perennial danger and insufficient mental equipment to take through life. We should certainly teach young people practical skills, but they must also take in our values: ethical, intellectual, and aesthetic. As we have already noted, no system of education, formal or informal, can exist value-free; even if children and adolescents were taught only technical know-how, such teaching would reveal the parts in the play we have assigned them. The Greeks and Romans made sure to teach their offspring not only practical skill for getting along; they made them memorize poetry commemorating the deeds of their mythological and historical heroes. They filled their children's minds with "useless" information, by rote, with one purpose among others: to make them members of a people, to make them one. We cannot view classical education aright unless we factor in this element of culture. Classics served the role of — to use the denigrated term of the day — cultural gatekeeper, a preserver of collective memories.

Where do we stand today? This idea of conserving culture has not been lost on all modern minds, nor have all those minds been politically conservative. Journalist Walter Lippmann, an influential voice for political and social liberalism, spoke to the American Association for the Advancement of Science in 1940 and described what he believed to be the state of American education. His perceptive words, raised to a higher power, likewise speak to our immensely greater shiftlessness today:

> There is an enormous vacuum where until a few decades ago there was the substance of education. And with what is that vacuum filled: it is filled with the elective, eclectic, the specialized, the accidental and incidental improvisations and spontaneous curiosities of teachers and students. There is no common faith, no common body of principle, no common moral and intellectual discipline. Yet the graduates of these modern schools are expected to have a social conscience. They are expected to arrive by discussion at common purposes. When one realizes that they have no common culture, is it astounding that they have no common purpose? That they worship false gods? That only in war do they unite? That in the fierce struggle for existence they are tearing Western society to pieces?

Lippmann observed that the modern world had "established a system of education where everyone must be educated, yet [where] there is nothing in particular that an educated man should know." Whether or not we agree with Lippmann's diagnosis, let alone his presuppositions, we can see that he saw a society that had already reached a critical fork in the road. We ought to mark the spotlight on commonality. "The emancipated democracies have renounced the idea that the purpose of education is to transmit Western culture. Thus there is a cultural vacuum, and this cultural vacuum was bound to produce, in fact has produced, progressive disorder." Lippmann described, in effect, the deliquescence of liberal education and the liberal intellectual ideal in America, the consequences of which could not be foreseen easily before America's entry into World War II.

T. S. Eliot, a poet and critic with much to say about education, was convinced that any culture worthy of survival must work unstintingly to preserve itself and resist the modern, ideologically driven tendency "to create bodies of men and women — of all classes — detached from tradition, alienated from religion, and susceptible to mass suggestion: in other words a mob," which is "no less a mob if it is well fed, well clothed, well housed, and well disciplined." He addressed the prickly matter in his *Notes Towards the Definition of Culture*, a book written in an uncertain postwar England. He too noted how much the fervor for educational reform assumed education to be "an instrument for the realization of social ideals" — which are not always the same as cultural ideals — quoting a leading thinker of the time, who said that the ideal most to be served is "full democracy." But education, Eliot said, has even more pressing tasks. Ignored by many would-be reformers were the higher purposes informing the liberal and Humanist traditions, in which Eliot himself had been nurtured and to which he appealed:

> It would be a pity if we overlooked the possibilities of education as a means of acquiring *wisdom*; if we belittled the acquisition of *knowledge* for the satisfaction of curiosity, without any further motive than the desire to know; and if we lost our respect for *learning*.

Most tellingly, and most damning to the scheme of course electives obtaining in American schools and universities, Eliot did not believe students competent to decide for themselves what they needed to learn. The lights of tradition and reason must guide them. "No one can become really educated," he wrote, "without having pursued some study in which he took no interest — for it is part of education to learn to interest ourselves in subjects for which we have no aptitude." Eliot advocated a prescribed curriculum. Out with the cafeteria style of course selection: we should not tailor our courses simply to our ease and ignorance (or laziness), but strive to grow into a state of mind which is the object of a more rigorous, commonly directed course of study set by minds more mature and wise. This was for Eliot the sanest of conservative tenets, the conviction that a debt is owed to the past and that, conversely, the past bestows a legacy on the present by teaching its lessons by a vicarious and finely sifted experience.

All of this, of course, violates dearly held modern beliefs in our self-sufficiency as well as the spirit of relativism in which all curricula are now arranged, or left unarranged, on a level plane. One course is as good as another. All are valid "in their own way." Rejecting set curricula, though, ravages not only the older regime of classical education, which prescribed heavily, but also any traditional form of liberal learning that has taken upon itself the splendid burden of pointing up the knowledge most worth knowing. Yet this curricular flea market also poses an aberration in the West. It is we, not they who have gone before us, who cut a poor and disjointed figure in the eyes of history. Indeed, Eliot blamed the disintegration of Western culture on a form of cultural liberalism that "tends to release energy rather than accumulate it, to relax rather than to fortify. It is a movement not so much defined by its end, as by its starting point; away from, rather than towards, something definite."

> By destroying traditional social habits of the people, by dissolving their natural collective consciousness into individual constituents, by licensing the opinions of the most foolish, by substituting instruction for education, by encouraging cleverness rather than wisdom, the upstart rather than the qualified, by fostering a notion of getting on to which the alternative is a hopeless apathy, Liberalism can prepare the way for that which is its own negation: the artificial, mechanized or brutalized control which is a desperate remedy for its chaos.

Here we have, in one dose, many of the modern world's ills told with vivid, discomfiting simplicity. And this is not, to repeat, a matter for political partisans only. Many political conservatives today fit the bill foursquare. We are all liberals of this kind now. Hardly can we avoid being so. This is the air we breathe.

■   ■   ■

The Greeks and Romans yearned for a common culture. *Paideia* is the Greek word customarily translated to mean "education," but "enculturation" better approximates its essence. *Paideia* was about instilling core values, enunciating standards, and setting moral precepts. H. I. Marrou, a French historian of ancient education, held that *paideia* signifies "'culture' — not in the sense of something active and preparational like education, but...of something perfected: a mind fully developed, the mind of a man who has become truly man." Modern views of education neglecting *paideia* scarcely would have been recognizable to the ancients; they would not have deemed them complete. Education applied a social glue, a common set of ideals and expectations. The larger culture carried supreme weight with the Greeks and Romans — often at the expense of the individual. Paradoxically, though, they thought the surest path to the healthy society to be a course of instruction that appears to us the most individualistic because it is inner-directed and speculative. Played to its finest pitch, that course seeks to foster contemplation, which is, according to Aristotle, "the highest form of activity because the intellect is the highest part of our nature, and the things apprehended by it are the highest form of knowledge." The vitality of any culture can be achieved only if there be enough souls to apprehend the Beautiful and the Good. Cohesion by other means risks Eliot's "mob." The object was to educate autonomous men and women: citizens, not robots.

One historian has said that the "history of education has been an interplay between conceptions of freedom and conceptions of value," and that by these conceptions we place ourselves within our society. Schools and their curricula have always reflected the values of the society they serve. They still do — and this should concern us. If a society be rigid and authoritarian, children are taught obedience; if it be equalitarian, they are taught first of their rights as citizens, secondarily of their civil obligations. Likewise, a vocationally minded, commercial society will betray its priorities by placing training-for-jobs above all else: getting on is the goal. The ancients recognized that a sound culture must strike a balance between rival claims of authority and liberty. Whenever we talk about education, we do well to keep this in mind. Any curriculum presupposes a vision of the good, well-run society.

Sir Richard Livingstone, a profoundly astute observer of cultural requisites, wrote, along with Eliot and Lippmann, amid the dislocations of World War II to apprise Britons of the vast challenges, political and social, awaiting them at the end of the war. Much of what he highlighted applied only to the Great Britain of his day. But we can see that most of what he had to say impinges upon us now. We can also see how much Livingstone understood *paideia* from the inside and could transpose it for modern life.

What purposes should education, at its most enlightened, serve? Livingstone listed three functions, to wit: to teach us to earn a living; to teach us to be good citizens; and to help us to understand the meaning of the good life. The first objective, he wrote, we understand all too well, and the second is treated with growing neglect. But the third is almost irretrievably lost. He was right. When we peruse today's jargon-laden manifestos that would tell us what we ought to teach and learn, we search in vain for the third criterion. But Livingstone realized that philosophical — even spiritual — formation is not extraneous to the task; it is central. Robert Hutchins wrote that a "system that denies the existence of values denies the possibility of education. Relativism, scientism, skepticism, and anti-intellectualism, the four horsemen of the philosophical apocalypse, have produced that chaos in education which will end in the disintegration of the West," though this was an outcome that Livingstone thought we can counteract. Spiritual matters press upon the secular world just as irresistibly as they do upon the sacred. They just go by different names. Spirituality, embracing the entire personality, cannot be severed from education. As we are about to see, the spiritual motive found an especial home in Humanism, which had evolved to meet Livingstone's second and third criteria. Humanism seeks to help us understand our rights and duties as citizens, but it also seeks to help us grasp the nature of human existence as it has been celebrated and lamented through time and perceived through literature, philosophy, and history.

Livingstone said that the finest education, before it can be judged complete, must give everyone — or everyone mentally able — "an intellectual attitude to life and a philosophy of life." It must foster a "right intellectual attitude" seeking "to find the world and life intensely interesting; to wish to see them as they are; [and] to feel that truth, in Plato's words, is both permanent and beautiful." Not that we mustn't work for a living. "The efficiency of a community will depend on its technical and vocational education, its cohesion and duration largely on its social and political education. But the quality of its civilisation depends on something else. It depends on its standards, its sense of values, *its idea of what is first-rate and what is not*" (my emphasis). Words that swerve further from current dogmas of educational theory would be hard to imagine. We don't speak the same language. Yet any man of learning of the last several centuries would have found himself simpatico with the ideals, even while finding them hard to live by.

What about the role of moral training in formal education? It's there in theory, as it remains today in secular practice — though moral concerns now creak with the weakened, politically approved language of "tolerance" and "respect for diversity." But even these aims, critical as they may be for the building of character, still fall short of another. "One is apt to think of moral failure," Livingstone wrote, "as due to weakness of character: more often it is due to an inadequate ideal. We detect in others, and occasionally in ourselves, the want of courage, of industry, of persistence which leads to defeat. But we do not notice the more subtle and disastrous weakness, that our standards are wrong, that we have never learnt what is good."

Here is the crux of Livingstone's critique of modern education. It is leery of seeking out and acknowledging distinctions between good and bad, better and worse. It does not teach the arts of discrimination. We suffer from an atrophy of the judging faculty. "The most indispensable viaticum for the journey of life is a store of adequate ideals, and these are acquired in a very simple way, by living with the best things in the world — the best pictures, the best buildings, the best social or political orders, the best human beings. The way to acquire a good taste in anything, from pictures to architecture, from literature to character, from wine to cigars, is always the same — be familiar with the best specimens of each." We must educate the head and heart alike: "The sight of goodness in life or in literature or history gives a standard and a challenge. If anyone has been able to compare the first-rate with the second-rate, his criticism will not be merely bitter and barren, but creative, born of a vision perceiving the good, dominated by it and desiring to bring it to birth."

We must train the intellectual and aesthetic judgment, without which life for reflective, educated people cannot be deemed whole, without which we cannot awaken "the mind of a man who has become truly man." And any judgment presupposes a standard, a guiding principle external to one's self — a principle, in Robert Frost's words, "to stay our minds on and be staid." Common culture, common standards. Those standards show us where we stand on the grid of human experience.

Livingstone and T. S. Eliot both stood at a crossroads in the cultural and intellectual history of the West. For theirs was the last generation to receive stout draughts of the old humanistic, rigorous, liberal schooling, bestowed as a matter of course on those privileged to attend the better schools. They would live to see that tradition dissolve. And with the passing of that tradition, a cultural ideal began to lapse as well. Here again, as we did before, we must distinguish, in Werner Jaeger's words, between culture as an *"anthropological* concept, which means the entire way of life or character of a particular nation, and culture as *the conscious ideal of human perfection."* A worthy complement we find in a phrase from Alfred North Whitehead, who wrote that "Moral education is impossible without *the habitual vision of greatness."* Both the conscious ideal of human perfection and the habitual vision of greatness speak to those acts and thoughts betokening the acme of human achievement, especially those so judged by successive generations of discerning spirits.

These are the seeds of humanistic endeavor: to climb the heights of human possibility, to reflect on man's will to know and understand himself, placed as he is in a turbulent world made all the more violent and chaotic by his passions and by his perpetual fight to free himself from their fetters. We are on this planet to rise above lower nature.

So far, so good. But what do we mean by Humanism? If we crack this nut, Greek and Latin in the Age of Microsoft might begin to make some sense.

■　　■　　■

Humanism has never enjoyed a sure definition. Nor has its anti-religious press, earned and unearned, done the word any favors. But if classical education is hard to understand without grasping the goals of liberal education, it is absolutely incomprehensible without a firm hold on this idea of Humanism. So what is it? To some it's an optimistic belief in the capacity of human beings to solve those problems uniquely theirs. Or, as Livingstone once wrote, Humanism is "the belief that man is more important than his environment or his possessions; and that his fundamental business is not to understand [physical] nature, though that is one of his problems, nor to earn a livelihood, though that is one of his duties, but so to lead his life as to make the best of human nature and above all of what is characteristic of, peculiar to, and highest in human nature; or, as the Greeks put it, to achieve the *arête* [or 'excellence'] of man." Critics have asserted its profaneness as a philosophy of secular power in defiance of a divine creator. Those especially who espouse certain religious tenets have made Humanism — in full dress as "secular humanism" — a term of pure denigration. Both understandings bear traceable roots. Yet none exhausts the word or the idea. The Fowlers' *Concise Oxford Dictionary* sums up the meaning most usefully as a "Devotion to human interests; [a] system concerned with human (not divine) interests, or with the human race (not the individual); Religion of humanity; literary culture, esp. that of the humanists," who are themselves defined as students "of human nature or human affairs; [they are students] (esp. in the 14th-16th cc.) of Roman and Greek literature & antiquities." The "devotion to human interests" endures in the popular mind, however little that idea can be said to mean certainly, as does the idea of Humanism constituting a kind of religion. But the emphasis on "the human race (not the individual)" represents the predominant modern view, conditioned, I believe, by the more outward-looking "humanitarian" impulse.

We can look back a couple millennia, though, and amuse ourselves to see that the confusions stretch back all the way to the classical world itself. The second century A.D. Roman Aulus Gellius, himself keen to capture the meaning of the Latin root *humanitas*, noted that common people understood it broadly, while those who spoke "pure Latin" — the educated elite — restricted its meaning:

> Those who have spoken Latin and have used the language correctly do not give to the word *humanitas* the meaning which it is commonly thought to have, namely, what the Greeks call *philantropia*, signifying a kind of friendly spirit and good feeling towards all men without distinction; but they gave to *humanitas* about the force of the Greek *paideia*; that is, what we call *eruditionem institutionemque in bonas artes*, or "education and training in the liberal arts." Those who earnestly desire and seek after these are most highly humanized. For the pursuit of that kind of knowledge, and the training given by it, have been granted to man alone of all the animals, and for that reason it is termed *humanitas*.

He went on to clarify the related *humanior* as meaning not "good-natured, amiable, and kindly," which was its "usual sense," but as applying to someone of "some cultivation and education (*eruditiori doctiorique*)." Someone, that is, who has learned not only from books, possessing "knowledge of letters," but also one who has taken on the cultivation that comes of the contemplative life. Thus, wrote modern philosopher and man of letters Irving Babbitt, *humanitas* "really implies doctrine and discipline, and is applicable not to men in general but only to a select few — it is, in short, aristocratic and not democratic in its implication." It faces outward, but inward first. *Humanitas* seeks to amend the self before amending the world around.

Babbitt's pivotal distinction arose out of the jumble he spotted between *humanism* and *humanitarianism*, two words that had come to mean — and still mean a century later —

practically the same thing in the popular mind. And his division illuminates. "A person who has sympathy for mankind in the lump, faith in its future progress, and desires to serve the great cause of this progress, should not be called a humanist, but a humanitarian, and his creed may be designated as humanitarianism." Peculiar mischief crops up from the muddle. "The humanitarian lays stress almost solely upon breadth of knowledge and sympathy. The poet Schiller, for instance, speaks as a humanitarian and not as a Humanist when he would 'clasp the millions to his bosom,' and bestow 'a kiss upon the whole world.'"

But the true Humanist, Babbitt said, "is more selective in his caresses." For he, like the eminently humanistic Cicero, knows that "what is wanted is not sympathy alone, nor again discipline and selection alone, but a disciplined and selective sympathy. Sympathy without selection becomes flabby, and a selection which is unsympathetic tends to grow disdainful." Set over against the humanitarian's, the Humanist's concern lies in "perfecting the individual rather than in schemes for the elevation of mankind as a whole; and although he allows largely for sympathy, he insists that it be disciplined and tempered by judgment." Tellingly, when Babbitt contradicted Bruntiere, who believed he had found the perfectly apt definition of Humanism in the Roman poet Terence's assertion that "I consider nothing human alien to me," Babbitt did so "because of the entire absence of the idea of selection." For here stands the "humanitarian busybody with whom we are all so familiar nowadays, who goes around with schemes for reforming almost everything — except himself." Selection was both a cultivated ideal and a counterweight to mere sympathy. Here the difference is sealed with wax. Humanism selects, humanitarianism doesn't.

Liberal education and the humanities, then, are not

synonymous terms, though the source of their confusion is not hard to spot. The goals of Humanism and the goals of any curriculum fairly called "liberal" have shot at neighboring targets. They aim to broaden, enlighten, deepen. Although Humanism did not don its familiar clothing until the Renaissance, its ideals took shape two thousand years before in the hands of the Greeks. They drew the blueprints for right education. The Romans finally codified the system, which they dubbed the "liberal arts." That legacy has been maintained to this day, though the muddy accretions of bad teaching and misdirected good intentions have covered over the roots.

"Liberal arts" derives directly from *artes liberales* and designates those activities promoting freedom and leisure, but we must add that, for Greeks and Romans, leisure carried none of our overtones of idleness. "Leisure" referred to those "arts" (even "techniques") reckoned conducive to the contemplative or reflective life, to an expansive freedom of mind. Opposed to the *artes liberales* were the *artes serviles*, the obligatory backbreaking work performed to earn bread and ale. *Artes serviles* were necessary for any society, *artes liberales* for a higher, more varied culture. The venerable Seven Liberal Arts of the Trivium (Grammar, Rhetoric, Logic) and Quadrivium (Astronomy, Music, Geometry, Arithmetic) were enshrined in the Middle Ages as those mental "arts" promoting leisure. But prior to leisure, or the liberal arts, came the articulation of the virtues. Moral muscle, being not inborn, must be firmed up before the Good Society can be achieved: goodness in the *polis*, but first goodness in individuals. The ancients knew that any society marked by unbridled appetites competing for control and satisfaction would quickly reduce itself to barbarism. The morally sound state was a prerequisite to the fruitful practice of the liberal arts. And the liberal arts required a measure of social tranquility.

Now for the sinews, the gristle, of those liberal and humane ideals.

■   ■   ■

The Greeks and Romans, while capable of great superstition, nonetheless placed great faith in the power of Reason, and it was the object of the *artes liberales* to discover truth. Yet they did not live solely in their brains. Plato believed in the fundamental unity of the Good. All the virtues amounted to *arête*: excellence, which signified the best quality appropriate to any act or actor, thought or thinker. It pointed toward the best of anything, to its perfection. Conduct should be informed by knowledge of the virtues, and evil comes naturally of ignorance. Morality is rational: it can be divined by the instructed mind; it isn't purely subjective; it is discoverable. Evil is a disease, a cancer of the mind and soul, healable by philosophy. One healed the soul by leading the mind to knowledge of values, which in turn leads to *aletheia*, or truth itself. Nothing short of this would produce the virtuous life, for the quality of life could be neither more nor less than the soul made it. How strange, said Socrates on the eve of his execution, that any citizen of Athens, "the greatest of cities and the most famous for wisdom and power, [would not be] ashamed to care for the acquisition of wealth and for reputation and honor, when you neither care nor take thought for wisdom and truth and the perfection of your soul." Socrates claimed his life's mission to be "nothing else than urging you, young and old, not to care for your persons or your property more than for the perfection of your souls."

The Western mind elevated this mighty philosophical aim into an ideal. The inner takes precedence over the outer, the mind and soul compose an inseparable whole, and both are fed or starved together. No option exists to train the mind *alone* without producing soul-deep consequences.

But how is the "inner" to be instructed? Here was the question posing the greatest challenge to Greek education, to *paideia*: How best to fit theory to practice? The Greeks also knew the tension between teaching for skills (training) and teaching for cultural and intellectual strength (liberal education). Aristotle, on the heels of Plato by a generation, admitted that "it is not clear whether pupils should practice pursuits that are practically useful or morally edifying." Still, the Greeks reached an impressive accord on the role of education in promoting virtue, one we see spun out richly in the works of Plato and Aristotle. They came to believe that education ought to change who the learner is. An operation such as this — and an analogy to surgery doesn't come amiss — must be undertaken with care. But the rewards were great and perdurable. Protagoras had proclaimed Man to be "the measure of all things," and an exploration into man's nature was proclaimed the highest pursuit we can make along our journey through life.

Certainly the most sublime work ever penned on *paideia* and the building of common culture is Plato's *Republic*, said by French philosopher Jean-Jacques Rousseau to be the "finest treatise on Education ever written." And indeed one cannot talk intelligently about education without having sat at the feet of Socrates and his companions as they wrestle with ways and means to build the well-run state. We need not detain ourselves with a detailed *précis* of Plato's thoughts, but we would serve our purpose with a glance at his view of the ideal state — for that is what the *Republic* describes, not so much a feasible political program.

Socrates gave his name to the Socratic method, a teaching device seeking as its object to make all knowledge personal by rigorous questioning, to make it more than a nod of lazy assent. The novice is thereby led through the bracken of his assumptions and biases to the clear light of knowledge. The teacher holds him responsible for all words and ideas he utters, pressing him to define them with greater exactitude. Just what do we mean by Justice, Freedom, Courage, Virtue? Are they achievable in this life? Or are they beyond the grasp of even the most righteous? And this method remains a cardinal means of testing intellectual mettle. The pupil isn't so much taught as guided, first to recognize his own ignorance, and second to spring from this illumination to true knowledge and understanding. Thus does knowledge rise out of ignorance. Thus can knowledge lead to wisdom.

How are human relations structured in this ideal world? Plato's view of humanity reveals distinctly hierarchical scaffolding.

The Republic of Plato's fancy is composed of three tiers. Living on the bottom are most of us, the great mass of people, from the poor through prosperous farmers, artisans, and merchants. They put food on the tables and keep the wheels of commerce turning but, by dint of their desire merely to make a living untroubled by higher aspirations, they are to exercise no political power over others because they have not been taught to wield power with justice and magnanimity. Next up come the administrators and the military, those charged with carrying out the policies set by the rulers on top. And the rulers, of course, are the "philosopher princes" who alone possess the knowledge and wisdom to rule.

This is not a democratic vision. It is guided by an assumed inequality throughout the populace. It is therefore shamelessly aristocratic: the rule of the best and most able. One abiding difference, though, from the more familiar and historical sense of aristocracy lies in the absence of any belief that the aristocrats — those who man the upper tiers — gain their ascendancy from inherited privilege. Rulers rule only after their characters have been judged meritorious. This idea, wrote Jaeger, Plato thought to be a principle "in harmony with nature and [which] is therefore absolutely inevitable in the state of divine perfection." The poor and laboring masses haven't had the education for enlightened rule. Yet, more significantly, the plutocrats out for nothing beyond lucre are also expressly forbidden power. Souls like these are also unequal to the task of ruling.

What curriculum must one complete before he is deemed worthy to rule over others in this theoretical state? Primary schooling stipulates a course of mathematics, literature, music, and gymnastics. Later, students learn logic. As adults, some set off into the upper reaches of philosophy. Significantly, not till they reach their thirties are they fit for leadership. Not till fifty or so will they be asked finally "to turn upwards the vision of their souls and fix their gaze on that which sheds light on all." For "when they have thus beheld the good itself, they shall use it as a pattern for the right ordering of the state and the citizens and themselves throughout the remainder of their lives, each in his turn, devoting the greater part of [his] time to the study of philosophy." Philosophy is "not a fine thing, but a necessity."

Plato claimed another tripartite split in human nature — one not surprisingly reflecting the three classes of the state. First, *appetite*, all physical and sensual wants, including avaricious desires for material gain; then the *spirited* element, which is formed by habit and will; and finally the *philosophic* element, which can perceive virtues like sympathy and selflessness and, if it's properly formed, can apprehend Goodness, Beauty, and Truth. Order, of whatever kind, is hierarchical. All this may strike us as fanciful. But the value of these ruminations to us resides in the theory, not the applicability. They crystallize. C. S. Lewis best summarized this model for the modern mind. "As the king governs by his executive," he wrote, "so Reason in man [the *philosophic* element] must rule mere appetites by means of the 'spirited' element. The head rules the belly through the chest — the seat...of Magnanimity, of emotions organized by trained habit into stable sentiments. The Chest — Magnanimity — Sentiment — these are the indispensable liaison officers between cerebral man and visceral man. It may even be said that it is by this middle element that man is man: for by his intellect he is mere spirit and by his appetite mere animal."

■   ■   ■

For devotees of this classical Greek view of the human mind and human nature, the supreme goal of education was happiness, which was conceived of as health of soul, the ultimate good man can hope to attain during his lifetime. And from this health of soul, they believed, would come *eudaimonia* (literally, "the good god within"), a harmonious balance of the whole personality. But once more: How to achieve it?

Early humanistic education began with the cultivation of character. Whatever intellectual feats a man might bring off, they were of scant value if he had not first achieved a goodness and tranquility of soul. Socrates had said that "according as the sons turn out well or the opposite will the whole life of their father's house be affected, depending for better or worse on their character." Character determined the health of the state. In this sense the purposes behind education were also political. Each man and woman would be of either the rulers or the ruled. And here the aristocracy must carry its own weight: a ruler must be distinguished from a subject by his superior character, not merely by the accidents of birth and wealth. Therefore his education must differ from theirs. He must care about supra-intellectual qualities. Jaeger explained the goal:

> The distinction between the two kinds of training extends even to food and regimen. The infant prince must learn to ignore physical needs and desires in order to fulfill urgent duties; must be master of his own hunger and thirst; must be used to short sleep, late to bed and early to rise; must not be afraid of hard work; must not be lured by the bait of sense.... Anyone who cannot do all that is a subject, not a ruler. Socrates gives this education in self-control and abstinence the Greek name for "training," *askesis*.

There can be no happiness without this *aidos*, this training in self-control, modesty, and reverence for that judged worthy of revering. Education began with principles such as these. People must first achieve the good individually before going on to serve the larger social good. The healthy society begins with healthy souls. And the healthiest souls are not formed without intellectual and, most of all, spiritual labor. We approach the heart of the matter.

The soul's quest for health began with the inculcation of right habits. Read Book III of the *Republic*. We see that the Platonic scheme, far from being over-intellectualized, approached the task with sobriety. The child is to be reared on music and gymnastics, both corresponding roughly to the training of mind and body. Many of us now tend to think of music merely as diverting entertainment. But to the Greeks, "music" formed the spirit. Plato believed that the soul needs training in the aesthetic and spiritual Good, and that music reflects those kaleidoscopic spiritual states — with melody, harmony, and rhythm — more readily than any other activity. It will either purify or corrupt the soul. The "rhythms of a life" must be "orderly and brave." Why? Because in just this way does "Good speech…and good grace, and good rhythm wait upon a good disposition, not that weakness of head which we euphemistically style goodness of heart, but the truly good and fair disposition of the character and the mind…. For in all these there is grace or gracelessness and evil rhythm and disharmony are akin to evil speaking and the evil temper, but the opposites are…the sober and the good disposition." One speculation holds that "education in music is most sovereign, because more than anything else rhythm and harmony find their way to the inmost soul and take strongest hold upon it…imparting grace." So anyone so trained would "praise beautiful things and take delight in them and receive them into his soul to foster its growth and become himself beautiful and good." The results for the student are indelible: "The ugly he would rightly disapprove of and hate while still young and yet unable to apprehend the reason, but when reason came the man thus nurtured would be the first to give her welcome, for by this affinity he would know her."

Near the end of his life, Plato expounded more broadly upon the theory of right education. "When pleasure and love, and pain and hatred, spring up rightly in the souls of those who are unable as yet to grasp a rational account," they will "consent thereunto through having been rightly trained in fitting practices: this consent, viewed as a whole, is goodness." The student is "rightly trained in respect of pleasures and pains, so as to hate what ought to be hated, right from the beginning to the very end, and to love what ought to be loved." This isn't just reading and writing and counting. This is *paideia*.

Likewise, Aristotle saw the cultivation of virtue first as a matter of encouraging habits, of learning to like what is worth liking, and reason and habit alike have roles to play. He thought of virtue as a mean, a midpoint, a balance of competing appetites and claims, which the well-directed mind develops over time.

> Moral virtue…is concerned with emotions and actions, in which one can have excess or deficiency or a due mean. For example, one can be frightened or bold, feel desire or anger or pity, and experience pleasure and pain in general, either too much or too little, and in both cases wrongly; whereas to feel these feelings at the right time, on the right occasion, towards the right people, for the right purpose and in the right manner, is to feel the best amount of them, which is the mean amount — and best amount is of course the mark of virtue.

At the same time, Aristotle sensed, as do we, the muddle of nature and nurture. Can such virtue be inborn? He had an answer.

> Some thinkers hold that virtue is a gift of nature; others think we become good by habit, others that we can be taught to be good. Natural endowment is obviously not under our control; it is bestowed on those who are fortunate, in the true sense, by some divine dispensation. Again, theory and teaching are not…equally efficacious in all cases: the soil must have been previously tilled if it is to foster the seed, [and] the mind of the pupil must have been prepared by the cultivation of habits, so as to like and dislike aright. For he that lives at the dictates of passion will not hear nor understand the reasoning of one who tries to dissuade him…. Passion seems not to be amenable to reason, but only to force.

Education is often compared to the cultivation of soil in ancient writings, as well as in those of the Renaissance. As plants are cultivated to grow strongly so as to be fruitful or beautiful, so must the human mind be pruned and weeded if it too is to become "cultivated." "Right habits," once planted, are not expected to form the soul on their own; those habits are products of vigilant husbandry. Saying much the same thing in a slightly different way four centuries later, Plutarch wrote of the responsibility of a tutor in this way: "Just as nurses mould [a child's] body with their hands, so tutors by the habits they inculcate train the child's character to take a first step, as it were, on the path to virtue. So the Spartan, when he was asked what he effected by his teaching, said, 'I make honorable things pleasant to children.'" The Roman Emperor Vespasian described the best teachers as those who "train the souls of the young to gentleness and civic virtue."

Aristotle said there are two kinds of virtue, intellectual and moral. "Intellectual virtue is for the most part both produced and increased by instruction, and therefore requires experience and time; whereas moral or ethical virtue is the product of habit (*ethos*)." A natural faculty, like sight and hearing, serves us without our exertion. There's nothing "natural," though, about the virtues: they come by effort and must be reinforced by habit. We acquire them "by first having actually practiced them, just as we do the arts. We learn an art or craft by doing the things that we shall have to do when we have learnt it…. Men become builders by building houses, harpers by playing the harp. Similarly, we become just by doing just acts, brave by doing brave acts." Here the political implications become most acute. "This truth is attested by the experience of states: lawgivers make the citizens good by training them in habits of right action — this is the aim of all legislation, and if it fails to do this, it is a failure; this is what distinguishes a good form of constitution from a bad one."

What was to be the result of all this strenuous philosophical effort? The wise citizen fit to govern first himself and then — and only then — to govern others. Precisely in this way does one become free through liberal learning: first, by acquiring right habits; second, by intellectual strain, by learning to apprehend the Beautiful and the Good with the mind. And the mind then confirms what the soul has already learned. One can become intellectually powerful, of course, without those right habits, but what good is that? The object of the ancients was not a programmable, ratiocinative machine. It was the cultured man or woman.

The Romans, taking their cues from the Greeks, built on this legacy. While they were a practical people, they also came to revere the philosophical bent. But, within their milieu, orators replaced philosophers as the cultivated ideal, men of speculative ability who yet matched that ability to a high sense of civic duty, of enlightened service to the state. Quintilian was the ultimate authority on creating the "perfect orator":

> The first essential for such a one is that he should be a good man, and consequently we demand of him not merely the possession of exceptional gifts of speech, but of all the excellences of character as well. For I will not admit that the principles of upright and honorable living should...be regarded as the peculiar concern of philosophy. The man who can really play his part as a citizen and is capable of meeting the demands both of public and private business, the man who can guide a state by his counsels, give it a firm basis by his legislation and purge its vices by his decisions as a judge, is assuredly no other than the orator of our quest.

Once more we find a tall order for the ideal citizen. And once more we find that skills are not placed above learning and moral rectitude. Character still helps to form the liberal mind: the mind, that is, with the ability to reflect upon its assumptions and sense impressions, a mind able to make sound judgments. When describing this ideal orator, Quintilian says he is "compelled to speak of such virtues as courage, justice, self-control; in fact scarcely a case comes up in which some one of these virtues is not involved." This ideal orator, this renewed paragon of the cultured mind, was to be placed on par with the philosopher because of his predilection and ability to reflect, to contemplate. This Roman synthesis stands in some ways as an even greater affirmation of the Hellenic vision than the schemes of the Greeks. For life is no longer framed within Plato's ideal garden, walled off from the world's squalor and chaos. The ideal takes on the trappings of a practical program. Philosophy gets brought down to the street.

Meanwhile, though, how fared the purpose of perpetuating culture in the Roman world? If we can answer this, we can also answer the question: Why Greece and Rome? And then: Why Greek and Latin?

■   ■   ■

As the sun set on the Roman Empire during the long decades of the fifth century A.D., the upper classes still possessed the confidence of a matured culture. They knew they had something valuable enough to preserve. Education throughout the vast bulk of the Mediterranean and in the distant northern places ruled under the eagle was, despite unevenness in practice, marked by extraordinary uniformity, a uniformity that had arisen out of the Hellenistic world. The civilizing net was cast widely during the latter years of the Roman Republic and stayed that way for centuries. Throughout the breadth of the

Empire, even as the world grew more and more unstable politically, the educated man was still honored. Just as important, he was recognizable. Culture held. Enough people agreed on what was vital to a thriving civilization. There was still a cultural faith, a belief in that intricate web of value and association drawing together diverse peoples and making them one.

Perhaps the greatest legacy of the Greeks was their belief in the goodness of what they were and what they had to give to the rest of the world. But it was the Romans, not the Greeks, who ensured the survival of that intellectual heritage underlying liberal learning and classical education. The Romans created much of the intellectual tradition we appeal to today. Rome too had emerged with a massive confidence in the strength and integrity of that tradition inherited from the Greeks — and the Greeks had no doubts about their cultural superiority. They could be skeptics, but they were not tormented by self-doubt; something new had entered the cosmos with them, and they knew it. Later, the Roman world was filled with many clashing nations. The unity the Romans achieved out of that diversity is amazing to ponder. As Marrou has observed, "Unity could come only from sharing a single idea, a common attitude towards the purpose of existence and the various means of attaining it — in short, from a common civilization, or rather, culture." Fighting armies alone did not create this unity. Unity was also engendered in those far-flung schools.

Early on in their history the Romans had no cultural center of gravity capable of attracting other peoples. They had little to envy. They were a rural people, living close to the soil and deriving their ideals of virtuous action from it. Although they would eventually dominate the Greek lands politically and militarily, they knew of their cultural shortcomings. Centuries passed before Romans could sport their own first-class literature and culture, but even as they did, they remained under the long shadows of Hellas. Cicero once asked, "Is there in fact a man among those Greeks who would credit one of [the Romans] with understanding?" Rome assimilated Greek things. The Roman poet Horace would one day famously concede: "Captive Greece took captive her savage conqueror and brought civilization to barbarous Latium." The historian Arnold Toynbee wrote, without exaggeration, that the Romans were Greek culture's "most celebrated converts and most effective disseminators." And this conversion brought with it a profound linkage of the two cultures. All educated people were to be versed in the treasures of both their languages.

Whereas the Greeks had learned only Greek, the Romans went on to learn both Latin and Greek — and the pattern was set: to be a fully educated, enculturated man in the Greco-Roman world, one had to know both tongues. It was not Petrarch in the fourteenth century who first insisted on a mastery of both Latin and Greek. Cicero did that, over a thousand years before. Quintilian later codified this proviso as holy writ, promoting this formal bilingualism pragmatically: "I prefer that a boy should begin [learning] with Greek, because Latin, being in general use, will be picked up by him whether we will or not; while the fact that Latin is derived from Greek is a further reason for his being first instructed in the latter." This linguistic approach to acculturating — assimilating — diverse peoples spread throughout the Roman provinces, making the classical world a truly cosmopolitan one. The learning of language leads to literature, and melding the high literary achievements of both the Greeks and the Romans helped to create a cultural unity.

"Letters are the beginning of wisdom." So one Greek maxim had it, with "letters" standing for knowledge of language, the ability to convey the complexity and subtlety of thought and sense with words. The Hellenistic age strengthened the consensus that mastery of language defined the highest reaches of cultivation. As Marrou has reminded us, when we speak of "classical education" today, we really mean "Hellenistic education." For it was during the Hellenistic age, roughly from the death of Alexander in 322 to the first century BC, that curricula throughout the Mediterranean congealed. The Word was in the ascendant. The cultivated man was, in a real sense, the literary man, the man of words. It was during this period too that the "conscious ideal of human perfection" made itself felt more widely as a culturally shaping force. One was moved, Marrou wrote, to recreate one's self from unmolded clay and "to produce from the childish material, and from the imperfectly formed creature one is born, the man who is fully man, whose ideal proportions one can just perceive: such [became] every man's lifework, the one task worthy of a lifetime's devotion."

Living contemporaneously with Plato, Isocrates might well be called the father of rhetorical — or "oratorical" culture — as opposed to philosophical culture. It was Isocrates who had pressed the importance of one cohesive Hellenic culture in a "multicultural" age, instructing people of his time that a culture must be built and maintained; it does not materialize out of ether. Images of building and tilling were native to his way of thinking; for him culture was a matrix of conventions, points of agreement, delicately woven and easily torn apart. Civilization itself emerges from a web of myriad laws, written and unwritten, creating unity out of disunity, social cosmos out of chaos. To live as an educated being in any higher culture is to act both as a builder of the house and as a weeder of the garden. Isocrates thought we must do two things primarily as a people: we must consolidate culture and we must educate our rulers.

We need rulers armed with a body of knowledge, a basis for common discourse and common sentiment, creating, again in Marrou's words, a "common devotion to a single ideal of human perfection, from the fact that they had all received the same kind of upbringing devoted to the same end." We need, in a word, an elite.

Reflexively disparaged today, an elite to the Greeks and Romans was not only inevitable in a sound society, but the desirable fruit of the highest thoughts, words, and deeds — thoughts, words, and deeds to which most of us are simply not equal. Again, a high culture reaches upward to the better and best. Distinctions arise. They are sought, not derided, as signs of intellectual and cultural health. Isocrates carried the day and, in a not too fanciful sense, set Hellenistic, and thus classical, education on its way. He stamped the template.

It was Isocrates, significantly, who gave traditional Western education its literary tenor. Some wise — or clever — sophists could teach without writing a word, their thoughts and spirits beheld forever through the prisms of others. After Isocrates, though, intellectual culture became scribal; it depended on books, written words, collections of which over time would form an authoritative list of *best* works. Culture meant books, because from books we learn about what is best. William James once wrote epigrammatically that the purpose of education is to help us to know a good man when we see him. Isocrates had some standards of his own: What does the man know? How has that knowledge changed him? And how common is that knowledge to that which is held by other knowledgeable people? Discovering the books that that man had read would tell us much. Other expressions of culture fade away. They're fragile. But the artifacts of culture enduring the longest come adorned with words, with those fleeting yet hard missiles of meaning that can keep alive a thought or feeling for millennia. Sometimes a word is worth a thousand pictures.

We too keep our memories. Until very recently, generations of American schoolchildren were made to memorize the Gettysburg Address, mainly for two reasons. One reason was the potency of the words themselves, for the speech is a masterpiece of eloquent brevity; it has literary value. But another reason was the belief that those words, furnishing the minds of young people, would confirm their citizenship, serving as a living reminder of what their country stood for. Memorizing them made for better citizens: "Reflect on the fortunes and accidents which befall men and kings, for if you are mindful of the past you will plan better for the future." History keeps the tablets. "Tell me what eloquence," Isocrates had said, "could be more righteous or more just than one which praises our ancestors in a manner worthy of their excellence and of their achievements." This routine wasn't just political; it was cultural. It claimed an inheritance. For, even then, the ideal was not just the freethinking man, but the truly cultured man, one who had earned, by knowledge and loyalty, a place within the ranks of those fit to be citizens — and perhaps even a seat among the rulers. Once again are we reminded that one cannot be born into a culture of the higher kind, automatically equipped with all its watchwords and prerogatives. One grows into it and is formed by it.

All of this is the stuff of humanistic culture. If we wish to discover the genesis of the West's civilizing ideal, as well as the origins of classical education, we look more profitably perhaps to Isocrates than to Plato and Aristotle, for it is Isocrates who represents "the original fountainhead of the whole great current of humanist scholarship." He is the source, as Werner Jaeger said, of this humanistic culture, calling attention to the

preserved verbal artifacts of his day as both defining and formative. He taught all who came after that anyone, before he can
be called civilized, has to read his culture's books. The curriculum of humane schooling began to take shape with Isocrates.
The idea of a canon arose for the first time: that is, a body of
written works acting as passwords to culture with which all of
the educated were expected to be familiar. Ideals became less
idiosyncratic and more public. For the Greeks and Romans
both, education was "essentially an initiation into the Greek
way of life, molding the child and the adolescent in accordance
with the national customs and submitting him to a particular
style of living — the style that distinguished man from the
brutes, Greeks from the barbarians" (Marrou). Theirs became a
bookish culture. And neither brutes nor barbarians can read.

Here we see that a key purpose of education is a fundamentally conservative — or preservative — one. Education should
preserve and transmit the past so that cultural memory
is lengthened, and so that descendents will not be left to
rediscover human truths already endured and expressed by eloquent forebears. This was the spirit of the Hellenistic age, a preservative epoch when "men's aim everywhere was...to keep
poetry alive [rather] than to challenge the great masters" (W. W.
Tarn). Originality was not prized so much as reverence. Great
libraries were established at Rhodes, Antioch, and Pergamum,
the greatest one at the Greek city of Alexandria in Egypt, containing hundreds of thousands of papyri rolls. Philology — the
science of language — was launched at Mytilene, textual criticism at Ephesus. The Alexandrians put in place the rules of
Greek accentuation that continue to ease our reading of the
texts. Men studied the admired works of the past and strove to
imitate them. Here, in this period of assimilation, the difference
between learning-for-culture and learning-for-skills is most

sharp. It's not that the ancients cared nothing for practical skills or for what we call "critical thinking." But anyone systematically exposed to the best that's been thought and said will also analyze it, cutting his intellectual teeth on the minds that brought it forth. Acquiring culture under this rigid regime, though, comes by the avenue of literary learning.

Universal agreement did not obtain on all vital matters. Isocrates argued with some in the Socratic school over whether virtue can be taught entirely. Plato thought it could. Isocrates did not, believing a "sound judgment" to be the proper and realistic aim; the best one could hope to do is to point up the finest examples in the annals of virtuous thoughts and deeds. (Later the Roman philosopher Seneca took Isocrates' side: the teacher cannot instill virtue; he can only prepare the mind for it.) Isocrates' plan, though, best perpetuated the memory of culture. It came to be called "rhetorical," as it aimed to train men who would lead people not by force but by moral suasion. This was a new aristocracy, the *aristoi* of the knowing and eloquent. The orators set out in turn to train "logographers," writers of speeches. It is speech, after all, that separates man from the beasts. By speech man is able to reflect and to relate his reflections. The power of words suits him for a life lived *sub specie aeternitatis*, for all time. Knowledge was not for him a matter of gnostic exclusivity but the sum of contemplated experience. And it was there to be told. One finds, Isocrates said, that "among our public men who are living today...those who give most study to the art of words are the best statesmen who come before you on the rostrum, and, furthermore, that among the ancients it was the greatest and the most illustrious orators who brought to the city most of her blessings." The Word reigned.

■   ■   ■

The Greeks and Romans not only gave birth to Western civilization, they bequeathed to us their categories of thought and models of action. They bestowed a vocabulary for the inquisitive and just mind. They laid the foundations of culture in Jaeger's second, fuller sense — *the conscious ideal of human perfection* — by defining more sharply the "good life" worthy of a free man, a man unfettered by servile obligations to other masters, one who had been trained to use his mind by ordering his affections, and by learning to ask the right questions of the world around him. This man, at once independent and civilized, became the model of the Humanist. Liberal education and its rational, humanizing ideal traces its roots back to the rocky soil of Attica and the straight ways of Rome.

"Man is an ideal-forming animal," wrote historian W. G. de Burgh, "stirred at every stage of his development by aspirations which transcend the level of his actual attainment; and his civilization, at any given epoch, comprises also the world of his religious, moral, and economic values, his intellectual outlook upon life, his personal beliefs as to his function and destiny, his standards of moral goodness and social welfare. It is in the light of such ideals, determining our conception of human progress, that we distinguish civilization from barbarism."

Or at least we used to. Life is unknown and unknowable without intellectual depth. And despite the changes wrought by centuries, the education of the free mind has changed little in form; it has kept its anchorage. Objectives have shifted through time — Man is the measure of all things in one century, God in the next. Yet two elements of this cultural legacy — one mental, one material — have been handed down to us in trust: first, the belief that the human mind is capable of apprehending the truth and second — though much was lost — a solid corpus of ancient writing that has ensured the survival of classical learning. It's all there for us to enjoy and pass on. This heritage has kept before our eyes *the habitual vision of greatness.*

The beacon shines still, though it flickers. We are not especially keen to preserve anything nowadays. Culture is cheap, where not completely degraded. We can only guess what the ancients might think of *us*. With our rockets shooting off to moons, planets, and other pieces of celestial driftwood, we might assume their breathless wonder. But W. H. Auden might have been onto something when he wrote that "the bewildered comment of any fifth century Athenian upon our society from Dante's time till our own...would surely be: 'Yes, I can see all the works of a great civilization; but why cannot I meet any civilized persons? I only encounter specialists, artists who know nothing of science, scientists who know nothing of art, philosophers who have no interest in God, priests who are unconcerned with politics, politicians who only know other politicians.'" For anyone who knows the Western tradition and the bright lights emanating from it down the centuries, Auden's guess would seem as plausible as any other. Somehow we are no longer large enough or whole enough to embrace so much of the world.

Diogenes Laertius, writing in the third century A.D., celebrated the value of a civilization that exalts the feat of individual cultivation as the highest earthly attainment in his oft-repeated tale of the Megaran philosopher Stilpo. Demetrius Poliorcetes wished to restore Stilpo's fortunes after the pillage of Megara, and he asked Stilpo to count up what he had lost. Stilpo replied that he lacked nothing that had belonged to him before, for he retained his culture, his *paideia*, and he was still clothed with learning and eloquence to see him through life. Quiet confidence such as that our anxious age seeks in vain. It's an echo from a stronger, clearer, bracing age. And it haunts us. Our curious view that changing times must always alter or overtake hard-won wisdom, of course, would have amused a man like Stilpo, who saw man's short sojourn on earth primarily as a time for cultivation; we're here to tend our gardens. He would have looked quizzically upon any epoch endlessly re-inventing the wheel, searching for happiness where better minds and spirits have already discovered it cannot be found. Stilpo might see in ours an accomplished world, but not a wise one. He might see a comfortable people, a smart and ingenious people, but perhaps not a free people.

TWO

Prospect from the
Castalian Spring

A usonius of Bordeaux, a Roman rhetorician and tutor
to the young Emperor Gratian, had climbed
Parnassus during his youth. The muse of Poetry had
lit upon this man of public affairs. Literary forms and images
arising from Greece and Rome bedecked his mind. The classical
legacy flowed through his veins. For even as a Christian, he had
taken a Roman rhetorical education of the old stamp. But when
his public fortunes declined after the murder of the emperor in
383, he spent his retiring years in sumptuous and quiet cultivation, nesting on the green banks of the Garonne, etching erudite epigrams, learned letters, and bucolic lines on the natural
beauty of his valley. While Ausonius was to be one of the last
men of letters to emerge from the classical world, the literary
and cultural tradition of that world held for many decades to
come. And culture held with it. That tradition, though, eventually retreated with the Legions. By the early fifth century,
Paulinus of Pella, a grandson of Ausonius, looked out on the
twilight of the Roman Empire and lamented a fate destined to

burden educated people down the many long centuries to follow. "To have to learn two languages at once is all right for the
clever ones and gives excellent results," he wrote, "but for an
average mind like mine such dispersion of effort soon becomes
very tiring."

His grumble echoes down the corridor of years. Paulinus
too wondered why this high threshold, this *doctrina duplex*, this
"ante-chamber of learning," as German reformer Philip
Melanchthon called it, stood before the gilded gates leading to
intellectual respect and renown. Sweating over these two languages seemed a high price to pay for civilization. The two languages of course were Greek and Latin, the one at that time the
language of high culture, the other the native vehicle of admin-
istration and law for a far-flung empire, yet a tongue that itself
had become a powerful literary language of great subtlety. Here
they stood, nearly a thousand years before the Renaissance, high
and columnar, already bearing up a fortified edifice of learning
and tradition.

Together Greek and Latin constituted a lingua franca for
the educated, one that endured for well over a millennium that
witnessed colossal turns in the life of the Western world. Indeed
they survived the very nations to which they had once given
voice. The classical languages stood as a sign — and, some
thought, a guarantor — of permanence. They must have seemed
sculpted from Parian marble. But by 1834, as another epoch
reconsidered this legacy and entertained more modern cultural
goals, the English headmaster *par excellence* Thomas Arnold
sounded alarms. "Expel Greek and Latin from your schools," he
wrote, "and you confine the views of the existing generation to
themselves and their immediate predecessors; you will cut off so
many centuries of the world's experience, and...place us in the
same state as if the human race had come into existence in the

year 1500." (If we bear in mind the desultory state of education today, this alternative no longer shocks us: we should be grateful now, and many of us would settle, for a historical memory reaching back so far.) Between these two statements of Paulinus and Arnold — one plaintive, one magisterial — lie fourteen centuries of civilized life, during which time the classical inheritance was set to performing divers tasks, both sacred and secular. That legacy proved to be elastic, but its value was little assailed. History offers few instances of such a consensus on intellectual aims, and therefore on cultural requisites. Only during the last few generations has that consensus broken down.

Whence came this bold and formidable idea, tempered by experience and confirmed by the ages, that a human being in the West must run his paces with these two difficult, archaic languages and their literatures in order to deem himself properly educated? Greek and Latin have played the troll under the bridge, jealously guarding access not only to classical learning but also to wider intellectual distinction. They lent the password. What were the sources of such belief and practice? With little amazement do we discover that the foundations were laid in the Greco-Roman world itself. What were those distant peoples trying to accomplish in their classrooms?

■　　■　　■

The Greeks and Romans steered their education by ideas we now condemn as regressive. School was a grinding, sometimes bitter experience, with nary a finger lifted to sweeten the pill. Children began their education at home, where training in literacy walked hand in hand, as we have seen, with the inculcation of cultural ideals and habits of upright character. Parents and tutors worked hard, as Plato wrote, so that "each child may excel, and as each act and word occurs, they teach and impress upon him that this is just, and that unjust, one thing noble, another base, one holy, another unholy, and that his is to do this, and not do that." And when the children have "learnt their letters and are getting to understand the written word as before they did only the spoken, [they] are furnished with works of good poets to read as they sit in class, and are made to learn them off by heart: here they meet with many admonitions, many descriptions and praises and eulogies of good men in times past, that the boy in envy may imitate them and yearn to become even as they." Children were not to be brought out of their shells; they were to be shown the consequential, the true, the beautiful.

Round about the age of seven they were carted off to school to learn their letters and numbers more deliberately under a teacher of grammar. Now came constant, pulverizing drill and numbing recitation, with no adult concerned apparently about a deadening effect upon a child's creativity or individuality. Later on adolescents went to a *grammatikos*, who built on these skills and raised his pupils to a higher plane, pounding into his charges the already familiar cadences and winged imagery of the greatest poets of Greece, Homer and Hesiod. Homer in fact was the first and preeminent poet learned. Deservedly had he been crowned as the "educator of Greece." To know Homer was to be a Greek, a Hellene.

Literary education — which classical education was from the beginning — naturally exalts poetry, the highest purpose for which words can be employed. But first one must pass through Grammar, which encompassed a good deal more for the ancients than for us, including not just the parts of speech, morphology, and syntax, but also the systematic study of literature. Still, we might ask, what about that pursuit we call "appreciation"? Literature, it may seem, simply is not literature at all unless it be appreciated and admired. How much latitude was the average student likely to be lent when responding to Homer? Very little. With the *grammatikos* students learned to understand and explain what they read, not to "respond" to it. Their opinions were worthless. Students were not to appreciate what they read and memorized, at least not immediately. Their job was simply to learn it, the guiding rule being that the best appreciation follows only upon sure knowledge, and from knowledge arises understanding. Merely subjective responses lacked the value assigned to them in our day. The student was too young and inexperienced to have a response any learned adult was bound to recognize; "right" response came with maturity. The teacher sought to make a student who could elucidate, not criticize. "The greatest part of a man's education," according to Plato, "[is] to be skilled in the matter of verses; that is, to be able to apprehend, in the utterances of the poets, what has been rightly and what wrongly composed, and to know how to distinguish them and account for them when questioned."

Here was brass tacks schooling, no-frills and rigorous, where the student was set to acquiring a body of knowledge — in this case, literary and cultural knowledge. No one bothered about what we call skills of "critical thinking," which came naturally to anyone successfully navigating this course of study. Critical thinking was a result, not a target, of classical education. As we know it today, criticism, social and otherwise, did indeed play a role in Greek society, and even a tightly controlled role in Greek and Roman education, but its wider practice remained the privilege of an august few. Criticism, of which our notion of appreciation is a distant cousin, was rightly viewed as "the last fruit of ripe experience," as Longinus wrote. It was a high calling and a high attainment. The student's job was to gather the seeds of culture and sow them. Over time, he would ripen his experience. The goal was to know and preserve. Just as it is now, Grammar was about skill, but this skill was not a superfluous one. Without thorough mastery of Grammar, progress in the life of the mind was unthinkable. (Today we think that thought with abandon.)

A training in Rhetoric, the art of persuasion and eloquence, might last until a young man's twenties, and its pursuit made up what we now call "higher education." It was the finishing school for the articulate. To speak well was the indispensable ability — and unmistakable sign — of the educated man, whose upper education had instilled *recte loquendi scientia*, the knowledge of correct speaking. A man donned his education with the words he used. We recognize classical culture now not only by alabaster images of stony ruins, but also through thick gauze of verbal brilliance. The men whose words and ideas we remember best were citizens of a republic of letters. They had learned to think and speak and write with precision and flair. They tried not to say something new; they tried to say something worthy, and to say it perfectly.

And such people ran the culture. Although the Hellenistic age saw the birth of the textbook and the codification of rules, ancient usage of language in the West was determined not by arbitrary dictates of grammarians but by the habits of the educated. This was the common route usage traveled through history till modern times, when latitudinarian ideology has sought to iron out all speech on a flat plane of equality. Intelligent men and women of the classical world did broaden the field of accepted usage with new words and new turns of phrase, and did so constantly, but not until they had learned the correct and accepted usage of the best authors. ("Correct" grammar and usage are always matters of consolidation. What distinguishes them in our time is their source of authority: namely, nearly anyone who opens his mouth.) The standard was set not by the man in the street, but by the man in the forum. Privileges of speech were public ones. Guardianship of language was needful for a cohesive culture where all wished to be both eloquent and readily understood. Cicero prescribed correct, aptly rhythmic speech, which he doubtless would have learned at the knees of tutors, and Seneca later referred to teachers as "custodians" of the language. The very purpose of these schools, in the words of M. L. Clarke, was to produce "men with a ready command of words, who could delight and entertain their listeners by their elegant style and mellifluous delivery." The result, wrote H. I. Marrou, was "an 'oratorical' kind of education, which in appearance is entirely a matter of aesthetics, whose one aim is to create 'wizards with words,' [and which] is in fact the most effective way of developing subtlety of thought." Standards of thought and expression, while evolving, were clear to all educated people; at least no one questioned the role of standards themselves. Culture requires them — even as it languishes without them.

Greek and Roman adults memorized their reading no less than their children. Scarcity of books may explain the origin of the practice, but such does not account completely for the literary passions of the educated. These were people always quoting someone, usually someone both wiser and more eloquent. Culture was clubby. "We have only to glance through the pages of the ancient authors," Marrou wrote, "to realize how real and all-pervading was the presence of the poets in the lives of well-read men. In conversation, in private correspondence, in the serious situations of life that call for 'famous sayings,' always and everywhere the right word could be found — it was expected, welcomed, and regarded as indispensable."

No doubt this aptitude and habit, this thirst and hunger for the *mot juste*, paid off. When and where copied material was not so easily procured, much of what was known collectively dwelled in people's heads, and that which they remembered made up the furniture of their minds. They lived with it. For those who memorize take permanent custody. And this custody confirmed their citizenship within that culture. Heroes defined virtues, poets conveyed beauty, and their examples were impressed indelibly upon the public mind by the words that armed and ornamented them. Knowledge became personal, intimate, not merely a dry intellectual exercise. Poetry could sing in their heads. Not only did they live with it; they lived by it. When we join this pedagogical attack to the yen for correctness in speech, we can divine how far, for better and for worse, we have swerved from classical ideals.

The routine of the classroom would not invite a modern temperament inured to softer methods. Discipline was harsh. The teacher was supreme in power before students; when not leading the class in unison recitation, he lectured authoritatively, even dictatorially. The study of a particular poem, for instance, would begin with a *praelectio*, a preface of explanation, perhaps a few words about the poet, his importance, and the virtues he exemplified. (This stage might also include a summary form of textual criticism where the teacher may offer corrections in passages when versions differed, as they often did in the ages before printing.) Next came the actual reading, the *lectio*, where pupils likely practiced declaiming properly, or reading aloud for mellifluous effect. Then came exegesis, or the *enarratio*, where the text was carefully explained, cases and conjugations examined, with the teacher providing glosses of unfamiliar words. Finally came the judgment of quality, *iudicium*, passed

by the teacher, usually taking the form not only of literary judgment — the literary merit may be assumed by the work's nest
in the curriculum — but also of moral reinforcement.

We may be shocked to discover that the original humanities course was marked by such relentlessly objective dryness.
Little wonder that classical education came to carry doleful associations of aridity. But once again, knowledge and refinement
were the pearls of great price, not soft exposures leaving the
poem perpetually out of focus, its value and significance forever
indeterminate. Students were invited inside the poem, but they
had to enter by doors already marked by wiser minds.
Experience knew best.

Quintilian once wrote that not even literary merit was sufficient to bestow value on a literary work, for "unformed minds
which are liable to be more deeply impressed by what they learn
in their days of childish ignorance must learn not merely what
is elegant," they must also study that which is "morally excellent." It was he — following the lead of Cato — who proclaimed the ideal Roman orator to be *vir bonus dicendi peritus*, the
good man skilled in speaking. An essay attributed to Plutarch
fastened upon the link between mental training and moral
behavior, asserting that "there must be a concurrence of three
things to produce right action: nature, reason, and habit. By
reason I mean the act of learning, and by habit constant practice. The first beginnings come from nature, advancement from
learning, the practical use from constant repetition, and the culmination from all combined. So far as any of these is wanting,
the moral excellence must, to this extent, be crippled."
Restraint was a moral good. Horace suited this idea in poetical
armor: "The poet fashions the tender, lisping lips of childhood;
even then he turns the ear from unseemly words; presently, too,
he moulds the heart by kindly precepts, correcting roughness

and envy and anger. He tells of noble deeds, equips the rising age with famous examples, and to the helpless and sick at heart brings comfort." Virgil described how a statesman might stand before a riotous crowd and, "with virtue and high service crowned," alleviate their distemper: "His words their minds control, their passions soothe." There was no divorce of the public and private. Sentiments like these children took in almost with their mother's milk. Their earliest lessons contained moral admonitions couched in precise, elegant language, examples of moral virtue matched to the finest expressions.

So the teaching was strict, the learning hard. But waiting at the far end of the journey would be civilized human beings, citizens who had learned what their culture was about and what it needed to conserve. It may be telling that we do not find many instances in the ancient world of pupils set to writing their own poems: their task was not to express themselves, but to bow humbly at the feet of others. They were apprentices. They were to know, not to be known. We can see why "classical culture did not know any romantic need to make all things new, to forget the past and be original," as Marrou put it. That is not where greatness lay. For "the purpose of living properly, what we need is not new and surprising ideas but established good sense, traditional wisdom." The boon of all this was not hidden in the bracken; such a schooling "imposed a standard literary culture based on a few recognized classical poets" who had defined and expressed the highest ideals of life and excellences of language. "The well-organized educational system of the [Roman] Empire," wrote historian R. R. Bolgar, "had for its main aim to teach the two literary languages and to inculcate in the minds of all its pupils the established methods and desirability of imitation." Here was not a recipe for an atomized society of self-centered individuals, but one for unity of culture, providing a form of education that made such elusive unity attainable, a reasonable prospect. Yet the method was sober in its high demands. When aims are pitched high, even a partial failure may lead to ultimate success. The climb itself builds muscles, even if we don't reach the top. Out of this disposition of mind classical education arose.

Classical education thus begins to reveal a few of its stony outcroppings. Underlying its method is, first, a certain belief that learning is a hard, intractable affair and resistant to attempts to smooth the edges in order to make it otherwise and, second, another belief that its fruits ought to serve more than the individual — while never doing less. Anything worth knowing comes to be known at a price, often an exacting one paid over many years. The consequences reach far. People have a common culture. And, as Jacques Barzun has written, a culture of the classical kind strives for "fixed grandeur, dignity, authority, and high polish; while in the individual it produces morality and peace by showing him that values are rooted in the universe, rather than dependent upon his fallible and changing judgment." This is the essence of classical Humanism.

We find contrasts to our own time to be unforgiving. They should not be shoved aside. For Greeks and Romans, the fully grown adult set the standard, not the child. For the ancients were marked, as Marrou wrote, by an "utter lack of interest in child psychology." Theirs were not "child-centered" societies, and because of this they violate modern dogmas. Yet perhaps the jury still sits. For we "should not be too much in a hurry to crow about this and dismiss the Greeks' [and Romans'] attitude as outmoded ignorance," Marrou has admonished us.

In a culture as refined as theirs, and which in so many other fields has given so much evidence of great creative genius, such apparent ignorance must be regarded as deliberate, the expression of an implicit, perhaps, but nevertheless quite definite rejection of what it did not include.... What is the point, they seem to say, of concentrating on the child as though he were an end in himself? Apart from the few unlucky children who are condemned to a premature death, the only point of childhood is that it leads to manhood, and the proper object of education is therefore not any slobbering child or awkward adolescent or even an up-and-coming young man, but Man, and Man alone; and the only point of education is to teach the child to transcend himself.

This may be to us a harsh, Draconian view, but it would not have seemed so to any sophisticated mind till recent times. It is wrong only by modern measuring rods, which history might yet judge to be faulty.

Classical Humanism held that a learned mind, however many or however few people social circumstance may permit to achieve it — and make no mistake, the classical world was a class society — was arduously cultivated. Its fruits were earned; they were not a right bestowed. Little wonder then that such a society should produce an elite: not all people could achieve the ideal. Subjected to a modern test of equality, the Greco-Roman world fails utterly. But if the highest exemplars of Humanism were with us in the flesh, they might judge us to be failing an even higher test. Our idea of equality they might see to deny human nature; most certainly does it deny cultural nature. A society unable to discriminate cannot judge the higher and the lower — and a "classical" culture requires "a unified collection of great masterpieces existing as the recognized basis of its scale of values" (Marrou). Classically educated people gain the power to ascribe value, simply because they have been exposed thoroughly, systematically, to the best.

"Or so goes the theory," we might say. Precisely. But there must be a theoretical underpinning to any widely employed regimen, for every intelligent practice a paradigm. To rebut this vision with the simplistic observation that it did not always work is puerile. Ideals are not elected, or ought not to be, by their guarantee of assured achievement: that is the demand of a slave, a vulgarian of whatever class. Ideals should be chosen according to what a society hopes to become, for man is indeed that "ideal-forming animal." Ideals determine, and sustain, culture.

■   ■   ■

The long odyssey of Greek and Latin down the ages had begun. They proved to be resilient conveyors of classical civilization. Latin, as the language of law and *imperium*, made for cultural unity, its lapidary grandeur raising it far above the regional tongues evolving throughout the Dark and Middle Ages. Latin acted as a pan-European language. The Roman Catholic Church baptized it as the language of faith in the West — a legacy made possible by the long arm of the Roman Empire — with momentous consequences for the future of classical letters. Ancient Greek, though destined for hibernation as the language of deep learning in the West from the end of the Roman period to the fifteenth century, had claimed the crown long before as the queen of philosophical and literary languages. The *koine*, or common, dialect was spoken by much of the Roman world, including many in early Christian settlements dotting the Mediterranean. The Gospels were penned first for that world in Greek, as were the Epistles of St. Paul. The early Church's councils were conducted in Greek. The Christian Fathers communicated naturally in this tongue that, despite

Roman power, served as the true international language of the Roman period. Greek-speaking Jews read their Scriptures in the (Greek) Septuagint. Centuries later, according to a nineteenth-century historian, Greek remained "the means of blending Oriental [i.e., Eastern] with Western modes of thought," wedding the exotic to the familiar. (The protracted loss of Greek cut off the West from first-hand fluency with its treasures, a loss not repaired until the floodtide of the Renaissance.)

Greek and Latin had chronicled the ascent of civilized life, recording its twists and turns, its triumphs and disgraces. By the fall of the Roman Empire, they provided a microchip storing the wisdom and folly of a thousand years. They told the tales later generations would repeat and embellish. So long as they survived, so survived the glories of the past. But their voyage through the centuries to come was choppy.

The Roman Catholic Church not only sustained Latin but also became the beacon of learning in the Dark Ages, preserving — and sometimes expurgating — classical riches, hoarding them away in distant monasteries. "Libraries were armories of the Church: grammar was part of her drill," wrote historian Charles Stuart Parker. But this was later. Early on the Church had not been so friendly to pagan knowledge. Educated clergy and laymen took sides in the tussle between secular learning and sacred purity. Tertullian, a Church Father of the second and third centuries, claimed the Scriptures as the only source of authority on spiritual matters — for which of course the scholar also needed Hebrew. Tertullian suspected the infections of secular philosophy and rhetoric; he could not countenance a Christian teaching in Roman schools, where the Christian teacher was bound to keep the feast of Minerva and to speak of scandalizing Greco-Roman mythology. His search for a middle way reveals the awkwardness that the wealth of classical learning presented to the Church. Nonetheless, this austere orator recognized the superiority of Roman rhetorical education. "How otherwise," Tertullian asked, "could anyone acquire human wisdom, or learn to direct his thoughts and actions? Is literature not an indispensable instrument for the whole business of life?" Gregory the Great, though also suspicious of classical knowledge, later made formal the idea that secular learning, while perhaps dangerous to Christian theology and morality alike, still helped the devout "to sharpen their spiritual weapons."

The compromise was bumpy at first. During the age of St. Jerome and St. Augustine in the fourth and fifth centuries, learned Christian men were of two minds, as though teetering between two worlds, which in a sense they were. St. Augustine complained of some men being more mindful of the rules of grammar than of the laws of God — an intellectual tilt Augustine himself shared before his own conversion. Christians, he said, must be "unafraid of the grammarian's rod": their comfort lay elsewhere. St. Basil proclaimed himself the disciple of fishermen, and therefore spoke and wrote proudly to the masses in simpler, less rarefied dialects. But the cultural imperatives still tugged. These were educated men. When St. Jerome retreated to the deserts of Syria to cut himself off from the dusty secular miasma in order to embrace pure contemplation, he lugged along books of classical authors. There he dreamed that, upon death, and when he was taken before God and he claimed the discipleship of Christ, God answered: "It is false. You are a Ciceronian. Where your treasure is, there is also your heart." But however much that nightmare might have gnawed at his conscience, St. Jerome remained enthralled to the beauty of classical literature.

Indeed the treasure trove of classical knowledge proved too

great to leave to dust and ashes. Not even the saints could deny its power and efficacy. Even after his conversion, St. Augustine had credited Cicero's (now lost) dialogue *Hortensius* with inspiring him to take the high road of philosophy that eventually led him to Christian faith. Paganism and Christianity might have been spiritual enemies when they first struggled for souls, but the intellectual culture of the pagan world found ready devotees in educated Christians intoxicated by its riches. The Catechetical School of Alexandria typifies this *rapprochement* between classical and Christian learning. At first a school to prepare new converts for baptism, it later came to offer a broader, more liberal course of instruction under Clement and Origen in the third and fourth centuries. The course began, according to one historian, with "a training in grammar and logic, followed by a thorough grounding in geometry, physics and astronomy, leading up to a comparative treatment of philosophy and especially of ethics...culminating in a careful study of the Scriptures." And the deal was struck. Except for the last item, this curriculum could have been found in any sophisticated pagan school in any civilized city in the Mediterranean in the closing years of the Roman Empire. Succeeding centuries would see the founding of many such schools. Religious faith was gradually joined, if shakily, to classical learning. Slowly were Christians integrated back into pagan culture, not to be reclaimed by paganism, but to reap the best that classical culture had sown. Christians christened the classical heritage. Secular learning, along with the crumbling manuscripts preserving it, was saved by the Church.

•   ■   •

Devotion to classical study did not cling solely to the sunburnt lands of the Mediterranean from which it rose from the cradle. The frontier reached to the ends of the known world. Making herself a most unlikely safe house for the classical inheritance, Ireland sheltered monks who copied manuscripts and trained the clergy destined to spread Christianity to other wet, craggy, and wind-whipped places within the British Isles, bringing in tow high literary culture as well. They discharged their duty with exuberance. The Venerable Bede wrote in his *Ecclesiastical History* of young scholars who spirited their enthusiasm and learning to the cold and rainy lands of the far north — indeed to the very edge of civilization itself:

> Since they were both deeply learned in sacred and profane letters alike, they gathered round them a band of disciples whose hearts they daily refreshed with the waters of healthful knowledge, teaching their hearers the rules of metric, astronomy, and the computus as well as the works of the saints. The proof of this is that we can find pupils even today [eighth century] who know Latin and Greek as accurately as their own mother tongue.

Latin coursed down the Dark Ages into the High Middle Ages as a flourishing language, in some ways just as vital as it had been when chiseled by the sharp styli of Cicero. The Catholic Church had long since made it a tool of unity amongst fragmented peoples with their own emerging vernaculars. But it was no longer the same tongue it had been in Roman times; it was growing and exfoliating. New words found their way into the lexicon, while some old ones got blotted out. Throughout the Middle Ages, wrote Parker, "Cicero did less to form style than Jerome; Plato was forgotten in favor of Augustine; Aristotle alone, translated out of Greek into Syriac, out of Syriac into Arabic, out of Arabic into Latin, and in Latin purged of everything offensive to the medieval mind, had become in the folios of Thomas Aquinas a buttress, if not a pillar, of the Christian Church." Not even theology escaped classics.

Theology, though, did not inspire every impulse to recover and learn. Pockets of men, here and there, partook of the sweetness of poetry. Many a monk in a placid, cloistered monastery garden across Europe in the ninth and tenth centuries would come to take delight in pagan fancies shining from newly rediscovered manuscript pages of epic and lyric poetry, such as that of Virgil, already redolent of august antiquity. Perspicacious minds came to see that the classical heritage was not only to be learned. It was also to be savored. Lyric poetry kept the scent on the rose of Latin. Thus we might trace Humanism, and the poetic sensibility that it fed, to the ninth through twelfth centuries rather than to the fourteenth through sixteenth. Here was a furtive renaissance. For even with the growth of Italian, French, German, Spanish, and English, Latin served almost alone as the language of culture during those early centuries. Latin was the language of churchmen, clerks, men at court, and consequently it was the official tongue of the universities born during the Middle Ages. Few knew it, by our standards, and fewer still knew it well, but it was the chief language to know. "Text-books were in Latin, lectures were in Latin...and the use of Latin was compulsory in all forms of student intercourse," wrote historian Charles Homer Haskins. "Thus in the Middle Ages," wrote Parker, "Latin was made the groundwork of education; not for the beauty of its classical literature, nor because the study of a dead language was the best mental gymnastic, or the only means of acquiring a masterly freedom in the use of living tongues, but because it was the language of educated men throughout Europe, employed for public business, literature, philosophy, and science.... [It was] essential to the unity, and therefore enforced by the authority, of the Western Church." That age producing the Gothic cathedrals and genius on the scale of Anselm, Abelard, and Aquinas — not to forget the vernacular glory of Dante — was no mean epoch, a glorious age by almost any measure.

Yet with the waning of the Middle Ages came a reaction to the newfangled Latin. Some saw it as a specialized language emerging neither out of Church nor court, but from the obscure metaphysical Scholasticism of the Schools, the great universities: Paris, Bologna, Orleans, Oxford, Cambridge. Latin had grown all right, but usage had become crabbed, rendering it even more inaccessible to the unversed. Intellectual ferment beset the West in the Middle Ages, and perhaps Scholastic theologians and students may be forgiven for running roughshod over the language of Virgil and St. Augustine in hot pursuit of an encyclopedic, metaphysical understanding. Grammar was neglected, logic exalted. And, as can happen readily whenever intellectuals hold the reins, an impenetrable jargon took hold amongst the educated that excluded all who had not read the same books and attended the same lectures. School usage had created a new language, one dense and inelegant and useless for conveying any idea or sentiment not sung with syllogisms. This language, many believed, was no longer aesthetically pleasing. Thus did some people come to view this period, despite the great watermark it left on the Western mind, as one of decadence marked by the opaque argot of tonsured scholars. *Oxoniensis loquendi mos*, the "Oxford way of speaking" in murky philosophical shorthand, became a term of reproach against a fallen standard of Latin.

Many thought that the linguistic house wanted cleaning. Poets and other stylists with bents more literary than philosophical gladly took up the job. A groundswell grew. Much was brought in, much swept away. For these house cleaners were to be the prime movers of the Renaissance, that luminous epoch viewed even today, however simplistically, through sepia-tinted lenses as a second springtime for the classical world, a rosy-fingered morning when ancient voices long stilled piped out for the first time since the sun had set on the Roman Empire.

■   ■   ■

Thus dawned the age of Renaissance Humanism. The Italian Renaissance has been labeled a time when classical education itself was invented. This is partly true, for it was then, with the birth of what came to be called the New Learning, that the classical pursuit took the shape it kept largely until the nineteenth century. But we must tread carefully. History is rarely that simple. Almost every fresh turn inspired by the likes of Dante, Petrarch, and Boccaccio — figures of the late medieval and early Renaissance worlds — finds some antecedent in earlier centuries. John of Salisbury, a cultivated man of the twelfth century, used incidents from ancient history to render moral judgments, an act typifying the Renaissance more than the Middle Ages in the common imagination. Nonetheless, a shift in sensibility sharpened in the fourteenth and fifteenth centuries. A bracing revival was afoot; it was not so much a bold step into the future as a look back over the shoulder to classical days, to what was considered a clearer, more humane age, a time far removed from the cloistered ways of the Schoolmen and the gritty internecine cruelties of warring Italian cities. Whereas before this period we can spot the bare beginnings of Humanism — in the Latin lyrics of itinerant scholars and in the zealous copying of secular manuscripts during the Carolingian

Renaissance — it was in the High Renaissance that the cult of antiquity, the "religion" of Humanism and classical culture, blossomed.

Whatever else we might say about the Renaissance, however humble and complex its origins, and however much education remained the province of the privileged few, we must not fail to recognize it as a wide-ranging, if not exactly popular, movement. Its fruits nourished many people beyond the libraries and *scriptoria* of scholars and clerks locked away in the Schools and monasteries, chopping metaphysical logic and — as some thought — butchering Cicero's Latin. Ancient writings were dragged from the cell to bask in the sunshine. The Greek texts of Aristotle began to be unearthed and read again in their Attic purity; Plato's dialogues again vibrated in men's minds. Other changes redounded to the benefit of the many. A vernacular language like Italian matured to near perfection in the hands of Dante and Petrarch. Literary life abounded. Architecture changed. But there is no doubt that this period, roughly from 1400 to 1600, saw the elevation of all things Greek and Roman in literature, thought, and art. The Romans had shown the way. For, as M. L. Clarke put it, "humanist education, with its emphasis on literature, oratory and morality, can be thought of as a return to Rome." And the journey home started in the schools.

The Italian Renaissance, that sunlit, colonnaded world of Leo Battista Alberti, was an unashamedly imitative era. Poets, scholars, and teachers set out to copy classical forms in the literary and plastic arts. And with imitation always comes prescription, those codified rules measuring the success or failure of any literary or artistic effort. We find in the enlightened precincts of Florence a turn from scholastic theology and metaphysics to literature, ethics, and politics. Man was the measure of all things once again. In the fifteenth century, Giovanni Pico della Mirandola wrote his *Oration on the Dignity of Man*, a paean to the God-given spirit dwelling within each human being, a view of humanity born of an optimistic age. And men of the Renaissance sought the purer texts of the ancients to support their intellectual and aesthetic conversion; they needed scriptures for the new faith. Along with their learned forebears of the Dark and Middle Ages, they strained to recover and edit classical texts lost for centuries in dusty stacks, seeking the complete originals instead of the copies and *florilegia* (anthologies) produced by scribes of prior days. They would drink at the wellspring. They were driven to collect, authenticate, interpret, and apply. They were out to reclaim a birthright.

Schoolmasters taught young people not only the ways of God, but also officiated over their initiation rites into the classics, making the classical inheritance a living presence in the lives of their charges. As the classical scholar R. M. Ogilvie once observed, in fourteenth- and fifteenth-century Italy, "the merchant class was seeking a new ideal: the ideal of a cultivated layman independent of the Church or of noble birth." To be fed were not clerical scholars only, nor even just the sons and daughters of the nobility, but eventually the children of the burgeoning commercial class. One could begin to escape the disadvantages of lower birth with a thoroughgoing classical education.

These new men dedicated themselves to rhetorical and literary pursuits. They didn't exalt the ambiguities of theological speculation; they stressed the attainable in human thought and action, that which could be learned by the talented — and the loftier their models the better. They rededicated themselves to the classical ideal of humane learning described by the likes of Cicero, Aulus Gellius, and that schoolmaster for all ages, Quintilian, whose complete treatise on education, the *Institutio*

Oratoria, was recovered in 1416. During these days "classical" education became synonymous with "humanistic" education, and the highest in human achievement inspired its curricula, courses of study which were rarely uniform from place to place, yet which often employed the same core of ancient authors and works. Petrarch hearkened to Roman criteria when in 1367 he proclaimed that, properly pursued, *studia humanitatis*, or the study of man, made the learner good, not just learned. Training the character once more became, in classical fashion, the guiding imperative of education, but now with a twist: union with God was not replaced, but enhanced, by the classical ideals of *virtus et fama*, virtue and fame. The gentleman who had learned the lessons — moral and stylistic — that the ancient world had to teach could build upon that capital, not as a huckster hawking his wares, but as an enlightened follower, a knight errant in quest of a lost world. Fame might greet the poet or orator, for this was a time when literary accomplishment might bestow a crown of laurel on the head of the man who had proved himself most deft with ideals and the words that clothed them. Once more, not originality, but mastery of formal, set tasks was the aim of able minds. Educated men were known by their ability not only to do the right things, but also to say the right things in the right way. New rules reigned over the court of play. The dimensions had been measured out, the lines chalked, the net raised; it remained to the student to perfect his moves.

The recovery of antiquity was underway. But that reclamation meant more than a rebirth and expansion of ancient knowledge. More was at stake. The best and brightest men of the Renaissance wished to promote the best in word and deed, trusting that models of thought and action would inspire a better world, one enamored with classical *paideia*. Devotees of *studia humanitatis* valued human achievement and the originality arising from the most talented of minds — like Petrarch's — even though they did not believe all people to be equally capable of contributing to their civilization's greatness. Yet no one possessed of intelligence was lost. Students who could not so contribute might at least distinguish themselves by imitating the best and the noblest from the past. Their schools were not nurseries for geniuses so much as workshops for the culturally competent.

What strikes us now, despite the high-flown rhetoric and noble ideals, is the *practicality* of the humanistic mind. Humanism was about *verba et res*; it involved itself with words and things. The humanist wished to be useful. And what could be more useful to the city than the virtuous citizen? Book learning did not stand on its own. The Humanist of the Renaissance wished above all to complete his personality. "Distinction in social life," wrote historian William Harrison Woodward, "was marked by power of conversation and by personal carriage, by resourceful leisure and dignified old age." Further, the Humanist sought mastery over both his fevers of soul and the passions of his body. "To be self-contained and yet to contribute some special or personal element to society was the double function of 'the complete man.'" Mind and body were to be perfected together. But the education of the complete man or woman had to begin early. After its first rounds in the home, it began in earnest at school, where students were to be taught the arts of freedom. For, Woodward also said, it is "one of the ends of liberal studies to make a man truly worthy of his freedom, to secure him against the tyranny of ignoble pleasures or of varying circumstance." Still, however practical they deemed their ideas to be, we should note that men of the Renaissance could also hatch their share of theory. Indeed they needed to theorize. They were trying to change the world, to tap roots, to start anew.

Early in the fifteenth century, Leonardo Bruni D'Arezzo

wrote *De Studiis et Literis*, a famous epistle — a heady literary form of the day — addressed to a young woman of the Italian aristocracy, Baptista di Montefeltro, advising her on what the educated man and woman should read and perhaps be known to have read. His treatise survives, and it is one of the finest and most revealing explications of humanistic education we possess. Tipping his hat to what everyone of the Renaissance came to know and believe — while also admitting the assertion to be redundant for a woman of her cultivation — Bruni claimed a "sound and thorough knowledge of Latin" to be "the foundation of all true learning," along with its being a "study marked by a broad spirit, accurate scholarship, and careful attention to details." The language must be learned completely. And, in doing so, educated men and women would also drink in "fine taste," for they must develop an intellectual and aesthetic sense of literary style. Style, for the Humanist, wrote Woodward, was "the indispensable condition of permanence, almost indeed of credibility, in a literary work." Style was "the obvious mark of the educated man." Bruni certainly so saw it:

> To this end we must be supremely careful in our choice of authors, lest an inartistic and debased style infect our own writing and degrade our taste; which danger is best avoided by bringing a keen, critical sense to bear upon select works, observing the sense of each passage, the structure of the sentence, the force of every word down to the least important particle. In this way our reading reacts directly upon our style.

Reading was not to be broad or "inclusive," but good: it should consist of the best. For the best authors, Bruni wrote, supply students with "tests of correctness." They show us what is rightly admired and wisely emulated.

The curriculum swelled. Students should study History, which "enlarges our foresight in contemporary affairs and affords to citizens and to monarchs lessons of incitement or warning in the ordering of public policy." From History "we draw our store of examples of moral precepts." And History leads seamlessly to Ethics. But Bruni placed Poetry at the top of the heap. Without the balm and armor of Poetry, no man or woman is entitled to be called educated. Here, at the feet of the poet, we learn literary form at its highest, most exquisite pitch. The object of such study is the citizen whose learning is "full, ready, varied, and elegant." Yes, the student must learn to hold commerce with the world of facts, for "proficiency in literary form, not accompanied by broad acquaintance with facts and truths, is a barren attainment." But beware: "information, however vast, which lacks all grace of expression" is thrown away. The student must have both breadth of learning and grace of style.

And the Renaissance reaffirmed the liberal ideal. Petrus Paulus Vergerius published *De Ingenuis Moribus* in 1404, a treatise that we may unfold even now as a map for liberal learning. Vergerius said the teacher should help the student achieve "soundness of judgment, wisdom of speech, [and] integrity of conduct." The inculcation of character still came first, but the duty of the talented to develop the mind with a liberal education was itself almost tantamount to a moral obligation. Liberal pursuits helped men breathe fresher air. "We call those studies *liberal*," Vergerius wrote, "which are worthy of a free man; those studies by which we attain and practice virtue and wisdom; that education which calls forth, trains, and develops those highest gifts of body and mind which ennoble men, and which are rightly judged to rank next in dignity to virtue only." Learning to think logically was not enough. Memory he exalted as one of the most precious of human faculties. Intelligence may be more important than memory, he wrote, but intelligence without memory is worthless. Therefore, training the intellect begins with training the memory. Books are, in essence, "memory made permanent." They store the cultural tablets. They may contain useful and transcendent knowledge, but they contain more than thoughts; they contain expression. Indeed, right expression can ensure survival to the thoughts. And thoughts must have "style." So the path from training for character to the revived Renaissance curriculum of History, Moral Philosophy, Eloquence, and Poetry is a smooth one.

But before reaching those heights, one must know languages — for which Grammar was the key unlocking their doors. Grammar bestowed, in the words of the fifteenth-century scholar Nicholas Perotti, *ars recte loquendi recteque scribendi*, the art of correct speaking and writing, and was therefore *initium et fundamentum omnium disciplinarum*, the beginning and basis of all knowledge. Grammar was not a job to be eased or escaped but a task to be mastered — and mastered before all else.

It was the literature of the classical world itself, of course, not Grammar as narrowly understood, that opened doors. But study of the one made possible an intimacy with the other, and since the languages studied were Latin and Greek, reading literature presupposed an exhaustive grammatical grounding. Grammar was the fount of eloquence. Another thinker of the fifteenth century, Aeneas Sylvius — Enea Silvio Piccolomini, later Pope Pius II — penned yet another epistle on the education of youth in which he held that no man or woman can be learned or wise without Grammar, for without it, literature is forever closed, a dead rumor. "Literature is our guide," he wrote, "to the true meaning of the past, to a right estimate of the present, [and] to a sound forecast of the future." Literature equips and completes the educated human being. The student must strive for "the well-stored mind," and the proper and eloquent use of words drew the surest sign of such a mind. We must safeguard the world against the man of "too ready speech." And to achieve eloquence of speech, one must have "Grammar to order expression; Didactic to give it point; Rhetoric to illustrate it; [and] Philosophy to perfect it," all together engendering, by graduated steps, the learned mind and the cultivated soul. Underlying this method was the assumption that wisdom can be attained through assiduous learning. So the Renaissance provided both an ideal and a curriculum designed to realize that ideal.

The path upward was steep but clear. One could see the summit, if dimly. The main piece of gear needful for the ascent was "a good and teachable disposition," and that was much. Men of the Renaissance, no less than the Greeks and Romans, did not credit the modern dogma that all people are educable; many are not, and the enlightened of the day were disinclined to spread pearls before swine too long. Aeneas Sylvius, taking a leaf from Plutarch's book, restated the three elements making for the educated mind: nature, training, and practice. Curiosity and effort supported training and practice, as together they were the great elevator. But nature was the great leveler. One must be born with an educable nature. "No master can endow a careless and indifferent nature with the passion for learning," wrote Battista Guarino, son of the great humanist scholar Guarino da Verona, in 1459. One had that passion or one did not. But if one were born with the fortune to be so gifted — and this may be what *gifted* means — the learner could commence the climb. The work could begin.

All of which brings us to the happy days of the Mantuan school of "Casa Giocosa" founded by the wise ministrations of Vittorino da Feltre, perhaps the most humane man ever entrusted with the grave task of teaching the young and passing on a high inheritance. He provides the most felicitous example of Renaissance schooling. Vittorino believed in opportunity for all — or at least for all of the talented. He too held that nature had not fit all people for learning. To get the most out of study, one needed not simply capacity for learning, but a "taste" for it; learning ought not to be forced upon a student unequal to its rigors and intellectual largesse. But once capacity and taste are discovered in a pupil, Vittorino believed that the young man and woman could be molded like clay into that ideal citizen, the complete human being formed along humanistic lines. Vittorino made as his object, according to Woodward, not "the pedant, the ostentatious rhetorician, [or] the narrower type of grammarian" at which some schools aimed. Although himself a scholar, he did not wish primarily to create scholars. He wished to foster in his students a soundness of mind and body — *mens sana in corpore sano* — that "Greek feeling for grace and harmony" sitting at the heart of the Humanist creed. Vittorino was wont to say that "Not everyone is called to be a lawyer, a physician, a philosopher, to live in the public eye, nor has everyone outstanding gifts of natural capacity, but all of us are created for the life of social duty, all are responsible for the personal influence which goes forth from us." Here was Humanism at its most outward looking, ambitious both for the health of the individual soul and the commonweal.

Few have been better suited for a life of quiet study. Once a teacher of mathematics, Vittorino had also studied, in the early decades of the fifteenth century, Latin Letters at Padua under the Ciceronian scholar Gasparino da Barzizza and Greek under the great scholar Guarino da Verona. He was appointed to the chair of Rhetoric at the university in Padua by the age of forty-four. But he decided to become a schoolmaster, choosing to serve not the isolated if vital interests of scholarship, but those of Humanism where it takes root best: within the young. Gianfrancesco Gonzaga, the Marquis of Mantua, had cast a net to find able tutoring for his children and caught Vittorino, who took up his duties at Mantua in 1423 with smiling, evangelical fervor. What began as an arrangement for the children of the marquis, though, became a famous school for sons and daughters of aristocratic rank. Vittorino eventually extended his tutelage to poor students of ability, paying their way from his own purse or with the charity of his benefactors.

Court schools like Casa Giocosa were the greenhouses for Renaissance Humanism. They fed and nourished it. The airy and civilized court of Federigo Montefeltro of Urbino in the fifteenth century — a high perch for civilization if ever there was one — stands unimaginable without them. For, once again, civilization does not happen spontaneously; someone must clear the ground for it. Schools like those found at Mantua, Ferrara, Vicenza, and Cremona taught the skills that later made the civilized man and woman possible. They sowed the seeds and, more importantly, watered the plants and kept the garden weeded. Although many of the commoners attending Casa Giocosa went on to Padua or Bologna to study Law or Medicine, Vittorino did not set out to prepare them for their professions. He set out to civilize and cultivate them. Anything less or other would not have squared with Humanist tenets.

The Humanist curriculum in Italy appealed to patriotic sentiments. Many Italians equated Italian history with Roman history; Rome had been Italy's golden age. Students read Livy, Caesar, and Sallust, thought then to be the major historians of Rome — Tacitus and Suetonius were not yet sharing space on the shelves — and memorized and recited shining passages. But patriotism does not explain all of this renewed, perfervid interest. For when they were ready, Vittorino's charges would also read Plutarch's *Lives*. Thus did History funnel their minds into Moral Philosophy, which purported to teach how good citizens ought to live. Once again, History was to do more than supply information about the past. History set out to provide moral precepts. The Humanists' admiration for ancient biographical portraiture does not surprise us when we realize how big they thought the subject of History to be. It was not merely a detached and clinical inquiry. One read of great men to glean examples of upright living and noble deeds; one read of evil men in order to learn from their evil deeds what the good man or woman must avoid. So the study of History at Casa Giocosa was "reverential in spirit rather than critical," as Woodward has written. For Vittorino, the pursuit of History added up to "the contemplation of notable deeds told by a master of words." As James Cleland, the author of an English treatise on education from the early seventeenth century, would write, reading History "should be the chiefest study of a young nobleman when he cometh to any perfection of speech and understanding."

But language took front seat. From the beginning Vittorino immersed his pupils, boys and girls alike, in Latin and Greek. The young scholar was expected not only to read the two languages, but to write in them as well. Composition in Latin and Greek was the pinnacle of the humanistic discipline. For while this was not the whole of the course to run — students also studied Geometry, Astronomy, Music, and nascent forms of natural science — the ability to write in those two languages, both in prose and verse, demonstrated to the utmost the polish students had attained through their schooling. Composition cut the benchmark of their achievement. And naturally students needed models of excellence.

Poetry reading in Latin began with Virgil, the chief of Latin

poets and *rhapsode* for the Roman myth. Students could recite
great swatches of Virgil with ease. Lucan followed close on.
Horace, Juvenal, and Ovid also lay on the banquet table, though
Vittorino advised that they be approached carefully in schools as
too difficult or, for the younger ones, too risqué. And there was
oratory and philosophy, the two arts of both the public and private citizen. Cicero reigned as the stately Roman philosopher,
and passages from his *Letters* and *De Oratore* constantly stood
before young students — especially the *Letters*, which they imitated in form and sentiment within their own compositions.
Early Latin comedy also played a key role in the humanistic
course. Playwrights Plautus and Terence were promoted quickly
in the curriculum for their value in teaching the art of Latin
conversation. We must remember that, by the fifteenth century,
students did not grow up speaking Latin; they spoke Italian.
Few had heard much Latin outside of church. Yet Humanists
insisted that their budding scholars learn to speak it. Latin was
not common or, to use the word of the day, vulgar — which is
what attracted those hot for brilliant articulation. It was the language of learning and a coin for the elite, and its use required
exacting care. Its vocabulary could make many fine shades of
distinction, while its syntax could render them briefly and
gracefully. If students could fly a phrase in Latin, they could fly
it in any other language. Latin was the bridge to eloquence, a
bridge students had to show they could cross. This all
Humanists of the era believed and practiced.

Most significantly, unlike other schools of the immediately
prior decades, Vittorino carted Greek into the curriculum as
well, upping the ante of cultivation even more, and for this reason he sits on the frontier of a new age in classical education for
the modern world. He linked the worlds of Paulinus of Pella
and Thomas Arnold. Many schooled Italians had not known

Greek at all fifty years before. Now, in the 1420s and 1430s, Greek was on its way to becoming once again a common possession of the educated, thanks mainly to places like Casa Giocosa. But Vittorino, no doubt like other masters of the day, treated Greek somewhat differently. Latin sat in the curriculum primarily for its value as a conduit for composition; Greek existed for its wealth of information and beauty in history and poetry and — in the days before Galileo, Copernicus, and Kepler — science. Although students went on to compose in the language of Homer and Plato, the value of Greek was "literary rather than linguistic" (Woodward). It still grazed in alien fields. Greek was mostly to be learned and read, not imitated. Indeed, Greek texts, reliable and unreliable, had just fallen into scholarly hands within the previous generation.

Yet once re-acquired, Greek stayed, and became again, for the first time since the Roman world, the other language the educated had to know. Reading in Greek probably began with history, not poetry or drama. Students started with Thucydides and Xenophon (and later Herodotus), and Geography — serving as a kind of preface to History — could now be taught from the pages of Ptolemy and Strabo. Plato and Aristotle were still rare acquisitions in the middle third of the fifteenth century. Aeschylus, Sophocles, and Euripides were yet to be re-discovered. Plutarch, of all these, was seen at this time as the greatest of the Greek authors, the one any conscientious Humanist would learn first. Alexander Hegius, who headed the College of Deventer in the late fifteenth century, had written, "If anyone wishes to understand grammar, rhetoric, mathematics, history, or Holy Scripture, let him learn Greek. We owe everything to the Greeks." The Greek language was still, in the age of Vittorino, about content, not form. But that would change.

■ ■ ■

The age of Erasmus followed hard upon the heels of the Italian Renaissance and consolidated its intellectual and aesthetic regime, creating a consensus largely undisturbed by the massive dislocations of the Protestant Reformation. Humanism became part of the mainstream of intellectual culture throughout Europe and, while some parts of it had to be picked at, the humanistic curriculum was blessed both by Catholics and Protestants in the West. Melanchthon and Johannes Sturm made Humanism acceptable to the Lutheran Germany of the sixteenth century. The Jesuits did likewise during the Counter-Reformation. All factions put dibs on the curriculum. Classical study was incumbent upon all who wished to rise above their stations in life by intellectual effort. Literary tools proliferated. Soon popped up a plethora of all the familiar apparatus of lexicons and grammars, those handbooks of correct and stylish usage. Grammar itself began its own transformation. For scholars of the Middle Ages, Grammar had been a logical, utilitarian business: learn it, know it, use it. Grammar lent a skill, nothing more. Spied through a medieval prism, the rules of language were knowable, identifiable. But Renaissance Humanism cared more about style than strict correctness and so enthroned the erstwhile usage of the best authors as the difficult though acceptable standard for educated men and women. Humanism prescribed linguistic rights and wrongs with ancient texts at the ready, not solely with sclerotic rulebooks. Man was not now so much the measure as the Better — and more eloquent — Man.

New measures could be just as arbitrarily strict as the old. Lorenzo Valla's *Elegantiae Linguae Latinae*, published in the fifteenth century, set the standard for "Ciceronianism," an ambitious if contrived approach to Latin by which only those words were admitted to use that had once appeared in the works of Cicero. The Italian scholar Bembo once dubbed Cicero *unus scribendi magister,* the one and only teacher of writing and, for the righteously pure of mind, there would be no other. The English scholar Roger Ascham later wrote that only in the works of Cicero was "the Latin tongue fully ripe and grown to the highest pitch of all perfection." Why, they seemed to ask, waste one's time with the second-rate? Why not go for the best? This was an age of standards, after all. Ciceronianism was a spirited enterprise for those thirsting for linguistic decorum. But it was also fatal for the future of Latin, rendering it forever unable to grow and to welcome new words for new ideas and things. Humanism, at full bloom, promoted this peculiar form of linguistic puritanism. Imitation like this indeed seems slavish to us, and Erasmus himself ridiculed the abuses resulting from a too-strict adherence to the canons of imitation. Francis Bacon later protested that reliance on Cicero "grew speedily to an excess, for one began to hunt more after words than matter, and more after the choiceness of the phrase, and the round and clear composition of the sentence...than after the weight of matter, worth of subject, soundness of argument, life of invention or depth of judgement." Ciceronianism became for many lilting and fecund minds a straitjacket.

But we must not neglect the point of it. Imitation established a pattern of "right language," an ideal destined to affect that epoch's sense of polish in verbal expression. The kind of language aspired to was not the "natural," spontaneous effusions of the street, mastery of which came to practically everyone. By and large, men of the Renaissance sought beauty, literary and otherwise, judged it a rare commodity, and wished to duplicate it wherever it was found. The standard was the thing. Usage was the key. This quest for stylistic precision — along with the invention of printing — extended the authority of Humanism far and wide. Beyond this somewhat artificial dependence upon Cicero, though, Valla's guide to good usage strikes us even now with its elegant simplicity: "I take as [grammatical] law whatever is pleasing to the great authors." The English Humanist Sir Thomas Elyot had deemed Grammar little more than a device to provide an "introduction to the understanding of authors." One had to be not just deeply read, but also widely read, in the best authors; their riches shined a light on proper Grammar and Usage. *Follow the best* was the principle.

Gradually the scope of classical learning expanded in depth and breadth as well-trained students became well-prepared teachers and as printers issued reliable editions of Greek and Latin works. Schools and colleges sprang up to dedicate themselves solely to humanistic study. Classical learning spread in a remarkably short time to parts of Europe till lately unaware of its existence. Indeed we cannot overestimate its thrust as an intellectual and spiritual force in the first decades of the sixteenth century. Many commoners could be educated like princes. Change came quickly. The books one generation had barely known by word of mouth the next generation read, studied, and memorized, perhaps scarcely realizing that the works had not been to hand continuously since they were composed a millennium or two before. The ink on the pages of Cicero, Demosthenes, Homer, and Virgil must have seemed always dry.

Desiderius Erasmus stood as the foremost impresario of Renaissance Humanism at its most mature, becoming an international figure — almost a celebrity — of deep and far-ranging influence amongst kings, clerics, and common men. He sailed the flagship. Rarely has a man been so confident of being right, and his proselytizing placed Erasmus at the center of the "Northern Revival" of classical learning. Born in 1466 of dubious paternity, Erasmus attended Hegius's Humanist school at Deventer, and might have been taught for a time there by Rudolph Agricola, the great early German proponent of the New Learning. Erasmus eventually entered Holy Orders as an Augustinian and, though he dedicated his most active years to promoting the cause of Humanism, he never lost his sense of the unbreakable bond between the Christian faith and classical knowledge. For Erasmus their marriage was complete. His life also demonstrates the late-fifteenth-century spottiness of that learning: Erasmus got no Greek as an adolescent, and his own Hellenizing did not arrive until after he reached the age of thirty. Learning, like religion, could come late to the duly converted. Indeed we remember Erasmus now not because of the profound originality of his thought, nor for the thoroughness of method shown in his treatise *De Ratione Studii*, but for the way he so zealously lit a fire of enthusiasm for the Humanist creed. "Within the two literatures of Greece and Rome," he once wrote, "are contained all the knowledge that we recognize as vital to mankind."

And as that knowledge grew in scope, so did the reading list, informed by the curricula of the Italians. Nonetheless, Erasmus boldly recommended authors theretofore considered hazardous for young minds. Erasmus reposed total faith in the efficacy of literature to guide the reader — with the aid of expert teaching — into all good things. He pressed particular ancient authors as essential to a true education. Amongst the Greeks, the student must read Aesop (with whom one usually began), Plutarch, Homer, Euripides, Aristophanes, Lucian, Herodotus, and Demosthenes, each author typifying especial virtues, literary and otherwise. The Romans presented him with Cicero (of course), Seneca, Sallust, Plautus, Terence, Virgil, and Horace, with a new place awarded in some quarters for

Quintilian, who had veritably defined the educated mind. The works of Jerome and Augustine made staples for the pious. All these classical authors took medals as the champions and they were welcomed to the arena, so long as they were read thoroughly and well. Like the ancients themselves, Erasmus never mistook skimming for reading. Careful method led the way to right, fruitful reading of the kind that nourishes, strengthens, and refines.

While swimming within the roiling intellectual maelstrom of Paris in the closing months of the fifteenth century, Erasmus met a good number of English students and, by the fall of 1499, he was supping with English humanists in London and Oxford, from which he would journey to Cambridge and alter the state of scholarly life and letters in England. The fever had crossed the English Channel. For this was the England not only of Sir Thomas More, who befriended Erasmus and welcomed him into his home. This was also the England of Grocyn, Linacre, Latimer, Colet, Foxe, Fisher, and Sir John Cheke, men who brought the Renaissance, and the classical learning extolled by it, into English courts, common rooms, and classrooms. And it is chiefly England — and America — to which this survey now turns.

■　■　■

By the early sixteenth century, Humanism had long ceased to observe borders. Germany had produced Johannes Sturm, who headed the Strassburg School upon which was based the *gymnasium*, the model of classical schooling applied throughout Germany and Austria for the next several centuries. France could boast the names of Budaeus, Ramus, Rabelais, Scaliger, and Casaubon. England traveled along the same road, if more slowly at first, and English scholars soon joined the roster of illustrious classical humanists. Humanism of its nature sought disciples. Linacre and Grocyn had sat for the Italian classical scholar Politian's lectures in Florence and brought home their enlightenment and ardor for the New Learning. They probably deemed themselves acolytes, but they were in fact an awakening elite, a new sort of secular priesthood, the likes of which England had never seen. And most of them knew one another. As a student, Thomas More had read Greek at Oxford with Linacre, who had himself learned at the feet of the greatest continental scholars — Politian, Chalcondyles — of his youth. Together these men transformed the syllabus in which the English gentleman was steeped, a syllabus that did not change substantially for well over three hundred years. The gentleman became, among other things, the classically educated man. Here the old martial ideal of the brave soldier was refined. Learning, not just manners, made the man.

Literary Humanism reached its apogee in the sixteenth century with the titanic figures of Erasmus and Sir Thomas More. These two men matched most perfectly the moral, intellectual, and aesthetic benefits of humanistic study to the discharge of honorable public service. Few other periods have afforded such giants of the human spirit and intellect. With their masterpieces, Erasmus's *Praise of Folly* and More's *Utopia*, these figures demonstrated better than any others of their time the promises fulfilled by the painstaking discipline of a classical education. If human beings prove themselves by their actions, the acts of Erasmus and More — literary, political, spiritual — shone forth for all to see. They were Humanism's best advertisements. But the humanistic ethos had to seep deeply into the fabric of English life if it was to thrive. It needed explicators.

Sir Thomas Elyot, a minor official who rose to Clerk to the

Privy Council, typified a strain of Erasmian Humanism pecu-
liarly English. Although closely allied in tone to Castiglione's
The Courtier and the Italian custom of courtesy, English
Humanism took on its own contours. Wishing to promote "the
knowledge that maketh a man wise," Elyot wrote the *Book of the
Governor* in 1530 in part to establish rituals for an education in
statecraft by which youth were to seek personal excellence. But
Elyot — who also compiled an authoritative Latin-English dictionary — sought as well to widen English vocabulary, aug-
menting "our English tongue whereby men should as well
express more abundantly the thing that they conceived in their
hearts, as also interpret out of Greek, Latin and other tongues
into English." Here was a new concern newly articulated. Elyot
wished to perfect the style of English. Like their European
counterparts, both noble English youth and those humbler ones
below were to strive after an aptitude for eloquent speech.

But they were to read Latin and Greek, not English, in
order to get there. Elyot advocated, in other words, a
Humanist's literary education on the classical model. Grammar
was of the essence. Nothing about the journey, he assured his
readers, could be made easy. While learning Latin, Greek, and
French could be made palatable with games and other playful
diversions in the early years, eventually the hard work of memorizing and practicing must begin. Still, the payoff would come
later in life when, the dreaded textbooks closed long before, a
man or woman might finally approach "the most sweet and
pleasant reading of old authors," when one's desire to learn
would be "extinct with the burden of grammar." Poetry — "the
first philosophy that ever was known" — again took the first
berth on the train, just as it had in the curricula of the Italian
Humanists. They all began with the quest for beauty. Once
more, though, hard work was the password to the good, refined

life. The proper aim of the Humanist was not intellectual integrity alone, but the ability to take delight in delightful things. A classical education was to enhance the soul. John Colet, founder of St. Paul's school in London, held a like faith that a proper education should, in Woodward's words, "dignify leisure."

Perhaps the most wise English work on classical education produced during the flower of the Renaissance was penned by Roger Ascham, a scholar of St. John's College, Cambridge, who once served Queen Mary as Latin secretary and the young Princess Elizabeth as tutor. *The Scholemaster* emerged posthumously in 1570 and went on to exert a penetrating influence on the English mind of the day, for it represented the most confident, settled view of education's aims and methods. It showed Humanism with an English face and itself remains no negligible literary production. Education, as always, began with character. Parents should wish to avoid the rearing of children who are "bold without shame, rash without skill, [and] full of words without wit," because children with these traits become adults with the same tendencies — plus the cleverness and guile to make the world suffer their deficiencies and vices. Virtue, like knowledge, may be "hard and irksome in the beginning, but in the end [is] easy and pleasant." For "where [the] will inclineth to goodness, the mind is bent to truth." But Ascham quickly brought the reader down to the mat.

"All men covet to have their children speak Latin," Ascham asserted. Facility with Latin certified a man's intellectual worth. A classical education in England told all people that a man's training had not been superficial, but strenuous, rich, and real. Even more, it told the world that he had not been taught skills merely. His mind and taste had been formed; his was not a servile mind. The value of practice and rote learning having been well established during the previous centuries, Ascham advised constant application to writing to be "the only thing that breedeth deep root, both in the wit for good understanding, and in the memory for sure keeping of all that is learned." Practice — even numbing practice — makes perfect. All begins with Grammar, for "we do not contemn rules, but we gladly teach rules...plainly, sensibly, and orderly," as knowledge springs from rules and regularity. The disheveled mind must be eschewed from the early years; the cultivated mind is the orderly one. As we might expect, Ascham dedicated much of *The Scholemaster* to recommending classical reading, and his pages are replete with the names of classical authors and works to be read and revered.

Ascham sounded another note. Although he concentrated on the value and use of Latin, we may note the ubiquity of Greek in this work: not just endorsements of Greek authors, but Greek passages — and untranslated Greek at that. Greek was a full partner in the firm again by the end of the sixteenth century, and in some ways it was becoming a more senior partner. As Erasmus, echoing Cicero, was supposed to have advised the erudite daughter of Thomas More, "You are an eloquent Latinist, Margaret, but, if you would drink deeply of the well-springs of wisdom, apply to Greek. The Latins have only shallow rivulets; the Greeks, copious rivers running over sands of gold." Doses of the two languages were to be meted out equally, and the Greek and Roman authors were not to be read for their academic or professional value only. For, Ascham wrote, "in the Greek and Latin tongues, the only two learned tongues which be kept not in common talk but in private books, we find always wisdom and eloquence, good matter and good utterance." Form got wed to content.

Humanists founded schools rapidly in the early sixteenth

century. Cardinal Wolsey started the Ipswich School in 1528 expressly to promote the new model. Then followed Christ's Hospital, Rugby, and Harrow, established largely to serve the same purpose. These were heady years for education. All things were possible if one learned the right languages and read the right books. Yet when we look closely at English school practice during the Sixteenth century, we see that these ideals were hard to live by. Mastery came slowly. Schools seem to us like factories for drudges, not academies of wisdom. But then this is what we should expect. The wisdom came, if at all, later. Prep schools lived up to their name: they were preparatory. Students in classics required long periods of intellectual gestation. As it had been for the Romans, school was about sweat. The grammatical grind early on in this new age, though, took the form of "appositions," exercises in which students challenged one another, often in a spirit of gamesmanship, with questions posed and answered in Latin. (They were rarely encouraged to speak in Greek, which remained largely a literary, scientific, and philosophical language, not one prescribed for colloquial use.) These exercises — relics of the Middle Ages — continued, and the Renaissance saw the advent of a more varied array of "helps" for beleaguered pupils. Lily's *Grammar* replaced the old guide of Donatus and became standard for English use. Later it would be said that Lily's was one of the three most revered and memorized texts in England, along with the Bible and the *Book of Common Prayer*. (Linacre had also composed a grammar textbook, but it was judged too scholarly for younger pupils.) Terence and Plautus remained as aids to Latin conversation, as did Erasmus's *Colloquies*; by the 1530s, the Spanish classical scholar Vives had produced his own *Colloquies*. Texts known as *Vulgaria* helped students to take their first steps with Latin composition, from which they graduated to sterner forms of letter writing on the model of

Cicero. Verse composition also became common and, though we may be skeptical as to how sophisticated school versifying was in the Tudor period, we can see that Poetry was paid more than lip service in English schools as the monopoly of History was eased in the Latin canon. Poets emerged. Virgil, Ovid, and Horace secured their places among the Roman authors.

Colet of St. Paul's wrote his own manifesto of sorts with his *Aeditio* in 1527, in which he explained succinctly and pragmatically the purposes and methods of teaching in the better grammar schools of his day. It's clear that Latin was spoken in the schools as well as written, as it's equally clear that the grammar textbook gave just so much guidance and no more. Grammar and Usage may be complementary, but they're not identical. Eventually Latin was to come to students naturally through classroom immersion. Ideally they were to learn it the same way people have always learned language — by the "direct method" of using it to communicate:

> Let the pupil above all busily learn and read good Latin authors of chosen poets and orators, and note wisely how they wrote and spoke, and study always to follow them; desiring none other rules but their examples. For in the beginning men spoke not Latin because such rules were made, but contrariwise because men spoke such Latin upon that followed the rules and (so) were made. That is to say Latin speech was before the rules, not the rules before the Latin speech.

While instructing teachers on their proper and most efficient roles in teaching these budding Latin scholars, Colet left no doubt about the source of authority to be used when defining "good Latin":

Be to them your own selves also speaking with them the pure
Latin very present to them and leave the rules. For reading of
good books, diligent information of taught masters, studious
advertence and taking heed of learners, hearing eloquent men
speak, and finally, busy imitation with tongue and pen, more
availeth shortly to get the true eloquent speech, than all the traditions, rules, and precepts of masters.

No hidebound blindness of hoodwinked drones here. These
men were out to achieve results, not merely to enforce mindless
routine.

The rise of Greek in the sixteenth century tells a shakier
tale. Like other such intellectual practices, the implanting of
Greek was a top-down affair. (Humanism was, at its roots, an
enterprise of the elite. Even Shakespeare was supposed to have
had "small Latin and less Greek.") Colleges at the two ancient
English universities — Corpus Christi at Oxford among them
— were founded to enthrone the New Learning in the life of the
English mind. Greek was held with almost religious awe by the
newly converted. The smallest concerns could take on a monumental weight, and some went beyond the canon of works to be
read, even to the fringes of minutiae. The Cambridge of the
1540s, for example, witnessed a very public spat over which
pronunciation of ancient Greek was to be affirmed the proper
one. One group tried to adopt the pronunciation agreed upon
by scholarly phonetic investigations, while another coterie
wished to settle for an imperfect pronunciation on the
Byzantine system acquired through Italian scholars. The quar-
rel was bitter, and it was not resolved till one of the parties to
the dispute, none other than the Chancellor of the university,
died. For Ascham and his scholars in sympathy, the episode had
"completely extinguished almost all the ardour we had felt

for learning Greek" at Cambridge. Humanists took their classics seriously.

Some of the troubles besetting the New Learning struck at
the fundamental tenets of Humanism. Professorships of Greek
had been duly established in the early decades of the sixteenth
century, and these chairs were sorely needed, as most native
English scholars of Greek had had to truck themselves to Italy
to be tutored in it. The professorships were welcomed in a country hungering for the full humanistic menu. But there arose a
faction at Oxford that stood against the teaching of Greek altogether: the language of Homer and Plato was a pagan pursuit
unlikely to aid the study of theology. And as Greek was deemed
chiefly a language of science and philosophy (as well as of poetry
and history), these men considered it too worldly; it was dangerous. One day Thomas More got wind of their efforts and,
with the king's support, pressed the university to protect the
study of Greek, reasoning that the language was essential to the
serious study of the ancient poets, historians, orators, and
philosophers. The works of these authors were, in sum, what
higher education had become for civilized men and women. His
was an eloquent defense of what was fast becoming the traditional Humanist creed and curriculum. The opponents were
shut down.

Nonetheless, despite its highly valued stock within the
precincts of the learned, Greek was sparsely taught in lower
school classrooms in the first half of the century. Colet called for
the teaching of Greek in a boy's schooling "if such may be got-
ten," which probably meant that Greek should be taught if a
stray scholar from Oxford or Cambridge could be scrounged up
to teach it. Its dissemination awaited not only qualified cohorts
to do the teaching, but also the grammatical texts (written, naturally, in Latin) to be composed, printed, and widely adopted.

These texts would in turn promote a more uniform set of expectations for Greek grammar and composition throughout the country. Three successive books — those of Clenardus, Grant, and Camden — wended their ways to acceptance and Greek slowly became a standard school subject, not an exotic plumed bird admired from afar. It was the other bridge more and more students had to cross. Once the pains of the grammar book lay behind them, students would customarily begin their reading with the Greek New Testament, followed hard on by Aesop (for moral reinforcement) and Lucian (for light dialogue). Teachers eventually found equivalents to the Romans they had been mastering for years. Demosthenes became the Greek Cicero, Homer the Greek Virgil, and Menander the Greek Terence. The works of Xenophon introduced many a young scholar to Greek historical writing, especially his *Cyropaedia* and (later) *Anabasis*, while Plutarch laid on more red meat for the historian and moralist alike. Euripides began to raise his head here and there, then Sophocles. Although few schools expected their pupils to master Greek conversation as they did Latin, Greek had come into its own in English schools and intellectual life by the beginning of the seventeenth century.

We must not imagine a picture of flat homogeneity in English schools at this — or at any — stage of classical education. Revolutions do not often overtake the academy. The first steps were tentative. Latin and Greek were taught neither widely nor uniformly well, and even some colleges at the privileged universities had to pick up the slack. St. John's College, Cambridge, made provisions for Greek beginners amongst its scholars as late as the 1570s. And adding to the academic turbulence, the extent and quality of classical teaching waxed and waned throughout the century with the fortunes of the English throne. Still, the trend was upward. Humanism had taught Englishmen that the present made an insufficient recipe for cultivation. They too began to see that the well-furnished mind was an achievement.

Throughout this period we spot one belief of the early Italian Humanists reinforced greatly over the years to come: Classical study, that child of Humanism, is practical. It qualified a man supremely for the world of public affairs. Sir John Cheke, the eminent classical scholar at Cambridge, said that a mastery of the Athenian orator Demosthenes would suit any intelligent young man either for politics or for the life of the cloth. But the bar was high. The bright and wise man would do well, if he read nothing else, to dwell "first in God's holy Bible, and then join with it [Cicero] in Latin, [and] Plato, Aristotle, Xenophon, Isocrates, and Demosthenes in Greek." The reading of all these, he said, "must needs prove an excellent man." An excellent man perhaps: certainly not a common man. As we saw with the Italians drunk with the first draughts of Humanism, the enlightened classes of England sought breadth and depth in their cultural life. "The gentry and city-men who endowed Colleges and sent their sons to them did so because they believed that *literae humaniores* [the Oxford classical course] taught wisdom and virtue," wrote Ogilvie, underlining the prevailing thirst of the sixteenth century for the intellectual benefits of Humanism. "It must be assumed that the Colleges in return provided a humane education."

The Renaissance ended amid embattled nations locked in bitter wars and racked with religious tumult. Human nature did not change; no Promised Land was reached. Yet the epoch closed with the Age of Discovery as lands across the seas fed the European mind with new fancies. Frontiers opened around the globe. These years left a bright residue upon the Western world that has never been entirely erased. The Renaissance fostered, in the words of art historian Walter Pater, a "love of the things of the intellect and the imagination for their own sake." The life of the mind was made safer for variety than it had been during the splendid days of the High Middle Ages. The world's historical memory lengthened. And in this drama classical learning — abetted by its ancient voices, Greek and Latin — played the leading role. The Humanist ideal was uttered for new listeners. More to the point, this period, through classical learning, bestowed upon later generations a recognized corpus, a body of expanded literary, philosophical, and artistic knowledge that, broadcast with the printing press, fashioned and maintained models of imitation designed for the pursuit of excellence. The educated man and woman were not merely educated. They were cultured. And their culture, such as it was, could be proved by the languages they knew and the books they read.

∎   ∎   ∎

The seventeenth century enshrined the classical inheritance. The Humanist furniture was itemized piece by piece, the vases were counted and tagged. That common cache of what educated people were expected to know was no longer up for grabs. It was an array of museum pieces whose value had been assessed on the upper end — though they were also museum pieces shining with use. By the time Shakespeare died in 1616, the revolutionary phase had passed. Humanism had become the orthodoxy of English high culture during the Stuart era. But it was not unalloyed. Puritanism also made itself a cultural force, one of great sophistication in certain hands, one obstructing here and there the Humanists' unfettered sway over curricula. Men of learning rose from both camps. Eventually, though their impulses differed, Humanists and Puritans came to agree on those things constituting the educated mind. Although

they did not always value the same classical authors and
works, they could share an outward looking — if not exactly
cosmopolitan — worldview when deciding what the better
schools should teach. We might even say that classics fostered
the social shifts prevailing well into the eighteenth century.
"Much of the credit for the gradual enlightenment of the upper
middle classes in the early Stuart period," Ogilvie has written,
"must be given to their Humanist education: it emancipated
them from a medieval acceptance of things as they were and
taught them to explore and to question."

Yet this age also saw shattering transformations in English
life. While Humanism might have ceased to be revolutionary,
revolution raged on other fronts. The Crown itself was threatened. Royal beheadings, plagues, and conflagrations upset social
equilibrium. The printing of books ushered in an age when
almost all literate people owned at least a few well-thumbed
volumes. No corner of life was left untouched. Science began to
transform people's view of their place in the cosmos. Galileo's
Siderius Nuncius and Newton's *Principia* were written in Latin so
as to be understood by men of learning in all Western countries.
Classics by then wore the stout armor of tradition, and throughout the century, education trumped scholarship. The widely and
deeply read man and woman still took precedence over the
scholar; what the many knew and read still mattered more than
what the erudite few discovered and edited. Universities might
have led the schools with their curricula, but schools did most
of the heavy lifting. And more people attended those schools.
Although this period was far from egalitarian, the reach of education extended a little further to those citizens less fortunate by
birth, with greater numbers of the sons of the nobility and gentry attending Oxford and Cambridge to receive a gentleman's
education — a brightening ideal now. By the ascendancy of

Charles I in 1625, ten percent of students matriculating at the two ancient universities were poor and aided by scholarships.

Greek and Latin still ruled the field in the century of John Donne, Milton, and Dryden. The languages extended their reach too, even to local grammar schools. The very term "grammar school" meant school for Greek and Latin, not English, grammar. Grammar-school curricula became more uniform as some texts were granted the authority of royal decree. But the two classical languages of tradition did not rule quite alone anymore. Hebrew found its way into more classrooms. Protestantism would have its scholars know both major languages of Scripture, not just one. Still, as it opened a door to but one piece of literature — however vital that one piece was to the spiritual life of the West — Hebrew remained to many a pious oddity and never became as common in schools as the tongues of the Greeks and Romans. The curriculum expanded to modern languages. Boys at Westminster school went so far as to compose orations in Arabic. As the language of diplomacy, French became obligatory for future men of public affairs. Well-educated people were more polyglot than ever. This too was a literary age. While we know him now mainly as the author of *Paradise Lost*, Milton was known in his day as an excellent composer of Greek and Latin, and the reading list of those classical works he taught shows him to have been a scholar of wide learning. Dryden trailed not far behind Milton. They both had cut their teeth on classical literary forms, and the greatest authors of English literature were to be armed with a classical education for some generations to come.

The seventeenth century saw Greek rise to equal status with Latin, perhaps because fewer pupils had to speak and write elegantly in the style of Cicero. Plautus and Terence, those revered aids to conversation, were removed from their pedestal. Senecan prose overtook Ciceronian in some English quarters as the model to imitate, making English prose tighter, less round, in the hands of some writers. Classical schooling became more epicurean. Verse composition in Greek and Latin came into its own as the exquisite accomplishment of the classically educated and chief measure of the intellect's cultivation. One could gauge a man's mind by the words — and meters — he used. Sir Simonds d'Ewes claimed to have composed 2,850 Greek and Latin verses while attending Bury St. Edmund's school. Teaching tools like the *Index Poeticus* and the *Encheiridion Poeticum* found their way into pupils' hands. The Dean of Westminster, Lancelot Andrewes, made composition the primary work of his students. One chronicler wrote of him that Andrewes would teach boys well into the evening, "unfolding to them the best rudiments of the Greek tongue, and the elements of the Hebrew grammar, and all this he did to boys without any compulsion of correction; nay, I never heard him utter so much as a word of austerity" among them. Westminster required its two top forms to compose verses on the fly. John Evelyn, upon a visit in the 1660s, saw feats of classical composition performed "as wonderfully astonished me in such youths, with such readiness and wit, some of them not above twelve or thirteen years of age." Headmaster Richard Busby brought Westminster to its highest pitch of achievement, ordering his students to observe rules of Greek accentuation. Standards became just as exacting for Latin verse composition. Dryden recalled that, under Busby, ending two consecutive lines of Latin verse with a verb earned the unhappy versifier a beating. These must have been tedious days in school for the dull ones — but no doubt invigorating for the diligent and able. Garlands were to the talented.

The Stuart and Caroline periods brought other changes to the syllabus endured by young people as shown by the witness of Charles Hoole, a minister and schoolmaster who wrote *A New Discovery of the Old Art of Teaching School* in the 1630s. The curriculum widened as new names took their place in the classical pantheon. Students of Latin, who for years had read the old standards of Cicero, Plautus, and Terence, were now set to Lucan, Juvenal, Persius, Seneca, Martial, Pliny, and (a favorite of the era) Ovid. Greek class brought them Pindar, Hesiod, Sophocles, Euripides, Aristophanes, and Lycophron. Classical interest in seventeenth-century England tilted ever further toward the purely literary. Hoole spied another shift in the classroom: some schoolmasters, blessed with this greater wealth of literary riches at their fingertips, began to assign less reading per author so as to accommodate more authors and works. He prescribed another innovation with verse composition in *English*. This method, however sparsely practiced, was less of an innovation than it appears, as students of classics had had to master their native language for many generations through accurate and stylish translation.

The absence of English instruction from English education at this time, though, should not send us down the wrong road. English was given its due in this ebullient stage of its life; the quality of English poetry and prose penned in this age should leave no doubt that this was a great age of English style. But the brightest minds thought that mastery with English — or at least mastery with English of the best kind — came by way of a classical training. The seventeenth century has been called the first great age of English translations of classical works (though North's edition of Plutarch had appeared in the century previous). This was the age of the Authorized Version of the Bible (1611). Chapman's *Homer* made for a moment in literary history. Dryden's *Aeneid* stands on its own as bona fide English literature. Classical schooling bore much on the quality of the

English rendered by translators. The rhythms and syntax of Greek and Latin formed the cadences of literary English to no small degree. Students might, for example, be made to translate a Greek verse into clean English prose and then into Latin verse. Variations were entertained freely, the harder — and more apparently nonsensical — the workouts the better. The aim of all these exercises was never merely to learn the languages and the literatures of the Greeks and Romans. Their value was not merely cultural. The point of this method was to stretch students' minds, to expand their capacities, to inure them to manipulating, to playing with, words and ideas. A literary high culture would have no need to justify this flagrant expenditure of its students' time and effort. These students were novices. They were not learning a trade; they were improving their mental natures.

Although the classical curriculum reigned supreme till the Restoration, dissenters weren't in short supply, and they hailed mainly from two factions. First, men of religion, especially Nonconformists, remembered (knowingly or not) the fears of St. Jerome from over a thousand years before in objecting to the non-Christian, pagan content of all these works. The Quaker George Fox warned in the 1650s that the classical languages and the liberal arts "were but the teachings of the natural man," not those of the New Man of Christ. The educational reformer Comenius wrote that classical works blandish "blind pagans and turn the minds of their readers from the true God." Anyone well acquainted with Greek and Latin poetry can understand these worries. The classical oeuvre can be earthy in the extreme. But the second group's objections were more formidable, at least intellectually, and they adumbrate the modern yen for utility. While John Locke claimed Latin as necessary for the well-edu-cated gentleman — a term fast becoming redundant — he thought Greek appropriate for the scholar only. Furthermore, Locke deemed the languages, though worth possessing, too long and hard in the getting and he primed a search for shortcuts. Theme and verse writing he found utterly useless. More remarkable, though, are the apparent apostasies of Milton, which a closer look shows to be only apparent. No scholar like Milton would jettison the curriculum that had tempered his intellectual mettle. He merely sought to highlight the "solid things" by making the classical syllabus more "useful" for the student. Milton would have him read the didactic poems of Lucretius and Hesiod, learn farming from Virgil and Varro, and improve his culture with Plutarch and Xenophon. He thought verse exercises a "preposterous exaction" that forces "the empty wits of children to compose themes, verses and orations" of scant value. Yet scholars and schoolmasters might have answered that those exactions were never meant to yield value — at least for anyone but the pupil. They were calisthenics. Filling and forming empty wits was the very task classical study had set out to perform.

■　■　■

"Those who say our thoughts are not our own because they resemble those of the Ancients may as well say our Faces are not our own because they are like our Fathers'." So wrote Alexander Pope with all the hauteur of the Augustan Age. Another era dawns when such a man of letters can link not only himself but also the entire society of educated men and women to the Greeks and Romans. With that rational and periwigged era of Pope and Johnson, the world has calmed. After the turmoil of the seventeenth century left in the wake of the Glorious Revolution of 1688, English life in the early decades of the eighteenth century takes on a conscious, genial tranquility. The air is once again suffused with confidence. Dr. Johnson tries with his *Dictionary* to corral the unruly English language, which becomes now less idiosyncratic and more decorous. Lord Chesterfield writes that English must be marked by "an elegant simplicity and dignity of style." Classics leaves the school and feeds English culture (English high culture, that is). Literature now shares the stage with other arts. Architecture and land-scaping spread the Greeks' and Romans' influence to sectors theretofore little touched by it, including those unable to read Greek and Latin — we might almost say especially those unable to read Greek and Latin. English citizens can see the classical legacy in the visible artifacts of the world around them. The timber scrabble that was the City of London from the Middle Ages to the eve of the Great Fire of 1666 gives way to Portland stone and the Neo-classical designs of the Georgian period. Inigo Jones builds new wonders. Vanbrugh leaves his play-wright's table to take up the drafting tools of architecture in these splendiferous days of the enlightened amateur. Sir Christopher Wren builds his churches, including St. Paul's Cathedral with its great dome, a structure itself ringing changes on the classical heritage.

The academic atmosphere was changing as well, even though this was also a conservative, rule-girded age. Good minds were out to preserve good things. Although the English Reformation and the *Book of Common Prayer* were already two centuries old, Latin still rang in English ears. The Church of England maintained the old language, at the universities at least, where Latin versions of the prayer book sat in the stalls and pews. University rituals were conducted in Latin; from 1660 to 1700 alone, Oxford and Cambridge published more than twenty volumes of Latin ceremonial verses between them.

Christ Church, Oxford, used Latin in prayer services till 1861. Students paid their dues with constant practice in morphology and usage. Masters at Eton taught from Lily's *Grammar* till the 1860s; Camden's old Greek *Grammar* — written in Latin — kept drilling up-and-coming Hellenists. No price was too high to pay for cultivation. Contemporary accounts of relentless schooling fill letters and journals of the day. When we read poet John Gay's lines about a time when pupils were "lashed into Latin by the tingling rod," we know we've entered an age of spirited sadism in English classical education. Yet enduring the rods and the endless stand-up recitations they enforced became badges of honor. Later in life the brightest initiates had few doubts that the achievement was worth the pain.

The epicures still steered the ship. At Eton Latin prose was sacrificed to poetry; Cicero gave way to Horace. (At some schools Latin prose was confined almost entirely to collections like the *Scriptores Romani*.) Poetry was the thing. Samuel Parr, once a schoolmaster at Harrow, made his pupils act out Greek plays in the 1770s, perhaps the earliest example of this practice that matured with the Victorians. More students could read Greek with some fluency, though the lazy or thick of mind had help as Greek works began to be buffered by translations — into Latin. (Apparently, if one couldn't read Latin, he had no business trying to drink at the springs of Hellas anyway.) Greek grammars were composed in Latin well into the next century. Rules were still memorized and recited. Overall, classical curricula in the better Public Schools kept travelling on the road they had begun under the Stuarts, becoming more intensive and concentrated, despite the burgeoning number of works available for school use. The aim became one of reading — and re-reading — a few masterpieces rather than many. It was better to be thorough than broad in one's classical reading. Students at

Winchester were expected to read all of Homer, Virgil, and Horace — twice. The languages became so natural to some that they began to think in them. Issac Williams of Harrow claimed that sometimes, upon being called to gather his thoughts in English, he had to compose them first in Latin, only afterwards translating them into his native tongue, just to make sure he had said what was on his mind.

Verse composition in Greek and Latin kept pace with meticulously graduated skills. Imitation ruled the Augustans preeminently. Schoolmasters conferred upon their charges no time to stop and appreciate. Parnassus made for an agonizing, if rewarding, climb. With each new plateau achieved, young scholars were put through ever more challenging runs with new poetic forms. Students were set to making Pindaric and Horatian odes, epigrams, and epics. Greek iambics were set more frequently. Composing elegiacs, called "longs and shorts," fast became, as M. L. Clarke observed, "the mark of the Etonian scholar." Not only could one not be learned without having done them — that was obvious enough — but also one could not hope to be a gentleman, which was a more important matter. By 1840 Thomas Balston, headmaster at Eton, would ask, with perfect poise, "If you do not take more pains, how can you ever expect to write good longs and shorts? If you do not write good longs and shorts, how can you ever be a man of taste? If you are not a man of taste, how can you ever be of use in the world?" (*Use* meant a different thing to these people.) Taking Horace or Juvenal as models, some students took a shot at satire. The orthodoxy was now ironclad. Classical education wasn't just about the literature and history and philosophy; it was also about mental formation. By the end of our period, the young Lord Byron was made to compose hefty numbers of Greek hexameters at Harrow. Nonetheless, all did not have to be ceaseless drudgery for the accomplished. A pupil of Shrewsbury school, one T. S. Evans, could find leisure "in recording boyish adventures, happy thoughts, or any entertaining trifles in Latin or Greek lines." While pleasure may not have been the point of all these convoluted exercises — and it certainly wasn't — delight could be a nice dividend.

And this dividend still provided an impetus to English letters. Poetry has perhaps never owed so much to a cultural impulse. Augustan poetry is unimaginable without those years-long apprenticeships in the composition of Greek and Latin poetry. The honor roll is a long one. Pope, Swift, Collins, Goldsmith, Cowper, Gray, Dr. Johnson: they were all formed by classical education. This is not a retrospective discovery: the best minds of the time knew it. Poets and writers strove to make themselves equal to the legacy, following classical models with almost religious fervor, and the schools had taught them how to go about it. This peculiar form of emulation required not only wide reading; it needed conscious, painstaking imitation. And imitation usually began with memorizing. The old classical training, according to Pope, obliged students "to get the classic poets by heart, which furnishes them with endless matter for conversation and verbal amusement for their whole lives." It made possible the genteel world of the heroic couplet. Nor was the classical literary influence confined to poetry. Prose was transformed as well. Describing Joseph Addison's training in Greek and Latin, one of his biographers added that "an early acquaintance with the classics is what may be called the good-breeding of poetry, as it gives a certain gracefulness which never forsakes a mind that contracted it in youth, but is seldom or never hit by those who would learn it too late." Upon a suggestion to Dr. Johnson that quoting classical authors was a sure sign of pedantry, Boswell wrote that the learned curmudgeon rejoined with typical trenchancy: "No, Sir, it is a good thing; there is a community of mind in it. Classical quotation is the *parole* [the promise or watchword] of literary men all over the world."

Indeed by the close of the Augustan age, the classical pursuit sailed with somewhat fairer winds in the schools than it did in the universities, the scholarly miracles of Bentley, Parr, and Porson notwithstanding. Greek studies suffered an eclipse at Oxford in the eighteenth century, though they fared better at Cambridge. Latin seemed to dry on the vine. A friend of the poet Gray said that the Oxford of the 1730s was a "country flowing with syllogisms and ale, where Horace and Virgil are alike unknown." This was probably annoyed exaggeration. For though the universities were still primarily places where one completed an education in logic, philosophy, and science, all first-year undergraduates at Oxford had been required since the 1630s to attend lectures on Grammar and Rhetoric, neither of which could be understood without a grounding in the languages along with large dollops of their literatures. Classical education was not neglected there: it was assumed. Robert Greene of Clare College, Cambridge, when told that the one year of classics he had proposed for a course of study was not sufficient, said that his proposal was, after all, "a course of University Studies, which always suppose Classics already taught"; the university begins "where the School ends." Greek and Latin weren't needed to get out of the university. They were necessary to get in.

■　　■　　■

Meanwhile, over the preceding two centuries, the classics had sailed as seedlings across the Atlantic to America. The roots weren't long in the taking. When we remember that the Pilgrims had set sail from Old England to New England in 1619, we can better grasp the extreme oddness, even quaintness, of a man from another expedition in the Virginian swamps hard at work translating Ovid's *Metamorphoses* in the year 1623. George Sandys, an Oxford man and treasurer of the struggling Virginia Company, set himself to the task. When he finally dedicated the book to Charles I three years later, Sandys averred that the work had "sprung from the stock of the ancient Romans, but [was] bred in the New World, of the rudeness of which it cannot but participate; especially having won wars and tumults to bring it to light, instead of the Muses." For creating rather less than a masterpiece, he should be forgiven. Yet, as the author of the *History of Classical Scholarship* has written, "'rudeness' cannot justly be predicated of a poem, which was admired by Pope, and was described by Dryden as the work of 'the best versifier of the former age.'" Civilization was hard to put down, even in the wilds of Virginia. Indeed it had been ordained. On the eve of one ship's departure, William Crashaw preached to the mariners with these words: "If the ancient Romans converted the ancient Britons to civility, let the English here repay the debt." Michael Drayton christened those bound for Virginia as "Argonauts."

John Harvard, an exile of Emmanuel College, Cambridge, came to Massachusetts soon after the Pilgrims and founded Harvard College in 1636, giving most of his possessions — half of his money and all of his library — to the new college at Newtown, later renamed "Cambridge" in honor of the many early colonist scholars and their former university in the Old World. John Harvard's library consisted notably of Homer, Terence, Horace, and Plutarch, a fairly worldly lot for an institution committed early on to training Puritan ministers.

(Volumes of Plutarch especially would prove a prophetic gift to the college and to the future of this new country launched under the umbrella of the English Crown. "It is fair to say," wrote Richard Gummere, "that Plutarch was to the rebellion what Cicero was to the Declaration, and Aristotle and Polybius to the Constitution.") Formal requirements for admission to the new college were rigid. The statute published in 1642 is straightforward:

> When any scholar is able to read Tully [Cicero] or such like classical Latin Author extempore, and make and speak true Latin in verse and prose...without any assistance whatever and decline perfectly the paradigms of nouns and verbs in the Greek tongue, then may he be admitted into the College, nor shall any claim admission before such qualifications.

Getting into Harvard then was not, we might conclude, the mystery it is today. Requirements were clear, regardless of family or wealth. One was a student of the classics, or he didn't matriculate. When the College of William and Mary was founded in 1693, Latin and Greek were the only keys to entry. Yale followed suit, making this proclamation in 1720:

> Such as are admitted Students into the Collegiate School shall in their examination in order thereunto be found expert in both the Latin and Greek grammars, as also skillful in construing and grammatically resolving both Latin and Greek authors and in making good and true Latin.

King's College, later Columbia, was founded requiring nothing more for admittance than Greek, Latin, and arithmetic. Thomas Jefferson, when planning the curriculum for his University of

Virginia founded as late as 1819, nodded to this bit of plain speaking from one of his associates: "It should be scrupulously insisted on that no youth can be admitted to the university unless he can read with facility Virgil, Horace, Xenophon, and Homer: unless he is able to convert a page of English at sight into Latin: unless he can demonstrate any proposition at sight in the first six books of Euclid, and show an acquaintance with cubic and quadratic equations." Anything less would make the place "a mere grammar school."

Classical learning seeped deeply into the new nation's culture, not only in public speeches and newspaper commentaries, but also in the diaries and letters preserved throughout the colonial era. Cotton Mather wrote original Latin verse. Richard Lee II of Virginia had a library armed with Homer, Horace, Virgil, Lucian, Ovid, and Cicero; Lee wrote his journal entries in Greek, Latin, and Hebrew. Jefferson proudly said, in a gust of rhetorical nonsense, that "American farmers are the only farmers who can read Homer." Not true, of course, but even the overstatement tells us something about what the best-educated colonials thought educated men should know. Benjamin Franklin, upon taking over editorship of the *Courant*, adopted a familiar policy: "Gentle readers, we design never to let a paper pass without a Latin motto, which carries a charm in it to the Vulgar, and the Learned admire the pleasure of construing."

Yet Sandys had been right. America was still a "rude" country. People had to be engaged in many more pressing tasks to secure the physical comforts and securities of life before larger numbers could divert themselves with classical letters and other salves of learning and culture. Although the colleges wielded inflexible requirements for their would-be scholars, much time had to elapse before classical customs took hold of more citizens; a century passed before a single Latin poem was published within the colonies. But take hold they eventually did, and, quite predictably, via translations. Perhaps the first classical work actually printed in America came in 1729: an edition of the philosopher Epictetus. Next came Cato's moral Distichs in 1735 and Cicero's *Cato Major* in 1744, both printed by Benjamin Franklin; the last Franklin touted as the "first Translation of a *Classic* in the *Western* [or New] *World*." By 1786 the country could find the *Lyric Works of Horace*, translated by John Parke, who had served once as a lieutenant colonel in the army of George Washington.

The die had been cast. To make "good and true Latin," as the Yale declaration had it, was as strong a pedagogical practice in America as it was in England and Europe at the same time. One both refined and proved his education with it. Early Americans, as classicist and historian Meyer Reinhold has written, "lived in the afterglow of the Renaissance." Higher learning to them, of whatever kind, had to be useful, not merely ornamental; it had to play a guiding role in daily life. Classical learning did. Americans were — and were to be — beneficiaries of the Renaissance without having to suffer the pains of its birth. Consequently, the thinking and governing classes as a whole possessed the classical vision from the days of Jamestown and Plymouth, and they did not allow its strength to flag in grammar schools and colleges. As we'll see later, because the country's very founding and growth coincided with an invigorating age of classical dominance in the life of the intellect, the ideals of the United States of America were to be profoundly, if not irreversibly, affected.

■   ■   ■

By the time American independence was achieved and the French Revolution had come to its violent close, the Augustan era of polish and decorum seemed to shut with the heavy thud of a sarcophagus lid. The tidier political landscape in England might have seemed in a state of total excavation during the first two decades of the nineteenth century. While Europe stood on the brink of the martial age of Napoleon, the Old World felt the tremors of new mass movements. The winds of democratic sentiment blew briskly. The Reform Bill of 1832 extended the franchise in England to more citizens, and greater numbers took a greater interest in public matters. The nineteenth century was the first great age of Utilitarianism. Industry mechanized itself. Old ideals held, but as the century marched on they were disjointed with the times. Progress took on a mystical air as Science promised all that was needful to improve life. Ideas had to start making sense to ordinary people. Prerogatives of thought and action were wrested from dons, court, and clergy. Richard Cobden would say by mid-century that one issue of the *Times* of London contained more useful information than all the pages of Thucydides — though his was a distinctly minority view.

Changes were not confined to the voting box, factory, and broadsheet. Deeper fissures tore citizens, educated and uneducated alike, from their past. The Romantic impulse in literature and art greased the skids for a new gospel of the liberated sensibility. Old certainties were shaken. People gave voice to atheism and agnosticism, articles of doubt and anti-faith themselves almost becoming points of dogma, badges of stoic heroism. Travel became more frequent as restless itinerants struck with wanderlust could settle the colonized globe. Changes in taste were inevitable. Here was a sterner age when classical works glowed with an urgent modernity and were invested with the supreme power to inform the conduct of all human affairs. Thomas Arnold would write in the preface to his edition of Thucydides that his effort was "not an idle inquiry about remote ages and forgotten institutions but a living picture of things present, fitted not so much for the curiosity of the scholar as for the instruction of the statesman and the citizen."

The Victorians searched out new images of freedom and strained their eyes for broad, resurrected vistas of the good life. Things Greek replaced things Roman in the educated mind. The liberty of Athens mesmerized men who had become weary of Roman order and its imperial corruptions — a vast, labyrinthine world perhaps too much with them during a time when the British Empire ruled the waves to enforce the Pax Britannia. Well-schooled Victorians wished to breathe freer air and drink of clearer ideas in the *stoa* of their imaginations, imbibing as they ambled the lessons of humility and the joys of simplicity. They yearned to be Hellenes. Plato and Thucydides replaced Horace and Virgil as the cultural ensigns. History and the wisdom of philosophy claimed equal places alongside the fancies of ancient poets. And English poets of the nineteenth century, despite their Romantic trailblazing, tended to be just as drawn and inured to classical learning as poets of the age before. Shelley was a formidable reader of the classics, as were Coleridge, Byron, Tennyson, and Browning. These were not men of feeling alone, but talents of trained sensibility.

The new cult of travel fed the conversion to Hellenism as amateur archeologists traipsed the rocky terrain of Attica and Arcadia to touch with their hands a world spied theretofore only in books and footnoted in arid lectures. Books like Bartholemy's *Travels of Young Anacharsis* in Greece sold briskly. Then these dilettanti wrote their own dusty travelogues to mark their adventures in the sunny lands of Greek legend, finding that what the professors assumed to be mere legend had been fact after all. Heinrich Schliemann dug back three thousand years and "gazed on the face of Agamemnon." If there hadn't been a Trojan horse, at least there had been a Trojan War. Classical times departed from the gray etchings of the mind and donned real colors. Grote's *History of Greece* sat in many a front room. This movement was redolent of romance. H. W. Williams wrote in his *Travels in Italy, Greece and the Ionian Isles* in 1820 of standing before a "city which was for ages the light of the world; where the unfettered energies of man had achieved the noblest deeds recorded in history; where genius, wisdom and taste had reached their highest perfection." That city was Athens.

The English preference for Greek stepped apace with those wider cultural yearnings within the privileged precincts of the Public Schools and the universities. By the end of the eighteenth century, Coleridge was admonished at school to prefer Greek to Latin as the truly literary language for those blessed with a higher sensibility. Although Eton and Winchester changed their curriculum little in the first decades of the nineteenth century, they too adjusted to satisfy new desiderata. The greatest schoolmasters of the period tended to be Greek scholars, and their erudition no doubt rubbed off on the enthusiasms of their students. Masters taught Latin as assiduously as before, but one senses a pro forma air hanging about their teaching; as before, Latin was an accessory for the gentleman, but it had lost some of its cachet.

Classical learning as a whole changed its trajectory. Scholarly detachment grew as a new professional paradigm. Statutes for the classical course in Literae Humaniores at Oxford, consisting of the stepladder from Honour Moderations to Greats, took effect in 1800; the Classical Tripos at Cambridge was inaugurated in 1824. The universities added a

Greek prose requirement to their examinations by the 1840s. Their curricula broadened as they became less exclusively literary. History was added to Literae Humaniores in 1830. Moral Philosophy began to dominate classics at Oxford, where lecture halls were filled with a routine that one contemporary called "Aristotle today, ditto tomorrow." Another man averred with frustration that at Oxford "four years are spent in preparing about fourteen books only for examination," volumes which are to be "read, re-read, digested, worked, got up, until they become part and parcel of the mind." But this experience, while tedious to endure, was the very idea behind the course; it was hoped that the tedium of the unbending curriculum would help to form vigorous intellectual habits. By mid-century Plato emerged as the author to take up at Oxford, shifting the university's philosophical gears and leading to Benjamin Jowett's massive translation of the *Republic*, which, for better or worse, entered the common bank of knowledge of all educated people in England; one scholar had said that the book single-handedly "made Plato an English classic." But a reading knowledge of the classical languages, while still a skill of comparatively few, became more than ever a coveted social — if not always intellectual — accoutrement. Macaulay defined an educated gentleman as a man able to read Plato with his feet before the fire. J. A. Symonds once spent an entire night plowing through the *Dialogues*: "It was as though the voice of my own soul spoke to me through Plato."

The fifty years between 1820 and 1870 ushered in more schools to serve the growing and prosperous country and feed the universities above: Marlborough, Cheltenham, Wellington, Clifton, Malvern, Radley, and Lancing, among others. And these schools, along with their conservative older cousins, made a few changes. They placed a smaller stress on exercises aiming at strict stylistic imitation and a greater one on substance. Content began to reach parity with form. Names and dates, along with grammatical mnemonics, filled more hours of a student's days. John Stuart Mill had argued for more history and philosophy in the classical curriculum. John Henry Newman went along, dubbing these adjuncts "enlarging studies" for those pursuing, as he had, a literary education of the classical kind. From history students could extract both moral and practical lessons they might later apply to public and private life. Yet matters of style didn't fade away. Form retained its nest in classical instruction, though it was taught differently. Whereas before students typically wrote original compositions in Greek, in the Victorian age we see more weight laid upon translating from established English prose (perhaps a passage from an essayist or historian) into clear Greek. "Every lesson in Greek and Latin," Arnold would say, "may and ought to be made a lesson in English." Yet the old defense of classics as the promoter of national virtue still obtained, and indeed grew stronger. "A high sense of honour, a disdain of death in a good cause, a passionate devotion to the welfare of one's country," wrote Edward Copleston, "are among the first sentiments which those studies communicate to the mind."

Now came the unimaginable age of the Headmaster as Hero. Two great spirits embodied two great strains of English classical education in the first half of the century. Samuel Butler and Thomas Arnold were revered schoolmasters who transformed not only the curricula but also the very ethos of English school life. From his appointment as headmaster in 1798, Butler shepherded the rise of Shrewsbury school to its status as the premier institution of pre-university classical instruction in the country. He produced hefty numbers of renowned classical scholars, including Benjamin Hall Kennedy, whose precocious erudition won him Cambridge's Porson Prize before he even left the school. (Kennedy himself went on to lead Shrewsbury, remaining for thirty years and earning the reputation, according to one chronicler, as "the greatest classical teacher of [the nineteenth] century." He also authored the famous *Latin Primer*, which became the standard Latin text of the day.) Ancient history and geography received more attention under Butler. Tacitus and Thucydides became classroom staples. Cicero's speeches re-entered the classical canon. While verse exercises were not set aside, Greek and Latin prose took precedence over poetry in keeping with new requirements to read more of the ancient historians and orators. Classical prose composition became in fact the major feature of nineteenth-century classical education. Anthologies of the ripest fruits were published to acclaim by the tonier schools: Winchester had its *Lusus Westmonasterienses*, Eton its *Musae Etonenses*, Rugby its *Vulgus*. The most lasting educational innovation of the century arrived when Butler launched formal and competitive examinations to determine the pecking order of young scholars' achievements, changing forever the relation between school and university. He awarded prize money to the most accomplished scholar-performers. English-speaking classical scholarship owes incalculably to Butler's service in bolstering academic standards and heightening the goals of learning. But the influence of Thomas Arnold, if not so deep scholastically, reached much farther.

Wedding the strictures of classical education to the austere Victorian ideal of the Christian gentleman, Arnold arrived at Rugby school in 1827 and led the institution during its headiest days, becoming the schoolmaster the entire country looked to as a model. Religion towered in this sober age. Students were to be soaked in "godliness and good learning." Education took on the grave sincerity of a mission. As did Vittorino da Feltre centuries before him, Arnold sought to help the unformed young to become complete men, intellectually and spiritually. "Learning to think" did not constitute an education to Arnold any more than to others throughout the previous centuries. "Mere intellectual acuteness," he once said, speaking of lawyers, "divested as it is, in too many cases, of all that is comprehensive and great and good, is to me more revolting than the most helpless imbecility, seeming to be almost like the spirit of Mephistopheles." Once again we find enjoined the humanistic training of mind and spirit both. That a boy should become a gentleman was more devoutly to be wished than that he should become a classical scholar, for the "mere scholar cannot possibly communicate to his pupils the main advantages of a classical education," some of which advantages transcend the bounds of intellect. The young need a compass above all else. "When the spring and activity of youth is altogether unsanctified by anything pure and elevated in its desires," Arnold wrote, "it becomes a spectacle that is as dizzying and almost more morally distressing than the shouts and gambols of a set of lunatics." Arnold was nothing if not in earnest.

Hard learning, though, was not to be shirked. While a student at Winchester, Arnold had developed a love and aptitude for Greek composition. Taking also to reading the Greek historians and orators, he was said to be able as an adolescent to construe Herodotus and render him into elegant English at sight. Declaring himself "quite tired of the pompous boasts of Cicero" as a student, Arnold preferred historians, the tellers of fact. Throwing a blanket over the epicurean delights of those exclusively enamored of Greek and Latin poetry, he opted for "things rather than words," the facts of history rather than notions. He was well fit for the new age. Nonetheless, he harbored no doubts about the "relevance" of commerce conducted with dead men and dead languages. Crediting the cyclical nature of history, Arnold viewed the study of ancient history as essential to judging modern action. "Aristotle and Plato, and Thucydides, and Cicero, and Tacitus, are most untruly called ancient writers," he once wrote, for "they are virtually our own countrymen and contemporaries, but have the advantage which is enjoyed by intelligent travelers, that their observation has been exercised in a field out of the reach of common men." Knowing the past allows one to be prudent in the present and wise in the future. Arnold believed also that the best classical teacher will know modern history and modern literature, so as to draw the appropriate lines between the ancient and modern worlds — lines he of course assumed to exist. History, like language, was a practical pursuit.

But his belief in the balms of Greek and Latin was full and uncompromising. Although modern history and other modern subjects (as well as mathematics) were taught with passion, all else in the curriculum of Rugby hung upon classics. "The study of language," he wrote, "seems to me as if it was given for the very purpose of forming the human mind in youth; and the Greek and Latin languages, in themselves so perfect, and at the same time freed from the insuperable difficulty which must attend any attempt to teach boys philology through the medium of their own spoken language, seem the very instruments by which this is to be effected." English was to be mastered but, as they had been made to do for generations, students were to take the long way round. Nor did the classical languages stay in the ghetto of the language class; students read Greek and Latin for history — Herodotus, Xenophon, Livy, Tacitus — and for Scripture and biblical history with the Greek New Testament. Students also had to achieve an intimate acquaintance with French. The upper forms read La Fontaine, Pascal, and Molière, as well as major histories of France and England in French. By the time students reached the sixth (top) form, they were reading Homer, Virgil, the Greek tragedians, and Aristotle's *Ethics* — and all this before matriculating at a university. Many alumni recalled in after years Arnold's zealous praise for the "luminous clearness" of Demosthenes, his armchair fluency with Thucydides, his pleasure when parsing Plato, and his elevation of Homer, whose poetry he deemed a "fountain of beauty and delight which no man can ever drain dry." Eventually he would bring Pindar and Aristophanes to Rugbeians. Here was more than a teacher: Arnold held the keys to the cosmos. Classics would never again enjoy such complete, undiluted confidence. This age was the high waterline for climbing the Parnassian heights of classical precision and eloquence. This was the world of Mr. Chips.

And that, some thoughtful people came to believe, was just the problem. The Victorian age had spread classical education throughout the country to the happy point where many modest grammar and preparatory schools, though they taught pupils bound almost certainly for careers in trade, were spurred to mimic, however imperfectly, the practices of the great Public Schools. When we keep in mind the classical curriculum's strict, painstaking, and time-consuming regimen, we realize that classical schooling probably had penetrated as far as it could go into the larger population. But if a more widely diffused classical education had been in the ascendant throughout the age, classical scholarship suffered. Although this period produced many valuable scholarly editions of classical authors — not to mention a monolith like the first edition of Liddell and Scott's Greek lexicon in 1843 — the nineteenth century is not now remembered principally for bringing forth many scholars on the order of Bentley or Porson. Aside from notable discoveries in the adventurous field of archaeology, much of it amateur, little new light was shed on the dusty quiddities of Greek and Roman life, literature, and history. But, as C. O. Brink has observed, men of this age didn't try to shed that light. The public wanted not scholars but "reasonably educated and civilized men of affairs and it got what it wanted." Benjamin Jowett's roundly ridiculed ideal of the well-educated, public-spirited gentleman carries an undeniable cultural heft — one better pondered in its absence. The educated, public-minded citizen is no mean achievement.

While the classical tradition held unabated till the end of Queen Victoria's reign, classical education had its critics, some hailing from within the ranks. Ancient texts remained unacceptably corrupt and, where those texts were reliable, men still failed to comprehend their historical context. Classical composition may be a fine way to train the sensibility, they inveighed, but it reveals precious little about the way Aeschylus or Horace actually wrote or what they really meant: only the philological critic and historian can do that. Classical education might indeed have been too successful. It hadn't stopped to take inventory of its acquirements and add to the body of classical knowledge. It hadn't tried to separate itself sufficiently from contemporary life. So some fought back. A. E. Housman, the poet and brilliant scholar — nay, dyspeptic oracle — who later held the Kennedy Chair of Latin at Cambridge, had come up to Oxford in 1877. There he indignantly walked out of the one and only lecture of Jowett's he attended because he was "disgusted by the Professor's disregard for the niceties of scholarship." Mark Pattison, another Oxonian of the time, bristled against Jowett's ideal of educated, enlightened public service as resulting in "the degradation of a University into a School," converting a place of higher learning into a "cramming shop" — a trend which some claimed to have been evolving since the honors schools' creation in the first quarter of the century. This criticism no doubt had merit.

Yet there couldn't have been the classical scholarship without the classical education. It helped the cause of classical scholars to inhabit a culture that breathed classical air. Without his own training in Greek and Latin, the acidic Housman might not have had his rapier wit to sharpen and exercise so lustily on his inferiors. For he too was a man of his time, formed in large part by the books he had been set to read. Had he been nourished on the militantly mediocre schooling of our day, he might have been nothing more auspicious than a journalist.

■   ■   ■

The sands were running out. There would be, after Housman, but one more cohort enjoying the windfalls of classical education in the flower of an elevated literary culture. The author of *A Shropshire Lad* had himself drunk deeply at lyrical springs. The generation born and educated between 1870 and 1920 — that of Albert Jay Nock, W. Somerset Maugham, R. W. Livingstone, Rupert Brooke, Ronald Knox, T. S. Eliot, C. S. Lewis, Evelyn Waugh, Robert Graves, Louis MacNeice, W. H. Auden — would be the last group whose early exposure to classical rigors at school allowed them as adults to be literary masters and gourmands. If these were not to be the last brilliant writers, they were the last seasoned ones. Their university years, whether or not they read classics especially, were not squandered primarily in learning languages, ancient and modern, but in savoring the literature, thus permitting that literature in turn to form their taste and judgment. But all this, so long in the making, was not to last. The early twentieth century was a time of swan song. The two decades after the death of Queen Victoria marked a last stand of classics as a pursuit lending as much faith to aesthetics and intellectual formation as to knowledge of facts. Never again would it all seem so effortless.

Much of that flower of England, of course, fell on the muddy battlegrounds of Belgium and France in World War I. But not before re-elevating one more author of the distant past to his highest throne in the pantheon. These great ages of classical education closed with paeans to the first and preeminent poet of the Western tradition, tying the bow on three millennia of greatness. Homer had not been common reading throughout the prior four centuries. He was better known than read in the straight-laced world of the eighteenth century as well as in the morally sober one of the nineteenth. One got him accidentally at the knees of the odd master or don inclined to the joys of Homeric epic. As late as the 1870s, Homer went completely unread at Winchester and Shrewsbury. It took stuffy, conservative Eton and its stout headmaster Edmund Warre to help turn the tide back to the greatest bard of them all.

The Edwardian devotion to Homer probably began as a bid for relief from the relentless elenchus of Plato and the moral pessimism of Thucydides. He delivered in spades. Not only did he offer snappy, engaging narratives amenable to schoolboys and spinsters alike, but he also conveyed rare lyrical beauty. His seemed a voice from the morning of civilization. To read Homer was to discover a new country different enough to provide escape but familiar enough over time to lend comfort to rainy days. Here was an atmosphere of heroic munificence ranged "far on the ringing plains of windy Troy." No longer was the payoff for years of sweat over grammar and word lists simply higher thought: Homer said high things beautifully. How appropriate that the period of classical guardianship over the Western intellect and spirit should end where it began — with Poetry. It seemed that the rational and romantic imaginations had finally met. Walter Bagehot, a much earlier devotee, once said that "a man who has not read Homer is like a man who has not seen the Ocean" — there is so much that one does not and cannot know. With poetry in their minds and on their lips, Rupert Brooke and other members of that last generation lit out from clean and dear homes to die on distant fields. Patrick Shaw-Stewart, an old Etonian destined to perish on those fields, went on reading Homer to his final days, the truth of the poetry perhaps coming home as the guns thundered ahead. Wounded during that same war, C. S. Lewis would later record his thought as the bullets and shrapnel struck: "This is war. This is what Homer wrote about." Homer had given all these young men a vocabulary for their agonies.

The war in fact closed off the foothills to Parnassus, perhaps for good. By the time the Armistice was signed in 1918, calls for commercial and "useful" knowledge on both sides of the Atlantic, combined with blasted ideals and the horror of those fine, educated young men now lying in foreign graves, carried too much firepower to resist. Heroism was dead, at least for the time being, as was the ideal of the gentleman. So was "useless" knowledge. A new world waited to be built. Time had run out for the niceties of learning the words of the dead. The prism of classics sharpened the colors of the world no longer. Tags of classical quotation began to fall on deaf, uninstructed ears.

The roots of the change reached down into the classroom. During the second half of the Victorian age, many of the less-privileged grammar schools began to lose classical ground to the posh Public Schools. Greek proved too hard to keep afloat, whatever its vogue in smarter quarters of English society, and by the 1920s Greek was no longer compulsory for all attending Oxford. Latin returned as the premiere — and, in some places, once again the only — classical language taught, but it became a shadow of its former self. The teaching of Latin began to sleepwalk. People forgot what the point of it was, or ever was. Trumpets for the lost cause summoned soldiers to the battlefield one last time. The first quarter of the twentieth century witnessed an efflorescence of desperate, last-ditch defenses of classics. Scholars like Gilbert Murray, J. W. Mackail, and Richard Livingstone became evangelists and hit the lecture circuit with the zeal of men on a military campaign. They didn't want to go down without a fight.

But the strategy was no longer the same. Instead of defending the purity of the languages and the fortifying benefits accruing to those who learned them, the last defenders surrendered precious ground. Briefs filed on behalf of classical education dissolved into forlorn, inchoate pieties on the glory that was Greece and the grandeur that was Rome. The popularizing had begun. Content was everything, form nothing. They didn't say so in so many words — and indeed the best apologists didn't mean this at all — but the message seemed plain to the Greekless and Latinless masses who yearned for membership in the bookish classes: work was no longer required. "Appreciation" replaced rigor. Scholars became salesmen. Translations of the great classical authors were no longer cribs; they were bestsellers. A. E. Housman finally got his way more than he might have hoped back when he was busy cleaning the texts of Manilius and attacking the gentlemanly presumptions of Jowett. By the time of Housman's death in 1936, classical scholarship, bolstered by a century of spectacular feats in German classical philology, had overtaken classical education. It had all become serious business, not child's play. No more rattling off of grammatical rules by rote from the age of seven; no more agonizing over senseless Greek and Latin proses. Credentialed science was to rule forevermore. Classics became the specialty Housman had dreamed of: the rare accomplishment of a dedicated few, not a fruitful province of the talented and cultivated. The amateurs were routed. The field belonged to the professional players who would brook no more meddling from dilettantes.

As often happens with lost causes, by the time those apologists had erected their buttressed defenses, the brave had fallen. It remained only to collect the wounded. Whereas once Latin and Greek, together with their literatures and all else they drew in their train, were thought to make the complete human being and lay a foundation for higher culture, now they were dead weight in a leveling age, millstones dragging down the new day dawning. People began to think that classical knowledge closed more doors than it opened; it shut out the light; it slowed the pulse of a quickening world. All things were to be made new. What good is climbing a Parnassus within when we can build skyscrapers without? The dikes could hold back the waters no longer. *Après nous le Deluge.*

THREE

Traveling through the Realms of Gold

The scene was Mr. Jefferson's University of Virginia. The time was 1931. Philosopher-journalist Albert Jay Nock had been invited by the Page-Barbour Foundation to deliver a series of lectures on the nature of American education. Here was a topic tame and soporific enough to soothe an academic audience. It was also quaintly appropriate, as Jefferson himself had been much engaged with promoting an educated citizenry for the new, fledgling nation. Perhaps only the friends and avid readers of this social iconoclast could have known what awaited his listeners. Characteristically ignoring the vested sensitivities of his auditors, Nock set out to tell the truth and damn the consequences. He was convinced that American education was all but doomed, and he used the occasion to burst the bubbles of the theorists then ruling the American academy and tinkering with the schools. For over the previous fifty years, Nock believed, they had ensured with their curricular experiments that the United States might never again see a generation quite like that of the Founding Fathers, whom many of them extolled with staid patriotic fervor. Together the philosophizing hucksters had allowed American education to sink far below the waterline of survival marked by civilized men over many centuries. He came to sound General Quarters.

Nock believed that the entire modern scaffolding of American education had been built on bad theory from top to bottom. The *telos*, or aim, was wrong. Is the vertical, Practical Man — that tool manipulated for other people's enrichment — the best we can hope to be? Nock sensed uneasiness in the land, and he believed he knew where it came from. We may write off our needling discomfort with our schools, he said, as a malady caused by a "vague notion that we ought to be gathering grapes from thorns and figs from thistles." His first task therefore was to light a path to "clear thought" and to reestablish the age-old difference between education and training. He began by drawing the traditional line between "instrumental" and "formative" education, even while granting that a thriving nation needs both. The first historically has been called vocational "training," not education; it's about showing us how to do, make, and change things. But the second aims to form the mind, to instruct the intellect itself, to clear and plow rocky fields so as to plant and grow fruits of intellectual strength. The truly educated mind is the formed mind.

And such a mind, Nock said, is the one thing needful for a healthy society. All but the mentally crippled can walk at least one of these roads. Some people are trained; some are educated; some are both. The distinction is simple enough. But it creates cramps for a democratic culture. Nock, like myriad deep thinkers before him, believed that most people's fields are barren, incapable of yielding the best crops of education, regardless of desire and effort. All can travel the first road of training, but few the second. This idea was not open to debate; random walks along any street proved its truth. Nock blamed uninformed democratic sentiment for the modern faith that all people can learn practically anything, while, he said, "relatively few are educable, very few indeed." Unfortunately, though, equalitarian drunkenness has outlawed this nod of common sense. The doctrine of equality in the social and political spheres, he said, we have "regularly degraded into a kind of charter for rabid self-assertion on the part of ignorance and vulgarity," serving it up as a "warrant for the most audacious and flagitious exercise of self-interest." But it gets worse. The modern, sentimental mind militates against truth itself.

> The popular idea of democracy is animated by a very strong resentment of superiority. It resents the thought of an elite; the thought that there are practical ranges of intellectual and spiritual experience, achievement and enjoyment, which by nature are open to some and not to all. It deprecates and disallows this thought, and discourages it by every available means. As the popular idea of equality postulates that in the realm of the spirit everybody is able to enjoy everything that anybody can enjoy, so the popular idea of democracy postulates that there shall be nothing worth enjoying for anybody to enjoy that everybody may not enjoy; and a contrary view is at once exposed to all the evils of a dogged, unintelligent, invincibly suspicious resentment.

Here are the thoughts whose names we dare not speak. Within them smolder the fires of class struggle and envy. Yet Nock claimed nothing more than Plutarch, Vittorino da Feltre, Thomas Arnold, and other enlightened spirits have claimed throughout history. C. S. Lewis, we recall, said that equality, so valuable as a legal fiction for a just society, still has no place in the life of the mind. Political ideals of equality, Lewis said, may be necessary. But he, like Aristotle before him, drew that valuable distinction between the "education which democrats like" and "the education which will preserve democracy." For close up they face the world differently. One allows us to recline and feel good about ourselves; the other quickens us, out of a sense of our innate unfitness and incompleteness, to climb above what we are and rise to that which we might become.

But surely Nock, some may say, was too hard on a country that had spread the blessings of literacy farther than they had ever reached in recorded time. Never had so many people been able to read, write, and count. Yet is that enough? Literacy is fine and well, Nock said, but in the long view it's not much. Knowing how to read and write may shore up a nation's social health, but it's the bare minimum for a higher culture — without which any society must be judged cheap and ephemeral. In fact, "the mere ability to read raises no very extravagant presumptions upon the person who has it." "Surely everything depends upon what he reads," Nock said, appealing to Humanist ideals, "and upon the purpose that guides him in reading it." Whenever we judge a culture, we must weigh "the general furniture of its mind," and that furniture is flimsy and getting flimsier. It's time, he thought, to refurnish. We need less plastic and synthetics and more mahogany and teak.

Such thinking is, of course, heretical. It violates tenets of a secular faith in our righteousness and self-sufficiency. It denies the new age. But Nock believed it to be true to both history and common sense. His ideas might have occasioned some gnashing of teeth at Mr. Jefferson's University, where professors still exhaled the pragmatic vapors of John Dewey. Yet he merely reasserted the vision of Renaissance Humanists and their vital ideals of selection and formation: the quality of the things we know is of greater import than their quantity. And the way we say things can often pack as much point as can the things themselves. It's better to have sat at the feet of our betters than to pretend we're those betters ourselves. *Better* people pay dues; they serve apprenticeships. Education was less like a tool and more like a medicine. Certainly Nock was not speaking out for the well-touted "Information Age" to come, the very thought of which would have sent him into paroxysms of terror. He was speaking out for higher culture — the kind that had made the likes of Thomas Jefferson and John Adams possible. He was speaking out for the formed, well-stored mind.

Education for the intellectually gifted needs to serve both the smart people and the larger society of the less smart which, he hoped, the smart would go on to lead benevolently. Therefore education for intellectually talented men and women should be literary and cultural; it should be classical. Studies should be formative and "disciplinary," not vocational. For even the intelligent are but mere cultural postulants before they grow up. They need to be intellectually nourished; their twigs need both bending and straightening. And the model for the stake had been inherited from antiquity, rediscovered by men of the Renaissance, and sustained by the brighter lights of the modern world. The curriculum, though having been duly modified, already existed. No one had to reinvent the wheel. It was classical education.

Here was no tired European screed against an American lack of refinement. For it had not always been this way. Describing the history of education in colonial America, Nock reminded his audience that America had once got it dead right. Curricula within a typical early primary or secondary school until the age of the Revolution were "fixed, invariable, and the same for all participants." They held no electives. "The student took what was deemed best for him, or [he] left the place; he had no choice." Instrumental knowledge, "knowledge of the sort which bears directly on doing something or getting something, should have no place" in such a school, which should have "as strict an institutional quarantine raised against it as cities raise against a plague." That knowledge we can get on our own, or — as with computers — be taught in short order. Formative knowledge is more valuable, but it takes longer. The disciplined mind requires years to gestate. And the ideal curriculum for the twentieth century was the same triumvirate that ruled in the seventeenth, eighteenth, and a goodly part of the nineteenth: Latin, Greek, and mathematics. All other subjects grew from them, even as they were distinctly secondary to them. We can see the disciplined nature of this training-leading-to-education; acquisition of these three subjects exercised the mind with the primary elements of words and numbers. Its formative character was secure and definite. A student of the ancient world, Nock said, possessed a passport as a citizen not just of America, but also of the West.

> The literatures of Greece and Rome comprise the longest and fullest continuous record available to us of what the human mind has been busy about in practically every department of spiritual and social activity.... The record covers twenty-five hundred consecutive years of the human mind's operations in poetry, drama, law, agriculture, philosophy, architecture, natural history, philology, rhetoric, astronomy, politics, medicine, theology, geography, everything. Hence the mind that has attentively canvassed this record is not only a disciplined mind but an *experienced* mind; a mind that instinctively views any contemporary phenomenon from the vantage-point of an immensely long perspective attained through this profound and weighty experience of the human spirit's operations. If I may paraphrase the words of Emerson, this

discipline brings us into the feeling of an immense longevity, and maintains us in it.

This is a very long view indeed. And such an education served to do even more than discipline and form the mind. It inculcated right habits of feeling. An education like this establishes "certain views of life and the direction of certain demands on life, views and demands which take proper account of the fundamental instincts of mankind, all in due measure and balance; the instinct of workmanship, the instinct of intellect and knowledge, of religion and morals, of beauty and poetry, of social life and manners." All this adds up to "the Great Tradition of a truly civilized society," which is in the end the only sort of society worth having and preserving. Anything less is just getting and spending.

Nock's lectures were a stunning attack. His Voltaireian indictment contained no original counts. It had all been said before throughout the ages. Yet it needed repeating. Education should not be, as he explained later in his memoirs, a preparation for making a living, but a preparation for living. Education should aim at fostering a certain kind of intellect and a certain kind of human being. It required a lot of time at the blackboard learning things others have judged worthwhile. It involved learning to think well and to appreciate the solid proposition and the well-turned phrase.

Nonetheless, Nock's battle was lost as he spoke. And he probably knew it. For by the end of the nineteenth century in America, the old ways had passed. The industrial machine was grinding and it required brawn to keep it greased. And, just in time, a new theory had spread within the academy like a virus: election had replaced selection. President Charles Eliot had installed the elective system at Harvard, lesser institutions followed suit, and there was no turning back. Democracy would ensure that we all got what we wanted, not what we needed. "The old régime's notion that education is in its nature selective, the peculium of a well-sifted elite," Nock wrote elsewhere, "was swept away and replaced by the popular notion that everybody should go to school, college, university, and should have every facility afforded for studying anything that anyone might choose." The doors of education had opened. Popular will had triumphed. The world was more equitable. But some people were left with gnawing doubts. They could only wonder how history might have rolled out differently had the author of the Declaration of Independence been schooled thus.

■　　■　　■

"The right word is a sure sign of good thinking," Isocrates once said. Education in any literate society must begin with training in language. Words signify acts and ideas. They serve as common currency for the literate and illiterate alike, because even the unlettered utter sounds so as to communicate. Words distinguish; they supply an index to the quality and capacity of their users' intellects. They provide the gold standard for the thoughtful mind. Ideas are shadowy and inert without them. But with words to clothe them, ideas take on form. They gain substance. They become measurable, weighable. Words can make those ideas a shared possession. Private wisdom may inform one's own life supremely, but that wisdom may never inform or inspire others until one can, in some grand or modest way, breathe life into those private perceptions with the power of words. The mastery of language, according to Aristotle, both fosters practical skills and enhances the enjoyment of leisured hours; it is eminently useful for the workaday life while cultivating the mind and soul. Language, wrote Milton, serves mankind as "the instrument conveying to us things useful to be known" — and language is a precision instrument, like a Swiss watch.

Language is, of its essence, speech. It exists to be heard with the ears. But when spoken words are transmuted onto parchment or page, language can serve purposes greater than those of utility and leisure. It can be transfigured into literature. For literature is, as one Humanist has put it, language in evening dress. It fronts the wider world, speaking not to a mob but to a multitude of individuals. Yet the written word is not language bedecked for show alone. It touches the hem of the timeless. "A written word," wrote Thoreau, "is the choicest of relics. It is something at once more intimate with us and more universal than any other work of art. It is the work of art nearest to life itself. It may be translated into any language, and not only be read but actually breathed from human lips; not be represented on canvas or in marble only, but be carved out of the breath of life itself."

Today we pay homage, if not to this ideal, at least to the practical purposes walking abreast of it. Two of the Three R's have to do with words. Language provides the most reliable rod for measuring the educated mind. Computing strikes us — rightly or not — as a more mechanical function; machines can do that. Words require a different kind of judgment for their right and proper use. Language, we say, is the key to communication; language allows us to express ourselves; we even believe that an ability to use words satisfactorily helps us to get better jobs. Maybe so. As Nock once said in a moment of rare understatement, "A just care for words, a reasonable precision in nomenclature, is of great help in maintaining one's intellectual integrity." This is all to the good. Yet such goals are utilitarian;

they promise wages we can spend. Gazed upon through these
lenses, language is merely a tool, like a hammer or saw, a cell
phone or computer. Lost in all the theory is the larger, less quan-
tifiable, and cultural aim of learning to use language well for its
own sake. Good language makes for good thinking. But it's also
more aesthetically pleasing than the vague and pretentious
dreck with which the half-educated fill the world.

Classical education was always literary education *par excellence*. The finest exponents of that education in the past never
forgot the inseparable link between words and thinking. The
lady and the gentleman spoke well. Everyone from Isocrates to
Cicero to Erasmus to Dr. Johnson understood that, while our
words may not count for quite as much as the acts we commit,
still our use of words affords the most certain sign of our mental cultivation. Although the ineffable quality sought through
it was one of the mind and spirit, education was, in one real
sense, visible. We could see who had it. Here lies one explanation as to why Greek and Latin were pressed for so many centuries after their clerkish and scholarly uses in daily life had
ended: they helped, through their rigor and beauty, to form
intellects, to develop minds — minds always ready, when the
guard falls, to lapse into sloughs of cloudy thinking and muddy
verbiage. Thus were the languages and their privileged perch in
curricula defended for all those centuries.

The best and brightest of our day have abandoned this "formation" argument. We can see why. It was always hard to prove.
One tended to take it on authority alone, even when it was
amply supported by experience. The cultural argument is more
congenial and it makes more sense to us. It's easier to say that
we, as a culture, should know our family tree. We should
approach the argument from mental formation with trepida-
tion. Formation does not provide the best possible defense of

classical education. Like other cases, pro and con, it's not air-tight. But of all the old pleas for classics throughout the cen-turies, it's the one most neglected and — when acknowledged — reviled today. We might justifiably suspect that the *zeitgeist* has made a sound, fair appraisal of its claims a dicey matter. Many of us now insist on viewing education exclusively as per-forming an informative, not a formative, role. Indeed, as Nock understood, formation is not a sympathetic idea in a democratic age; it looks like yet another means of closing the club doors. It's also a more slippery notion to apprehend. One's aptitude with mathematics — that other tool for training the mind — can be tested; so can that with rules of grammar. But the "formed mind" cannot be so easily tagged. It inhabits an ineffa-ble universe.

Nonetheless, the formation argument for classics deserves more than a touch of the toe. Too many brilliant people in the past accepted it for us to ignore it. Indeed, some of them deemed it the only real case for classical education. So let us examine the hardest case, the one that was dismissed summar-ily from the court of enlightened — or at least certified — opin-ion eons ago. A classical education is, and by all rights should be, a disciplinary pursuit. It ought to be at least as much about form as it is about content. Let us indulge ourselves with a win-some exercise in this bit of pedagogical incorrectness.

■   ■   ■

Erasmus once wrote that there exist two kinds of knowl-edge: knowledge of "words" and knowledge of "truths." While knowledge of truths may come first in the pecking order, one cannot get at those truths without the knowledge of words. Classical education sought to provide a training in words so as to grant an entrée to those truths. And the training began with Grammar, Usage, and Composition. Notice we say "training" here, not "education." For education, rightly understood, is launched with training and drill. The educated mind must first know how to do, how to form and build, something. Education is the result; training is the method. Grammar, Usage, and Composition lend the starter sets for constructing that educated mind; they are the bricks and mortar, hammer and nails. But master architects draw the plans, not amateurs. Quintilian defined proper usage in language as "the agreed practice of educated men." Time and experience have validated his judgment. For centuries men and women of discernment have seen the claim's truth played out daily. To speak, write, and think well, one must learn from those who have expressed themselves better than had others throughout history. One learns how to think well by constant exposure to the greatest thoughts expressed with the finest, most apt words. Literature was the treasure chest; Grammar and Usage were the keys unlocking its lid.

This isn't exactly an obvious point now. We moderns prefer matter to form. We elevate the world of things because we can see and touch them. Material things are real. They can be molded to our designs. "Real" things belong to the "real world." Yet intellectual and aesthetic strengths are also real. They too help to determine who we are and what we're capable of. If we possess a soul prone to be formed and informed by a mind so strengthened, that mind can share in the timeless. It can rise above itself. For modernists, then, formation means little; for Humanists, it's almost everything. Here was the educational faith not only of the Greeks and Romans, but also of the Renaissance and of all in the modern world guided by its ideals and practices. The finer lights of these periods saw the best education as a duty served to great and good things — things, in other words, demonstrably better and higher than one's self. Reality was hierarchical. Schooling was meant to help pupils climb ladders to those better and higher things.

Yet they had to start at the bottom. They had to wipe their eyes and clean their mental lenses. The purpose of intellectual education, according to John Henry Newman, is "to remove the original dimness of the mind's eye; to strengthen and perfect its vision; to enable it to look out into the world right forward, steadily and truly; to give the mind clearness, accuracy, precision; to enable it to use words aright, to understand what it says, to conceive justly what it thinks about, to abstract, compare, analyze, divide, define, and reason, correctly." The education of the intellect should be, in short, "a discipline in accuracy of mind." And the maxim that ought to guide us, as every "sensible tutor" knows, is "a little, but well." Or, as Pliny, the first- and second-century A.D. Roman author put it, *Multum non multa*: Not many things, but one thing — and much of one thing. That one thing, as we've already discovered, was the right and proper use of words. Most of the plagues assailing the mind, Newman believed, could be traced to a person's ignorance of Grammar.

"Much writing breedeth ready speaking," Roger Ascham wrote in the sixteenth century. We should mark well this axiom. It contains a principle. Perfection comes from practice; the pupil must put in his time. Perhaps not all people are capable of eloquence, no matter how well instructed — but all of ready intelligence can be taught to recognize eloquence when they see it. They can learn to see its shape. They can learn to feel its power. But first they must be submerged in it. They must be schooled in eloquence — and not for intellectual purposes only. They should learn to take pleasure in it. Throughout sixteenth-century England, all future men of affairs had to learn to control words and ideas, so while they were young at school and university, they were set to developing "a fit, sensible, and calm kind of speaking and writing." This marching order may not sound exacting, but it's a tall order indeed. For there can be no "fit, sensible, and calm" use of language without mental formation. Eloquence extracted a price. The mind's formation required that one possess a "will to take pains." It was work. Yet the reward was massive. Most people, Ascham wrote, are "content with the mean"; the average suffices for the vast majority. But if we would be great, we must spend time with great things. We must learn the anatomy of style.

But do not Greek and Latin, as their critics have alleged, betoken a munificent waste of time and energy? We have traced the schemes and accidents of history giving rise both to those two tongues and to the system of schooling that sustained them for two millennia, so we can already answer these questions partially. Now we can see how they played their disciplinary role.

■   ■   ■

Greek and Latin carry in their long wakes an entire world of thought and feeling. But they do more. They give us codes of clarity and fluency. This is as true now as it was in fifteenth-century Italy or nineteenth-century England. Yet it would seem contrary to common sense. Would not a thorough acquaintance with one's native language do the trick much more efficiently? Surely the best way to learn, say, English is to read and write English? The answer of the ages is simple and direct, though it has rarely satisfied the maniacally literal mind: Greek and Latin were so taught for so many centuries *because* they were not native. Their very strangeness and dissimilarity to modern languages made them a unique, irreplaceable tool of teaching for those who would comprehend the workings of language *en tout*. The object was to gain an understanding of words from the inside, affording the learner an intimate familiarity with their separate and diverse natures. Thus could we own language in a new way; we would take it on board. We would learn to be both precise and graceful with the words we use. But as thinkers saw from ancient times till the day before yesterday, precision and grace are not a gift; they wait at the end of an arduous climb. The long way round is the shortest route home.

"Diligent translating," Ascham also wrote, "shall work such a right choice of words, so straight a framing of sentences, such a true judgment, both to write skillfully and speak wittily, as wise men shall both praise and marvel at." Translation is the logical place for the study of an alien language to begin, and perhaps also the natural place to end. No sense of history or mastery over literature obtains without the ability of a student or a learned adult to read the words that the old authors wrote and centuries of scholars preserved. Instilling this ability is no doubt the chief academic reason for learning Greek and Latin. It makes for scholars. But scholastic ability isn't the only reason. Exercising their words upon our own minds lends knowledge of that anatomy of style; it helps to bestow an expertise with the charm of felicitous phrasing. "Framing sentences" — a term Newman also used — in those languages sharpens our skill with "choice of words." It hones judgment. Such effort for the most fortunate of students provides abundant recompense, even though these beneficent results begin with dry, painstaking work. *Nil sine magno vita labore dedit mortalibus.* Life gives nothing to us without tremendous work and sacrifice. *Vincit qui patitur.* One who suffers also conquers.

So now we can spot some of the practical, if not always equally visible, advantages of learning Latin and Greek. Let us concentrate on Latin, as, of the two tongues, Latin has been the language most consistently taught through the ages. It has stood exposed against the firewall of ignorance and prejudice, taking the whitest heat from the stupidly zealous. Latin has become over time a symbol of an old guard to be fought and dispatched. It has taken most of the blows from smiling philistines and scowling reformers. Certainly the classically educated man and woman must have both Greek and Latin; to have only one is almost to have not even that. Ascham claimed that a Latin scholar without Greek is like a bird with one wing. But if we be allowed but one of them — and this I say as an unreconstructed Hellenist — we should choose Latin.

Advocates for Latin in the past have often sung its mental advantages to the exclusion of all else. According to legions of these priggish, schoolmarmish stiffs, one didn't learn Latin so as to read it, or even in order to gain entry into the upper reaches of Western literary culture. One learned Latin to help one's English — end of case. The argument worked passably well for a long time. And it ought to have worked. We can accept it. But it takes us only so far. This belief in Latin-as-an-aid-to-English was a diluted strain of the brave old *argumentum ad formam*. Suffice to say that the case eventually broke down, mainly because smart people recognized that learning modern languages could yield some of the same benefits, with the added advantage that they could be used to communicate in the modern day. They were not "dead" languages; at least we could use them in restaurants. Many also saw that, for purposes of mental training, mathematics was ready to hand as well, with the same advantage of being useful in an ever more calculating, technical world. These two observations — along with Latin's inherent, unavoidable, and cussed difficulty — shut down its supremacy in school curricula. Perhaps this had to happen: the case for

Latin had become weak because tired. Its defenders had become complacent and their weapons were dulled. Yet they always had a point. They still do.

James Russell Lowell, one of America's finest poets and essayists, once spoke before the Modern Language Association upon the inborn difficulties inescapable in the training of the mind. Translating from one language into another, he said, is the point where intellectual education begins.

> In reading such books as chiefly deserve to be read in any foreign language, it is wise to translate consciously and in words as we read. There is no such help to a fuller mastery of our vernacular. It compels us to such a choosing, and testing, to so nice a discrimination of sound, propriety, position, and shade of meaning, that we now first learn the secret of the words we have been using or misusing all our lives, and are gradually made aware that to set forth even the plainest matter as it should be set forth is not only a very difficult thing, calling for thought and practice, but is an affair of conscience as well. Translation teaches, as nothing else can, not only that there is a best way, but that it is the only way. Those who have tried it know too well how easy it is to grasp the verbal meaning of a sentence or of a verse. That is the bird in the hand. The real meaning, the soul of it, that which makes it literature and not jargon, that is the bird in the bush.

And it is the endless quest to find that "real meaning," Lowell said, that trains the mind. That's the very point of reading.

The American classicist B. L. Gildersleeve once said that any student "who learns among his earliest lessons to weigh and value words has made a great advance in habits of sober and cautious thought." Sir Richard Livingstone wrote that no one might truly be deemed educated who does not possess "some idea of the nature and laws of language." High thought and deep expression pulsate within language. Livingstone believed that Latin taught those laws better than any other tongue. A thorough training in Latin does encourage mental discipline. It helps us to think well. And indeed it helps us to understand English better than we would understand it without Latin. This one-two punch alone should justify its place in any good school. Let's begin to describe the gifts Latin brings in tow with the well-known boon of vocabulary.

English, as we have wearily heard repeated in dreary textbooks, takes about sixty percent of its words — either directly or via modern romance languages — from Latin. Any student who has invested strenuous years with Latin, both reading and writing it, will own an obvious edge with English over those who haven't. Not only has that student learned what the words mean, he has learned what they have meant; he has seen them jostling and lounging in their original habitat. They've gamboled at his feet. "Liberty" never means the same thing after our backs have been burdened with the full Roman weight of *libertas*. Nor does "constancy" convey quite the same quality as *constantia*. *Pietas* comes clothed with a baroque wealth of exalted overtones. And *gravitas* means more than "weight" to those who have rubbed elbows with it. If people have family trees, so have words, and tracing their branches through time and place reveals the complexity of their characters. Memorizing them, as we must do when learning to use a language, stretches the mind. Our brains become more capacious: the more we memorize, the more we can memorize. We begin to feel at home with those old words, and thus we feel more at home with their descendants in our own tongue. Once we have seen and used them, they're strangers no more. They're tactile; we can roll them in our hands. Commerce with them becomes easy.

Over time advantages arise from this commerce. One is mental expansion. Not only do our minds become better stored, but they also become more pliant, better able both to embrace new ideas and to judge old ones. They can analyze and synthesize on command. Our intellects graduate to a hard-won independence. They can cut through thickets of official obfuscation and doubletalk. Classically educated people are not the prime consumers of propaganda. Another advantage is confidence. We don't use words merely to impress; we don't need to. We use them to communicate and adorn. The modest weight of learning we drag along prevents us from being racked, as are some of our fellows, with an anxiety to look smart. We don't listen in our cars to cassette programs designed to increase our vocabulary — the vocabulary we learned neither at home nor at school — while we're trapped in rush hours in order to beat the competition in a corporate meeting with new, spiffy words. Our apprenticeship has already been served, though it doesn't inspire smugness. We yearn to be precise. And the precision we achieve, such as it may be, breeds a quiet confidence in our ability to say what we mean. Along with all the big and precise words we've learned to use well, we feel equally comfortable — and confident — using the small, non-Latinate words. Journalist Alistair Cooke once said that, because he had endured so much Latin in the classroom years ago, he doesn't now need to put on airs by using "circumlocutory" when he merely means "roundabout." He doesn't disdain the former; he simply saves the right word for the right moment — the word and moment the experience of his literary education had taught him to recognize. Cooke came, in more ways than one, from the old school.

If reading Latin can take us far down this road of mental expansion and confidence, Latin prose composition can take us even farther. We should not need to defend the practice of composition in any tongue we're learning. It fixes the grammar and syntax of the language in our heads while lending special insight into the genius of the nation from which it arose. As with speaking in a language, if we do nothing but beg directions, the act of writing in it affords possession; it makes it ours. This is readily conceded for modern languages. But why spend time learning to write sentences, paragraphs, and essays so few others can read?

Composing in the language of Cicero and Seneca, once again, can transform the way we use our own language. Writing in Latin especially spurs us to speak and write in complete sentences containing complete thoughts: a complete sentence *is* a complete thought. Here is a gain none too small these days when we're beset with verbal clutter and half-baked notions parading as serious thinking. Latin composition encourages us to structure the things that we have to say before we say them. It teaches us to communicate efficiently and well with finely tuned clauses and well-considered words. The practice of Latin composition helps to eradicate loose thinking and feeling. We learn to be responsible both for the words we use and the thoughts we broadcast to the world. Practice with Latin composition tightens expression. We learn to be brief. If Seneca, a Roman philosopher and statesman of the first century A.D., could shave a worthy thought down to a line or two — *Non qui parum habet, sed qui plus cupit, pauper est* (It isn't the man who has little, but the man who craves more, who is poor) — what right have we to prolixity? "What is written without effort," wrote Dr. Johnson, "is in general read without pleasure." A classically educated man, as well as one who had composed much in Latin and Greek, Johnson also believed that Latin teaches us how to strive toward economy and flair with our words. To paraphrase Johnson, nothing concentrates the mind so well as one hour spent on a Latin composition, either prose or verse. The work can be excruciating, the pleasure intense. But the composer, in the tested fashion of Humanism, improves his mental nature.

■   ■   ■

A classicist by the name of Isaac Stuart, upon being appointed to lead the Department of Classical Literature at the College of South Carolina in 1835, was summoned by the trustees of the college to define his mission before the governor and a joint session of the legislature of South Carolina in December of that year. Leaving aside a delicious rumination on the unlikelihood today of a governor and state legislature gathering to hear an address titled "On the Classical Tongues and the Advantages of their Study," we can see that the classical argument for intellectual formation lived a hearty life in nineteenth-century America. Claiming that Greek and Latin literature had — by then — served for three centuries in America "to form, refine and polish the minds of rising generations, and to nurse the inspiration of genius," Stuart avowed that they "continue, by common consent, to lie at the foundation of a manly, liberal education." His first justification for their maintenance was that "the study of Classics disciplines the mind," and he wasn't out to utter simple pieties about antiquated glory. His account of the exactions required for mastering Greek and Latin during that youthful time when classical splendors begin to enter the mind's bloodstream makes for a remarkable, one-hundred proof paragraph. It's worth quoting at length. The student of classics naturally begins with acquiring the languages.

In its first stage — that of Grammar — attention, memory and reflection are mainly concerned. These faculties, severely exercised, are continually increased in power, till the tyro [beginner] reaches the second and principal stage of his study — that of translation. Here first the meanings of words are to be settled. This cannot be done without an accurate knowledge of the parts of speech, without a nice appreciation of grammatical relation, and often without careful comparisons with the context. In the earliest and simplest process of translation, therefore, there is increasing necessity for the exercise of faculties already in training, and a new demand on the powers of judgment, comparison and deduction. Follow the student as he advances to involved and difficult sentences. Here words have greater variety of meanings. Their meanings, beside, as independent or relative, are often at variance; and often depend on the nicest inflections, or place in the order of inversions. Clauses multiply and require a greater number of relations to be investigated. Idioms occur, and demand the labor of noting peculiarities. The sense may poise on a particle seemingly indefinite and expletive. Attention, memory and reflection are now therefore more severely tasked. A more extensive collation of parts demands a nicer exercise of judgment and comparison, and gives fuller employment to the reasoning power, in discerning and applying results. In a word, an entire work of analysis and synthesis, its noblest employment, exercises fervently the whole understanding. But follow the Classical Student farther, from single sentences to sentences combined, and on to paragraphs combined. Beside now analyzing and recomposing the relation of words, his mind analyses and recomposes the relation of sentences; beside comparing the parts of a single thought, it compares entire and different thoughts and groups of ideas, and traces through them all the unity of a reigning subject. From particulars it has now proceeded to generals, and is exercised on a grander scale. A whole train of thoughts is to be pursued. Any loss in the train is to be corrected by greater vigilance of attention and memory — any imperfection in ideas, by intenser application in the reinvestigation of sentences; till finally the mind becomes prepared to make its general appreciation of the subject of translation. This last most difficult and important process, on which, as directed to various subjects, all excellence and success in life depends, is thus the final and constant duty of the Classical Student, and with him is guided and made effective by his preliminary discipline. His reflection in this case operates upon particulars well understood, well arranged. His conclusions, therefore, are not too hasty, nor founded on partial observation, and for the same reason his mind appropriates with happier selection and more permanent memory.

And what was the issue of all this to be over the long haul of life? "Certain valuable habits of mind," Stuart said, six in number. Classical study "forms the habit of settling the signification of words," by a method we can clearly divine. This was a most important habit to acquire, he said, "when we reflect how much of the error and heated useless disputes of men result from verbal ignorance or misapprehension." Next, classics "perpetually accustoms the mind to acquire and apply true principles" by way of "correct standards — a discipline, the paramount importance of which is conclusively shown by the abounding misery which results from false judgments." Classical study also "forms the habit of easy expression," as "fluency and ease are the consequence of an increasing vocabulary and repeated use." We also form the habit of "correcting and correctness," for "indistinct and imperfect ideas always at first accompany difficult translation." With all this we form "the habit of appreciating congruity," which "results from the constant necessity of understanding concord and government, the adaptation of word to word and clause to clause, till a thought be fully expressed."

Finally, classical study "accustoms the mind to form and direct its own trains of thought" through "the force of discipline and imitation, on a mind long engaged in pursuing trains of thought in others" — and pursuing them in two difficult and alien languages, greatly removed from us in both sense and time.

These are not bad things for a roomful of politicians to hear — and no doubt some of them would have grasped and praised every word, as they themselves had once been ordered to climb Parnassian heights. Politicians could be then, in South Carolina as elsewhere, the hacks many of them remain. But some could also be statesmen, due in no small measure to their having sat at the feet of good teachers and, as they grew older, great rhetoricians and poets through the books they read. Not by votes alone had they earned the privilege of leading others. We do not know how this address came off to the governor and members of the South Carolina legislature on that winter's day in 1835, but we ought not to expect to see anything like this soon entered into the *Congressional Record*.

■   ■   ■

Here are fine general observations. Together they make a certain theoretical and historical sense. But how precisely does this formation, this acquiring of right mental habits, work? What are the greasy mechanics of classical training?

Let's take a stout, high-sounding example of one sentence. We wish to say in Latin: "Hadrian governs the State, not as circumstances demand, but as if he were setting an example for the rest of mankind." *Hadrianus* is our subject. We now begin by breaking down what we mean by "state." The Romans thought of the state as a *respublica*, an amalgam meaning — depending upon the context — "nation," "constitution," "public affairs," and even "the public good." (Here's our first occasion to dwell on the variant meanings of words and ideas.) *Respublica* is a compound, from *Res Publica*, "public things," so the *res* bears an equal brunt of inflection along with *publica*. Together they make the direct object for the first clause. We now need a verb for "governs" in the present third person singular. We look in a dictionary to find *administrare*, meaning to manage, serve, do, or execute — in a word, to govern. (Here again we gain a new sliver of insight into one English word and its ramifications.) So far we have *Hadrianus rempublicam administrat*. We go on. For the sake of simplicity, we retain the order of clauses, though we need not do so, as Latin does not depend upon word or clause order in the way English and other modern languages do. "Not as circumstances demand": we find the verb *postulo* for "demand." A negating prepositional phrase beckons. *Res* — a factotum word, we discover — can carry the sense of "circumstances": *non sicut res postulat*. We enter the final turn with "as if he were setting an example." We switch a little complicatedly to the subjunctive mood, which presides over notions like intent, potentiality, desire, uncertainty, and anticipation. We see an imaginary idea: "as if he were setting an example for the rest of mankind" — but he isn't. *Quasi* allows us to construct a comparative clause (this, just as that). Last verb: "setting" an example can mean the same as "being" an example; let's use the proper form. Two words can serve for "the rest of mankind" — note the savings in words — *reliqui* and *ceteri*; we opt for a properly inflected form of the latter. Applying all the prescribed formulas, we tumble across the line. *Hadrianus rempublicam administrat non sicut res postulat sed quasi ceteris ipse futurus esset exemplo.*

We've cut the length of our sentence by a third while saying the same thing. This is a simple illustration. We could have followed other paths to the same meaning, and this is but a partial explanation for one possible rendering. Notice, though, what has happened. Although we have played in slow motion the steps one learns to take in seconds, we have shoveled a lot of coal for one sentence. And the effort has not been in vain. Running these heavy paces forces us to define our terms and decide what we mean; it makes us think. The thought does not stand alone as the one thing needful. Form and matter come together — as always they must. The procedure elevates us above our slack habits, transporting us out of our loose, lazy ways. We utter not what pours forth haphazardly in awkward spurts of inarticulacy, firing scattershot in the general direction of a target hoping we'll get points for proximity. Instead we think through the idea, and then we convert it into the right words. We strain through an intellectual exercise; we're sweatier for wear, but stronger. Were we to have an attentive audience for that one-sentence thought, rendered in whatever language, we might find our listeners quietly grateful for the pains we've taken, even if they were taken behind the scenes — and perhaps because they were taken behind the scenes.

Prose composition protects us from the dry bane of mere grammar for its own sake, a condition to which classical teaching has been tempted in the past. Writing animates any language. It keeps us active, engaged in the stuff of our material. We buy shares in any language we use.

We can readily see what a tremendous help a practice like this confers upon us for reading the works of Roman authors. We get inside the sanctum. But it does still more. Francis W. Kelsey, an American classicist from another era at the University of Michigan, wrote that work like this teaches us "exactness of observation, accuracy of discrimination, and carefulness in drawing conclusions," skills more than a little useful in the adult world; they help us approach not just verbal but mental "self-mastery." Every lesson in Latin is a lesson in logic. R. M. Wenley, a colleague of Kelsey's, illustrated the rigors entailed even in simple translation from an example lent by a former teacher of his, George G. Ramsay. Taking the simple two-word Latin sentence *Vellem mortuos* ("I would that they were dead"), Ramsay observed that understanding this sentence aright requires fourteen intellectual turns. "A student must know (1) the person, (2) tense, (3) voice, (4) number, (5) mood of the verb *vellem*; (6) that it comes from *volo*, meaning (7) 'I wish'; and that (8) the subjunctive has here a particular shade of meaning. As to *mortuos*, he must know that it is (9) the accusative, (10) plural, (11) masculine, from (12) *mortuus*, meaning (13) 'dead'; (14) the reason why the accusative is necessary." Wenley concludes: "A student who slips up on any one of these [steps] is bound to make a lovely mess when he comes to translate." As has been truly said, "In Latin you must be absolutely right, or you are not right at all." But the faultless moments, the ones when the winds fill our sails and the words blow perfectly in all their weight and beauty, are the ones we come to live for. They take us halfway up the mountain. We begin to look down on clouds.

Can anyone seriously maintain that such a stiff training in just expression leaves no salutary marks upon the intellect of someone who, having successfully run its gauntlet, becomes captive to the habits of the precise mind?

Yet such aren't the musings of Humanists alone. Successful people from the professions have borne witness in the past to the advantages of Latin, benefits we can easily recognize for those whose primary matter involves words, like lawyers, ministers, journalists, and teachers. One lawyer has written that the hard studies like classics and mathematics, those requiring accurate thought and performance, are the ones we need most, simply because they are hard: "It is the severe studies which, by steady grinding, bring out from the rough stone the diamond." But even those from the technical vocations have spied the benefits of learning the classical languages. Herbert C. Sadler, once a professor of naval architecture and marine engineering who received his classical schooling in the later nineteenth century, laid his cards on the table in pushing youthful classical study for would-be engineers. "The niceties of translation, the importance of gender, number, and case, the proper use of moods and tenses, and the demands of the relative clause, compel the mind toward a certain definiteness which is lacking in many of the subjects taught in the early stages of education." And what better training in that "certain definiteness" of mind can we gain other than by means of languages and mathematics? Another engineer agreed, while adding that modern languages cannot perform the functions of greatest value. "It is not the purpose of the study [of language] to learn how to speak [it]; the purpose is to understand its structure, and thereby understand the structure of our own language, and incidentally to acquire facility of expression." (Note the afterthought.) These people are the ones we want building our bridges.

"The sheer difficulty of Latin and Greek," wrote the *Nation* editor Paul Elmer More, "the highly organized structure of these languages, the need of scrupulous search to find the nearest equivalents for words that differ widely in their scope of meaning from their derivatives in any modern vocabulary, the effort of lifting one's self out of the familiar rut of ideas into so foreign a world, all these things act as a tonic exercise to the brain."

. . .

The glorious struggle is all a part — and an indispensable part — of climbing Parnassus. Thus do we learn both to freshen and strengthen our minds so as to be worthy conduits of high thought, eloquence, and, at the very least, clarity: not bad for one minute's, one hour's, or even one lifetime's, work. We are changed by it. For such training and toning, either with translating or composing, is more than the sum of "framing sentences." It's mental horticulture. We plant, and even weed, a small garden patch of the mind when we compose in this taut, conscious way, placing words and clauses with the same care we might expend on planting delicate seeds or transplanting mature stalks. That care becomes not only an exercise in exact thought, but also a loving act. We know we're doing something worthwhile. For one fleeting moment, we push back the chaos and make way for order. *Ad astra per aspera.*

We return to an old principle of Humanism. Words matter. Examples like these composed or translated sentences could be multiplied for profit and — for some of us — pleasure. And they were. For many years young students of the classics searching out precepts for choosing the right word for the right idea or sentiment wrestled with their *Gradus ad Parnassum*, a handy but thickly forbidding lexicon designed for composers of Latin. Within its pages novices found guidance for spotting and re-creating good, clear, and stylish usage; the *Gradus* showed them the footholds for the ascent. By using it they made themselves comrades in arms with untold generations of thinkers, dreamers, scholars, and other philosophical and literary spirits. Their climb too was hard but exhilarating. Schoolmarms were always right when they said that the strain of Latin composition was good for us, but they erred immensely, perhaps fatally, by not balancing the bitter doses with the blessed assurance that it could also bring great satisfaction. *Hoc praestamus maxime feris, quod loquimur*. Now the old adage that we differ most from animals in our ability to speak, to frame the world with words, begins to come home to us. Nothing quite takes the place of composing a Latin sentence for making one feel immortal.

What's true here of Latin is equally, though differently, true of Greek. Laying aside the obvious difference of Greek script to the Roman — along with all the extra apparatus of accents, breathings, particles, reduplications, and vowel lengthenings — we notice on a cursory glance that other differences between the two are formidable and far-reaching. Greek is a more supple language than Latin; the tongue of Plato doesn't tend to lay marble slabs and erect domes the way that of Cicero and Virgil can. But its suppleness makes it more elastic. It stretches. A Greek sentence breathes in a way a Latin one rarely does. To say that the poetic mind prefers Greek while the prosaic one opts for Latin would be simplistic — and in some signal cases baldly wrong — though some so claim, and a truth may lie somewhere amid the dregs. Greek nouns chime a bit more brightly; prose rhythm is smoother and usually swifter. Sounded from clear pipes, the melody of Greek intoxicates. (Still, the verbs can madden the impatient and untidy.) Many of the advantages of Latin composition obtain for Greek as well. Composing in either language forces the mind to reach beyond itself. And Greek verse composition may have an edge over versifying in Latin for the sheer rigor and nimbleness of the gymnastics, intellectual and aesthetic, we're made to endure. "More than one well-trained man," wrote Kelsey, "dates his awakening to the importance of accuracy in all things from his teacher's correcting of his accents in elementary Greek exercises."

"Not to know Greek is to be ignorant of the most flexible and subtle instrument of expression which the human mind has devised," Livingstone wrote, "and not to know Latin is to have

missed an admirable training in precise and logical thought."
He harbored no doubts about the formative value of Latin and
Greek composition. "Prose Composition, with its precision and
its compulsion to think hard and clear, is the best of medicines"
for those of us ailing from modern fads, ambiguities, and the
slipshoddiness of the marketplace. Composing in the classical
languages provides us with "singularly unerring tests of [the]
intellectual ability" residing in those who practice it — and in
those who have practiced it. "It is a perpetual discipline of
accuracy in thought and word and a rod for the back of journal-
istic chattering."

John Burnet, a Scot and eminent Oxonian classicist, once
sounded his own alarms, not for education in general as Nock
did almost thirty years after him, but for the classical pursuit
itself. Early in the twentieth century, Greek and Latin were in
danger, and so was their long-running role in forming intellectual strength and aesthetic vision. Speaking before the Classical
Association of Scotland at St. Andrew's in 1904, this feisty
scholar gave fair warning of the dreadful days to come, when
classics would become just another swab on the academic deck,
not the flagship of the line it had been for centuries. The practical people were on the move. Hordes of reformers clamored for
that "useful knowledge" to be taught in the schools — and
where it wasn't useful, schools were to make it easy and somehow *relevant* to modern concerns. Give us not the ancient languages, they said. Give us the history and archaeology and soci-
ology of the ancient word, and anything else we can easily
digest. Many classicists were ready to oblige.

But the essence of classical training, Burnet said, must not
be sacrificed to expediency. "It will not do to shirk the advocacy
of classical education," he told his audience, "as above all a
training in form, and to defend it mainly on the ground of the

interest and importance of its subject-matter." For "classical
education is essentially a formal discipline" — not, that is, a
discipline of content. He warned that "it is the substitution of
matter for form that is killing the study of the classics. A man
who has been taught the origin of the legend of Aeneas will not
read Virgil in later life; a man who has been taught to write
hexameters will." Therefore, not only must we retain prose composition in Greek and Latin, we should also retain — and
increase — composition in Greek and Latin verse, an exercise he
thought the highest literary training in form. Verse composition is "the easiest and best way of fixing in the memory" all the
grammar we need in order to know and use the language. After
all, it isn't "easy to forget a Latin perfect infinitive that has once
fallen neatly into its place in the second half of a pentameter."
Burnet recalled his own school days in the 1870s.

> I remember very well that, when I was eleven years old, we used
> to do elegiacs in the High School of Edinburgh. We did not carry
> them very far, I know, but it is all I remember of what I was
> taught then. The geography of Asia, the dates of the kings of
> England, and all the so-called 'useful knowledge' has disappeared
> from my mind completely, but I can remember some of the first
> Latin verses I ever made, and I feel that training, elementary as it
> was, to be a real part of me now. [Students] have no matter of
> experience that is worth expressing, but even a baby of a few
> weeks rejoices in rhythmical form…. I may be wrong, but I hold
> very strongly that the growing neglect of form in classical teach-
> ing is depriving it of most of its value, and I think that, unless we
> go back boldly to the traditions of earlier days, we shall find that
> our subject has become merely one branch of study among others.

That day of course has long since arrived. Classicists now share professional status with accountants and proctologists. They're just another group of careerists performing just another job. But our desperate, debilitating hunger for intellectual and aesthetic formation abides. Our twigs still need bending.

■   ■   ■

W. H. Auden was one of many writers of the last great generation of classically educated men and women upon whom an early classical training made indelible impressions, intellectual and otherwise. Those boyish classroom exercises had formed his very sensibility, and he lived to see the stupid, numbing consensus arise that a classical education holds scant value for the modern world. "The modern revolt against centering the school curriculum around the study of Latin and Greek is understandable" in an age of hyper-utilitarianism, he wrote, though it's "deplorably mistaken." "It is, no doubt, a pleasure to read the Greek and Latin poets, philosophers, and historians in the original, but very few persons so educated in the past 'kept up' their Greek and Latin after leaving school." The real value of classics, though, is "something quite different. Anybody who has spent many hours in his youth translating into and out of two languages so syntactically and rhetorically different from his own, learns something about his mother tongue which I do not think can be learned in any other way.... It inculcates the habit, whenever one uses a word, of automatically asking, 'What is its exact meaning?'" Auden's case for classics was not so much the cultural one but the case from formation. The pursuit of classics *per se* is worth all the devotion we can lend it. Classical knowledge provides keys to understanding Western civilization. But the habits Greek and Latin instill are worth at least as much.

The passing of classics from our schools has in fact crippled the larger culture. Here Auden cast his net far and wide. "The people who have really suffered since classical education became 'undemocratic' are not the novelists and poets — their natural love of language sees them through — but all those, like politicians, journalists, lawyers, the man-in-the-street, etc., who use language for everyday and nonliterary purposes. Among such one observes an appalling deterioration in precision and conciseness." How ironic that those democratic fears of "elitism" should ensure that those born without the privileges of the educated classes will remain permanently disabled, victims of others' good intentions. The signs of rot surround us. "Nobody," Auden wrote, "who had had a classical education could have perpetrated this sentence...in *The New Yorker*: 'He [a film director] expresses the dichotomy between man and woman in the images of the bra and Dachau.'" One would hope not. That's the murky, self-important lingo emanating from the lit. crit. seminar in English departments. It doesn't exist to communicate anything to the cultivated mind. It exists to confuse and impress easily bamboozled, uneducated, fee-paying sycophants. It pretends to profundity, but it's tripe. Language like this is not hatched for civilized people.

Perhaps we can have "culture" of a kind without bestowing classical education upon a goodly number of intelligent men and women. We may doubt whether we can have a *literary* culture whose roots run deep.

Novelist Evelyn Waugh paid tribute to his own classical training. Here we see plainly that the oft-heard cry that students retain little of their Latin misses the point. A classical training, thoroughly conducted along humanistic lines, changes the shape of the mind for the better. It stays with us.

My knowledge of English literature derived chiefly from my home. Most of my hours in the form room for ten years had been spent on Latin and Greek, History and Mathematics. Today I remember no Greek. I have never read Latin for pleasure and should now be hard put to compose a simple epitaph. But I do not regret my superficial [superficial for the time perhaps] classical studies. I believe that the conventional defence of them is valid; that only by them can a boy fully understand that a sentence is a logical construction and that words have basic inalienable meanings, departure from which is either conscious metaphor or inexcusable vulgarity. Those who have not been so taught — most Americans and most women — unless they are guided by some rare genius, betray their deprivation. The old-fashioned test of an English sentence — will it translate? — still stands after we have lost the trick of translation.

We should note here as well the starkly limited curriculum. His school's masters might have chosen to clutter the classroom with far shinier subjects than it did in the second decade of the twentieth century: commercial French, for one thing, or aerodynamics, or wood shop. That world was *changing*, after all. True enough. But that didn't mean that the well-constituted mind had changed; the intellect still required molding. The better schools then — as they ought to be now — were eager primarily to form the student's mind, imparting solid knowledge mainly as a by-product of sound teaching. As with the Greek and Roman schools so many centuries before, the curriculum of Waugh's school was also marked, as H. I. Marrou wrote, by a "definite rejection of what it did not include." What it didn't let in was of equal importance to what it did. Any school, we might conclude, with more than four or five subjects doesn't know what it wants to be — or, we may shudder to think, perhaps it does. Most public schools in America now strive to be cut-rate educational malls for the intellectually lame — whether or not students first darken the school doors that way, so most of them leave — while even some private schools pose as little more than colorful felt boards for the earnestly shallow, commonly confusing pious or patriotic piffle with real education. Neither set up makes for a school any educated human being is bound to respect.

Schools of the best kind have always aimed high while keeping feet to the ground. They didn't try to do too much; they tried to do the most important things. Those who ran them knew that we educate ourselves with the tools imparted by good teachers. All else was up to us. The old schoolmasters didn't profess to teach everything worth knowing. Indeed they professed the opposite. They shaped their curricula narrowly and wisely. Information alone is not knowledge, as they knew. Still less is it wisdom. Schools can accomplish much more when they recognize squarely how little they can do. Yet how much more can be done when our gaze remains steady, our head sober, our aims high. No results are guaranteed. But the effort pays off. Formed minds and tempered souls are no small gifts to the world.

Let's see one more example of how good schooling goes bad through wishful-thinking pedagogy. Perhaps the school should be, as we might say now, a challenging place. It should be hard. The work enjoined upon us should help us to develop, not only by its content but also by its method, the mind capable of teaching itself anything. It's not so much an informed mind we seek — the one full of "information" for an Information Age, making us little more than worker bees — but a certain *quality* of mind, a mind at once agile and civilized, one able to place the society to which it belongs into some scheme of history. We want not only a well-stored mind but a well-leavened mind as well. So what of it? This may be a good enough idea, as ideas go. Yet we must emerge from school doors knowing something. But what should we know? An answer sits at the ready. We should learn how to appreciate the "better things" of life.

And so we should. The snare here, the snake in the grass waiting to bite, is that this idea has led us down some false paths. "Appreciation" squares with Renaissance ideals, but, as conceived by us moderns, it's miles away from Renaissance methods. Today we don't lack teachers and theorists wishing to help students pull off an enhanced quality of mind. Many have tipped their hats to this principle by designing courses whose purpose is to help those students not so much to know but to *appreciate* the world around them. Yet this isn't the learning Vittorino da Feltre knew. We don't need, under this regime, to learn the hard things about poetry or music or art; we need only to appreciate them as poetry, music, or art. We need only to acknowledge their value. While it's easy to make fun of this attitude, we should recognize that, in the ablest hands, the quality of mind sought is a decent goal, and doubtless it's some-times achieved. Poetry, music, and art were not created, after all, to provide fodder for tests in school; poetry is more than scan-sion and difficult words, music more than scales and arpeggios, and art more than cracked vases and spatial perspective. All three were made to delight. They were meant to please us in some deep or diverting way. This we must acknowledge. But, however good the object of helping young people to take easy delight in the fine things around them, this approach to form-ing the rough, formless mind is also profoundly wrongheaded. C. S. Lewis helps us to see why in a little-known essay called "The Parthenon and the Optative."

"The trouble with these boys," said a grim old classical scholar looking up from some milk-and-watery entrance papers which he had been marking: "the trouble with these boys is that the masters have been talking to them about the Parthenon when they should have been talking to them about the Optative." [The "Optative" is one of the moods of the Greek verb.].... Ever since then I have tended to use the Parthenon and the Optative as the symbols of two types of education. The one begins with hard, dry things like grammar, and dates, and prosody; and it has at least the chance of ending in a real appreciation which is equally hard and firm though not equally dry. The other begins in "Appreciation" and ends in gush. When the first fails it has, at the very least, taught the boy what knowledge is like. He may decide that he doesn't care for knowledge; but he knows he doesn't care for it, and he knows he hasn't got it. But the other fails most disastrously when it most succeeds. It teaches a man to feel vaguely cultured while he remains in fact a dunce. It makes him think he is enjoying poems he can't construe. It qualifies him to review books he does not understand, and to be intellectual without intellect. It plays havoc with the very distinction between truth and error.

This is what school has become for us over the haul of three or four generations. It's become not so much about knowledge as it has about "experience." The teacher doesn't teach; the teacher "facilitates." Instead of providing solid instruction, for instance, about the Cathedral at Chartres, about its religious significance and dates and place in French geography and dimensions and Gothic architectural principles — the things, that is, we can really *know* about it — the teacher is now just as likely to stand before a class with a photograph of the cathedral and ask students to "respond" to it: "What does it make you think of? Would you want to walk into a building like this? Are all these statues beautiful or ugly? Would a woman be comfortable here? Write a paragraph on what you think it must have felt like to stand in front of it."

I jest, but only a little. Here is how we are set on the high road to the "Parthenon" kind of education — the kind that will, by its very method, allow us later to think we know more than we do. These questions might not make a bad exercise for kindergarteners, but they're unfit for anyone older — one year hence the student's time will be better spent memorizing Roman numerals. Yet much schooling today, even high schooling, has become every bit as vapid as this whimsical example suggests. Here, before the young can know the dangers of soft teaching or the seductions of ignorance, non-knowledge gets planted and watered. And left unchecked, as it usually is, it will spread like bamboo. Lewis goes on:

> And yet, education of the Parthenon type is often recommended by those who have and love real learning. They are moved by a kind of false reverence for the Muses. What they value, say, in Literature, seems to them so delicate and spiritual a thing that they cannot bear to see it (as they think) degraded by such coarse, mechanic attendants as paradigms, blackboards, marks and examination papers.... But there is a profound misunderstanding here. These well-meaning educationalists are quite right in thinking that literary appreciation is a delicate thing. What they do not seem to see is that for this very reason elementary examinations on literary subjects ought to confine themselves to just those dry and factual questions which are so often ridiculed. The questions were never supposed to test appreciation; the idea was to find out whether the boy had read his books. It was the reading, not the being examined, which was expected to do him

good. And this, so far from being a defect in such examinations, is just what renders them useful or even tolerable.

Lewis sees learning, in a word, *objectively*: if progress in learning can't be measured, for purposes of schooling, we have no way of knowing if it's happening at all. Knowledge can be measured; appreciation cannot. Furthermore, trying to test pleasure or approval may prove hazardous even to the soul itself:

> Tell the boy to "mug up" [study up on] a book and then set questions to find out whether he has done so. At best, he may have learned (and, best of all, unconsciously) to enjoy a great poem. At second best he has done an honest piece of work and exercised his memory and reason. At worst, we have done him no harm: have not pawed and dabbled in his soul, have not taught him to be a prig or a hypocrite. But an elementary examination which attempts to assess 'the adventure of the soul among books' is a dangerous thing. What obsequious boys, if encouraged, will try to manufacture, and clever ones can ape, and shy ones will conceal, what dies at the touch of venality, is called to come forward and *perform*, to exhibit itself, at that very stage when its timid, half-conscious stirrings can least endure such self-consciousness.

If the tenets of formation ought to guide method in our schools, we also see what content must be. It must be hard and intractable, its import significant, its substance learnable. Content is, in one sense at least, the bar we use to pull ourselves out of ignorance; the formed and forming mind is the muscle we use to pull. "Appreciation" may be properly valued above solid knowledge; the best kind accompanies us into our sunset years. Appreciation, inward apprehension and assent, touches upon the spiritual in our natures. It is indeed to be sought vigorously.

The only real quandary is how to get there. And Lewis, like so many before him, knew that, while the long way round — the Way of the Optative — may not guarantee arrival at the port of our desires, nonetheless it is the one way that weather-hardened, sea-legged mariners have tested and found to be not only reliable but, given the winds tossing us, safe. *Multum non multa.* This is the one chart we can trust.

■   ■   ■

Appreciation brushes the hem of the Aesthetic. Classics, as taught by Humanists, gave untold generations canons for taking in the Beautiful and Sublime. Classically educated people learned what was seemly. Education at its higher reaches should be, according to English classicist R. C. Jebb, a matter of aesthetic revelation. Auden's example of the renegade *New Yorker* writer is much to the point when we come to ponder the effect that Greek and Latin and their literatures have had on Taste and Style in the history of the Western world. For when he pointed to the pseudo-sophisticated crudity of the contemporary educated mind, he spoke not of a lack of logic and clarity alone. Not only had the writer Auden cited not learned to use language to good and proper purpose, he also hadn't learned to use it stylishly. That man's thought and the words transporting it were, to use a proscribed word, tasteless. Thought and utterance alike were inept and ugly. Much to that writer's disadvantage, though, he probably thought he was being quite stylish and sophisticated: certainly enough so to write for the *New Yorker* — and apparently his editors at that revered magazine concurred. And, in one sense, he was right: canons of taste have changed. We may no longer say, as Auden did, that that man was wrong to write that way; we may only say that his writing is or isn't to our *taste*. Taste is, after all, a subjective matter, a fact that there's simply no escaping, especially today, when the arbiters have fled. But it wasn't always thus. Once educated people could pronounce upon Taste and Style, and by and large the education they had received had granted them the license to do so. Standards ruled. This never meant that all educated people always agreed about what was tasteful and stylish, only that they had canons to which they could appeal when disputes arose. They had benchmarks. That day also is done. But we should not allow our excursion to reach its terminus without touching upon the subtle power of aesthetic precept that the Greek and Roman classics lent to the Western mind.

Taste and Style, as we have already seen, were primary aims within sight of Humanists for centuries. Heraclitus once said that "masses of knowledge do not instruct a mind." The civilized person had not merely to be knowledgeable; he had to own and wear that knowledge in a special way. Knowledge was as much a courtly acquisition as an arrow in a quiver with which to combat and conquer the world. A person's inner nature had to be transformed. We might say that this vision is a "construct." It is *artificial*. Of course it is. But we err if we thereby conclude that men and women, say, of the Renaissance did not know that Taste and Style were artificial. They did. So, they would have said, were manners. So was piety. So was an ability to dance a minuet or to sing a madrigal — or to parse an ode of Horace. So was any sense for the finer, more profound things. All of these had to be learned. They had to be constructed, made and re-made from the raw materials of mind, heart, and body. As Humanists saw it, we enter this life naked and hungering and brutal. We need civilizing. Such artificial attainments — such "constructs" — made and strengthened the very sinews of culture. The world certainly would have been survivable without them. It also would have been a lesser place.

Those elusive things called Taste and Style, though, must rest upon not-so-elusive standards. One must choose the norms by which he'll be guided. Will one follow fashion and the personal whims of the moment? Or will one take his cues from what has been established as the *best* the world has to offer? Aesthetics is not an easy field to joust on; neither of these questions is easily parried. Personality will play a role in the struggle, and genius, as has been said, is a law unto itself. Yet those schooled along classical paths knew that they had been given an education as much aesthetic as it was intellectual. Humanism made sure of it.

Our disquisition here has embraced the literary realm only. But of course we must recognize, if only in passing, that the aesthetic reach of the classical world extends far beyond literature, philosophy, and history — far beyond, that is, the realm of words. It has also put an ineffaceable stamp upon the world we perceive through our eyes. I cannot pretend to expound upon these. Yet when we gaze at the Capitol of the United States, or the White House, or the Supreme Court building — not to mention some of our other public buildings, banks, museums, and college and university campuses — we can see how completely indebted we are, not only as a nation but as a culture, to Greek and Roman ideals as filtered through their art and architecture. Thomas Jefferson — a student of Palladio and his *Four Books of Architecture* — suggested the Villa Rotunda as a pattern for what became the White House, and for the Capitol he urged "the adoption of some one of the models of antiquity which have had the approbation of thousands of years." These models were not only apt; they were beautiful. Jefferson wished, he said, "to improve the taste of my countrymen." Southern antebellum architecture owes the vast part of its sublime dignity and splen-

dor to Neo-Hellenism. Jefferson consulted the Roman Pliny in
designing the gardens and passageways at Monticello; he
planned a burial ground complete with a Greek temple, urns,
and an Aeolian harp. All this is as much a reflection on the classics' political influence as it is on a consideration of Style and
Taste — though Americans, for example, might pause to imagine what Washington, D.C. might have looked like without
classical arches, domes, and straight, broad avenues. Surely to be
ignorant of the civilization that brought them forth is to be
ignorant of one's origins, a quality of mind not safely or wisely
recommended to educated people.

When he stood that day before the governor and legislature
of South Carolina, Isaac Stuart claimed that through the bap-
tismal study of Greek and Latin, "Taste and Style are best
formed." Greek and Roman classics "exhibit most that knowledge of what is truly natural, in which is comprised 'the beginning, the middle and end of every thing valuable in taste.'" This
would seem a lofty claim indeed, but we've seen it before. How
do they do this? "Principally," he says, "according to the judgment of the most competent directors, *by the study of correct models*" (Stuart's emphasis). Here is Renaissance Humanism
adjusted not even slightly to the exuberant American temperament. It's pure and unadulterated. A study, he said, that "brings
the mind directly in contact with those very excellences of
which it is in want," that which "inspires it with knowledge of
principles and execution, and prepares it for its own independent action," is most to be sought by those who would be both
educated and cultivated. Classical learning may be help enough
to the rest of us, but perhaps the talented benefit most. There
they find standards. For "fervent genius, relieved from delay and
wanderings, often fruitless, in search of Truth, here, in the study
of correct models, enters her very Paradise — scans her heavenly

proportions and drinks in the harmony of her looks, in her very presence — sends his eye, new lighted with joy and wonder, far over the magnificence of her possessions and on each individual splendor, in the very spot of their dazzling existence, and leaves her abode penetrated with Truth's own divinest influences, bewildered and overpowered by that Enthusiasm of Perfection, which only abates to stimulate and guide one unceasing effort in the self-production of excellence." Furthermore, classical models "correspond most perfectly in style to the nature of emotions and passions. With all the freshness of youth, they show the guiding judgment of manhood. They spring out of a period when men saw and felt, and wrought and described, without 'the spectacles of books,' free from the endless and confusing associations of a world full of knowledge, free from the metaphysical restraints of language, free from the carp and chain of criticism." Classical models, in short, "form emphatically a natural intellectual Eden. Poetry, history, eloquence, philosophy, colloquy, each has its department, and architecture, painting and sculpture are in finished excellence." Once again, much of the value of the classical pursuit obtains not despite its remoteness from the modern world, but because of it.

The classical world bestowed upon all who served their youth in its purlieus a kind of parallel universe. It was at once a lens through which to peer and a code to break. Within its rich and peopled precincts we find personalities, high and low, and conditions, glorious and desperate, that serve as cultural compasses, showing us the distance we have still to travel before the flowering, the realizing, of our supreme ideals. They show us our proximity to perfection. No wonder the pursuit of classics was for so many centuries an erstwhile rival to religion — and why so many religious spirits bridled against it. Classics established yet another guide point, set another lodestar in the firmament, by which to steer our lives, intellectually, aesthetically, spiritually. Classical literature, thought, and art showed us the best of which we're capable.

But what finally about this idea of Taste? Were the classics a source of Taste because they were naturally "tasteful" — or was classical literature automatically considered tasteful because it was classical? Certainly not the latter. Many judicious people over the centuries have excluded the *Satyricon* of Petronius from the ranks of tasteful works, as well as some of the poems of Catullus, to name but two authors. Not every work of classical literature has been roundly embraced through history, as we saw with the English Puritans of the seventeenth century. Greatness is not always tasteful. So what accounts for this association of Taste with classics? One explanation is practical: classics have been veritably defined as that which has survived. So the conflation of classics with Taste isn't all that far-fetched when we recognize the high degree of *selectivity* involved in both the formal and informal sifting of classical literature. The sad fact is that most of what the Greeks and Romans wrote has been lost. What remains is the list of Greatest Works, those pieces and fragments that successive generations of critics, scholars, and lay readers deemed worth preserving. The *crème de la crème* had risen to the top and been scraped off, leaving us with the best they had thought and said.

Yet this account isn't quite complete. Certain qualities of character, good and bad, were thought to inhere within those Greek and Roman shards that two millennia of discerning spirits have considered to be the best of their kind. The jury is already in; judgment was passed long ago. Within Greek literature we find, along with all the mayhem of petty wars and nastily destructive domestic jealousies — all the meanness and pettiness of mankind — footprints of those grander traits of humanity: *nobility, restraint, balance, harmony, proportion, generosity, grace*. And these traits are aesthetic as well as ethical. Within the lines of Greek epic and tragedy, man finds the place assigned to him in the universe by the gods, a place he transgresses to his peril; the man or woman beset with *hubris* finds redemption in calm, opened-eyed resignation to fate. Later, the Romans showed us how man can acquit himself with dignity, even majesty. Chronicles of noble quests for order fill their pages. The long, straight Roman road is itself a telling symbol of the high destiny the Romans sought to fulfill. By the very nature of the task, wrote T. S. Eliot most tellingly, close reading of Greek and Latin classics over many years tends to engender "maturity of mind, maturity of manners, maturity of language and perfection of the common style."

There's no escape: our aesthetic vocabulary has grown from the classical sensibility. It would not be far off the mark to say that the Greeks and Romans have best taught us how to think and feel. Their greatest medium was their words. And to weigh words in our hands is to measure both their logical power and beauty together. It is to know what they mean, and can mean, at full thrust. For Jefferson, the classics provided "models of pure taste in writing." To Greek and Latin, he said, "we are certainly indebted for the rational and chaste style of modern composition which so much distinguishes the nations to whom these languages are familiar."

"The remains of the ancients," said John Witherspoon at the College of New Jersey in the eighteenth century, "are the standard of taste." Well enough. But of course we need not take up Greek and Latin in order to acquire models of Taste and Style any more than we may for their intellectually formative ones. This aim is almost unheard of now anyway. Content is quite reason enough to sustain interest and justify their nest in schools' and colleges' curricula.

The point we might make, though, is that one *can* do so —
and that these goals of intellectual and aesthetic shaping were
more commonly pursued over the past several centuries than
were the more scholarly ones of simple philological and historical inquiry. After all, the probing of chronological, sociological,
and linguistic problems, however weighty and vital they may be
for the life of scholarship, does not alter our mental natures.
Forming the mind does. Perhaps a renewed ardor for the formation of mind and soul will once again give us a pass for making
deft and shrewd aesthetic judgments. We may not be put off
thereafter when someone says that any response of ours to a
piece of literary or visual art is "just" our "opinion." An opinion
built upon established standards, after all, is not quite the same
thing as a mere feeling. Such an opinion may be well or ill-
founded, right or wrong, but it isn't *mere*. It never was.

■   ■   ■

"You have separated yourselves from the throng who grope
in the night of ignorance, scarcely conscious of the possession of
intellect," young colonial graduates at the College of William
and Mary in Virginia were once told upon finishing off their
classical education. They were thus "entitled to that homage
which the awakened intellect universally commands."
The Founding Fathers of the United States, as we saw before,
hailed from a society enthralled to classical ideals and models.
Greece and Rome exerted multiple influences — intellectual,
historical, aesthetic, spiritual — upon this greatest of all
American generations. How could contemporary readers fail to
be impressed by the immense, indelible watermark left upon
the founding American mind whenever they read the accounts

of the Philadelphia debates of 1787 over which constitutional form of government best suited the new nation that had already outgrown the Articles of Confederation? These men had read and digested Polybius, Aristotle, and Cicero, and they used the ancient luminaries to frame and illustrate their ideas before the assembly. Jefferson had not dubbed this conclave "demigods" for slight reason. These heated yet erudite debates, along with the *Federalist Papers*, fairly pullulate both with subtle classical allusions — with which Madison, Hamilton, and Jay assumed readers to be tolerably familiar — and direct references to the leagues — Amphictyonic, Achaean, Aetolian, Lycian — formed by the ancient Greeks in order to achieve political and physical security. To say the Founders possessed accomplished, if not monolithically educated, minds would be superfluous. To say that their trained intellects had enabled an already blessed generation to give wings to their wisdom during deliberation would not be an undue reckoning. They might have been the wisest, best-read public servants to preside over any government since ancient times.

Americans view the Founding Fathers *in vacuo*, isolated from the soil that nurtured them. They're whitened statues, existing out of time, locked in greatness. But little doubt can there be that the years those men had invested at school and college with Greek and Latin — along with smatterings of modern subjects — had prepared them optimally for the role they would play on history's stage. They deserve their press. English philosopher Alfred North Whitehead's observation sharpens the point: "I know of only two occasions when the people in power did what needed to be done about as well as you can imagine its being possible. One was the framing of [the American] Constitution. They were able statesmen; they had access to a body of ideas; they incorporated these principles into the instrument without trying to particularize too explicitly how they should be put into effect; and they were men of immense practical experience themselves." The other occasion, Whitehead said, "was in Rome, when Augustus called in the 'new men' of new ideas." Here is a comparison the Founders would have appreciated and probably, in their expansive hours, accepted. Yet it wasn't fanciful.

A *festschrift* on the sharp impress of a classical education on the conduct of public life in early America is a goal too big to reach here. We must also say that Americans of that generation are not the only people we could point to as fine exemplars of classically educated, public-spirited statesmen; a small book could profitably be devoted to Gladstone's scholastic grounding. But America's Founding Fathers provide the best and tightest picture of that impress at its most penetrating. Never have so many of the wise and well-read come together to do great things; never have book learning and practical experience combined to show the ignorant and cynical forevermore what the human mind and spirit can do when properly formed. Such wisdom cannot be manufactured for the moment — nor can it be aped. It must be cultivated. And it has to come from somewhere. For the Founders it came principally from two places: the pulpit and the schoolroom.

America is a religious country. The fabric of our polity is soaked with a piety we cannot shake out, even if we would. Winthrop's "shining city on a hill" is, among other things, a religious image. We look in the mirror and see our country as the Romans saw themselves, as people of a divine destiny: it was ordained that we be here. The primarily commercial designs of the first Virginian settlements do not vitiate the sacred identity stamped upon the American character by the Puritans and Pilgrims of New England. That legacy is real and it abides. But simplistic schooling over many decades has obscured the intellectual foundations of the American Republic. Early Americans didn't simply pray; they read books. These men were not, all of them, the purely narrow religionists of legend. They were conversant with the world of ideas in ways few college graduates today could rival. They were also cultured. We forget — perhaps because we were never taught — that even some of those fierce, fiery preachers of the seventeenth and eighteenth centuries who pounded Bibles had also once pounded Latin paradigms in class.

The Boston Latin School lends a paramount example, if not of what every grammar school was in America in those centuries, then certainly of what the best ones aspired to be. This school, like all of its kind, existed to feed the colleges, and the colleges centered their curricula on classics and mathematics. Headmaster Ezekiel Cheever became the standard-bearer of classical education in America in the same way Thomas Arnold would do in nineteenth-century England. Cotton Mather had been one of Cheever's pupils and honored him poetically: "Do but name Cheever, and the Echo straight / Upon that name, *Good Latin* will repeat." Another man paid tribute to him later as "A rare Instance of Piety, Health, Strength, [and] Serviceableness." Cheever composed for school use his *Accidence*, the *Short Introduction to the Latin Tongue*, in which he tried to simplify Lily's *Grammar*. By the first decade of the eighteenth century, Boston Latin had boys reading the orations and letters of Cicero, the Latin Testament, Virgil, Horace, and Juvenal, and the best were converting the Psalms into Latin verse. When they took up the *Aeneid*, they would translate passages aloud, write them out, and then translate them back into Latin — in different tenses. Greek grammar they learned from Cambden's *Instituto Graecae Grammatices Compendiaria*, going on to Homer, Hesiod,

Isocrates, and Xenophon. From schools such as these the
Founders arose. The schooling most of them endured was not
soft; they had had a classical education of the strictest kind.
They made themselves smart stock.

The founding generation can boast a cadre of deeply learned
spirits. As well-read men, these denizens of the Age of
Enlightenment were much engaged with modern thinkers, particularly Locke and Montesquieu, but the Greek and Roman
classics made their common coin of exchange. South Carolina's
Charles Pinckney had shone with Homer, Virgil, and Ovid at
the Westminster school in England, going on to Oxford to read
classics. James Wilson, before taking up politics, taught Latin
and law at the College of Philadelphia, and once at the
Convention, referring to the tremors of Shays's Rebellion,
quoted a line all present would have recognized from Horace:
"We walked on ashes concealing fire beneath our feet." James
Otis practically framed his thoughts in Latin, and he once published a manual on Latin prosody. Alexander Hamilton topped
off his classical training at King's College and later read and
copied great swatches of the *Lives* of Plutarch, paying special
attention to the makers of states: Theseus, Lycurgus, Numa
Pompilius. James Madison kept a commonplace book in which
he transcribed lines directly into Latin whenever he didn't cotton to a particular translation he'd read. A stroll through the
intellectual and aesthetic lives of Thomas Jefferson and John
Adams, though, tells volumes not only about what wisdom
looks like, but also the way in which wisdom is tempered —
made stronger and more articulate — by a tough intellectual
training. Despite the rabid political disagreements dogging
them earlier, Adams and Jefferson shared more in common than
their love of country as they aged. They shared a love of the classics perhaps more thoroughgoing and lasting than that of any of

their colleagues.

Adams came of modest origins. His struggling father had sensibly decided that a proper schooling was the only certain path to success, and he was determined to see his son succeed. One day the young Adams got fed up with Latin lessons and told his father boldly that he would cease to attend them, to which his father responded by ordering the lad to dig a ditch. After two days, the boy relented and went back to his paradigms and vocabulary and syntax. His mastery of Latin — he'd also learned Greek, but largely lost it later — whisked him through the Harvard entrance examinations and he spent three fruitful years there reading, re-reading, and studying his beloved authors from antiquity. He was caught for life. Yet his classical interest was not strictly political or historical; Adams cared about the well-employed word. Once claiming that Milton's *Paradise Lost* did not equal the best of the classical epics, Adams said that "The Aeneid is a well ordered garden, where it is impossible to find any Part unadorned, or to cast our Eyes upon any single Spot that does not produce some beautiful Plant or Flower." His classical learning wasn't merely for show; much of his zeal and understanding he saved for his diaries. There we find a passage from Virgil, translated by Adams, from 1758: "'He nurses a Wound in his Veins and is consumed by a blind, hidden fire,'" a line that might apply to any enemy, foreign or domestic. His diaries are filled with these. When he saw the approach of inevitable war for independence from England, he quoted from Horace: "'it is sweet and becoming to die for one's country.'" Adams's personal library would come to include Homer, Herodotus, Thucydides, Xenophon, Plato, Aristotle, and Epictetus among the Greeks; Tacitus, Sallust, Livy, Ovid, Lucretius, and Cicero among the Romans — all heavily read and annotated over many years. Here indeed was a man whose mental nature had changed. At the end of his days, Adams freely acknowledged his debt. "If I have gained any distinction," he said, "it has been owing to the two days' labor in that abominable ditch."

The aim of all this devoted reading was mainly delight. Adams's correspondence with Jefferson suggests as much; both men reveled in the riches of classical literature. But another object of the classical pursuit was — we return to Humanism once more — usefulness. Greek and Latin were useful to both private and public life. Adams spent most of the early years of the American nation on the move abroad on diplomatic assignments, with and without his family, and it was imperative that he hire a good tutor for his sons and guide him according to Adams's wishes. "I would not have them put by any longer to the Master of Fencing or Dancing," he wrote to one tutor. "Let them attend the Drawing and Writing Masters, and bend all the rest of their Time and attention to Latin and Greek, and French, which will be more useful and necessary for them in their own Country, where they are to spend their Lives." Useful and necessary, we may say, for the sake of the vistas these subjects would open to those boys as they became men — and as one of them became President of the United States. Adams wrote with the gusto of a father's ambition to his son, John Quincy. "My Wish at present is that your principal Attention should be directed to the Latin and Greek tongues.... I hope soon to hear that you are in Virgil and Tully's [Cicero's] orations, or Ovid, or Horace, or all of them." Such was exactly the fare enjoined upon any man who would also become, as John Quincy Adams did, a professor of oratory. His father never skimped on his advice. When John Quincy served in the United States Senate in 1806, his father, fearing that his son may be working too hard and jeopardizing his health, admonished him by letter that "Aristotle, Dionysius

Halicarnassensis, Longinus, Quintilian, Demosthenes, and Cicero, with twenty others, are not easily read and studied by a man of the world and a senator of the United States." Today this reading list might still pose a chore for United States senators — especially if they could not identify the authors. But isn't this, Adams might have asked with glinting eye, the very stuff on which the intellectual teeth of presidents and senators ought to be cut?

"When the decays of age have enfeebled the useful energies of the mind," Jefferson once wrote, "the classick pages fill up the vacuum of ennui, and become sweet composers to that rest of the grave into which we are all sooner or later to descend." Jefferson was much given to the rhetorical flourish and his praise could be fulsome. But whenever he wrote about his debt to the classics, his words came from a full heart. As had Adams's before him, Jefferson's father insisted on his son's taking a classical training from a tender age, and later Jefferson was unstinting in his gratitude: "I thank on my knees Him who directed my early education, for having put into my possession this rich source of delight; and I would not exchange it for anything which I could then have acquired, and have not since acquired." Here Jefferson spoke specifically of his ability to read Homer in the original Greek. For Greek was to him "the finest of human languages," and Homer was the "Father of Western Literature." Jefferson both understood and endorsed the dependence of the schools upon Latin, but he regretted the relegation of Greek, which provided the best training, he believed, in sound and sense together. Greek was, in a word, beautiful. And Greek and Latin together afforded the only training in language any educated man and woman needed — meaning, among other things, that the formal study of English by English-speaking peoples is facile and redundant. When we are young, he wrote, "any composition pleases which unites a little sense, some imagination, and some rhythm, in doses however small. But as we advance in life these things fall off one by one, and I suspect that we are left at last with only Homer and Virgil, and perhaps with Homer alone." Jefferson proffered his own advice to his grandson just setting out for college; already we can sense that the boy's schooling had not equaled that of the grand old man. "Your Latin and Greek should be kept up assiduously," he wrote. "By reading at spare hours; and, discontinuing the desultory reading of the schools, I would advise you to undertake a regular course of history and poetry in both languages." Once again, we see that this generation was not so entranced with politics as we now assume. These men knew when to set aside their disputatious natures and taste of the manna free to all educated people. Classics, to Jefferson and Adams both, produced acutely profound pleasure.

To read the letters passed between John Adams and Thomas Jefferson over nearly half a century is a liberal education in itself, as the two statesmen range far and wide over matters ancient and modern. Their missives provide a window into the accomplished, humane, and civilized mind. Those letters also show us the light and reasonable charity and forbearance possible between two brilliant, high-minded men of vastly different temperaments. Adams was a Stoic, Jefferson an Epicurean; Adams was a New England Federalist, Jefferson an agrarian Anti-Federalist. They spent their White House years as political foes leading opposing camps. Yet together they exemplify the best America is capable of producing when it recognizes that neither sentiment nor knowledge alone makes for the citizen best fit to pilot his fellows.

Classical words, phrases, and allusions pepper their pages. They raise Hesiod's admonition to pay the gods due honor. They discuss Seneca's warnings about civil discord and apply them to the new nation over whose birth they had presided. They graze over nonce words arising from the classical lexicon, approving some as seemly and blackballing others as barbarous. Adams inquires into the historical propriety of the Latin word *gloriola*; Jefferson cites its use in Cicero to mean "a little bit of glory." The reading and composition of classical verse exercise their memory and judgment. They strain to find agreement on the identity of the *aristoi*, the truly good and noble people best suited to govern; they weigh the competing claims of aristocracy and democracy.

Jefferson wrote to Adams in 1813 that he, a former president, had "given up newspapers for Tacitus and Thucydides, Newton and Euclid"; Tacitus they shared as their most favored historian. They conducted a long epistolary conversation on the Stoic philosopher Cleanthes, citing rival Latin and French renderings of Greek lines. Jefferson once wrote that he was loath "to enter the forest of opinions, discussions, and contentions which have occurred in our day." He then quoted, in Greek, a passage from the pastoral poet Theocritus in which a woodcutter looks out upon a sea of timber and wonders where to begin: "'What first shall I gather?' he said, gazing at the thousands of trees." "But I shall not do it," Jefferson responded. "The summum bonum with me is now truly Epicurean, ease of body and tranquillity of mind; and to these I wish to consign my remaining days." The prudence of a rational age had become, in these hands, wisdom indeed.

Not all of the Founders, though, had felt the force of the parental rudders steering Adams and Jefferson. Most notably, George Washington himself lived his great and active life without the boons of a formal classical education — a fact inspiring more than a couple reforming spirits over the years to

show definitively that those boons have been overrated. Yet
what the clever overlook is that humble side of Washington's
greatness that could and did acknowledge his own shortcomings. The greatest Founder of all revered the classical inheritance as much as any of his generation — perhaps more than
some did for having missed its rigors. Washington was a man of
Roman nature; he was the American embodiment of
Cincinnatus. He imbibed the spare, republican ideals of Joseph
Addison's play, *Cato*. All this his fellow countrymen could see.
But, most significantly, when the time came to provide for his
own stepson's schooling, Washington made sure the boy would
not suffer his stepfather's classical poverty. For the eight-year-
old Jack Custis, Washington bought editions of Sallust, Horace,
Eutropius, Cornelius Nepos, and Terence, throwing in a cache
of Latin grammars and lexicons. The young soldier would be
well equipped for the long march through life. Washington
talked proudly of the boy who started studying Latin practically
"as soon as he could speak." And while he preferred that the
child learn French instead of Greek, Washington dubbed Greek
"no bad acquisition." His stepson would have what he did not.
As with so much else in his life, Washington's actions write eloquent epigrams of their own.

Cultivated Americans once understood the value — including the practical value — of Greek and Latin classics, till the
tides of democracy swept them away after the Age of Jackson in
the second third of the nineteenth century. But even among
those of the founding generation, the vote for classics was not
unanimous. Benjamin Rush, a Philadelphia physician and
signer of the Declaration of Independence, spoke out early for
"useful knowledge," that knowledge and those skills helping
their possessors to do, make, and sell things. America, he
thought, should be a nation entirely devoted to rendering its

citizens useful, but not in the Humanist's sense of utility. When Rush submitted a "Plan for a Federal University," Latin and Greek were nowhere to be found in its curriculum. His designs were nearly messianic — though one might hesitate to call them Virgilian. "Should this plan of a federal university or one like it be adopted, then will begin the golden age of the United States. While the business of education in Europe consists in lecturing upon the ruins of Palmyra and the antiquities of Herculaneum, or in disputes about Hebrew points, Greek particles, or the accent and quantity of the Roman language, the youth of America will be employed in acquiring those branches of knowledge which increase the conveniences of life, lessen human misery, improve our country, promote population, exalt the human understanding, and establish domestic, social, and political happiness."

What can this full plate possibly lack? Note the bent of the rhetoric. We are to have a noble citizenry: but how exactly are citizens to be ennobled? Manifestos canvassed for the reform of education have run thus ever since. They depart from the hard, specific, and achievable so that they may embrace the soft, indefinite, and ungraspable. While spraying sunny ideals with high-sounding words, their advocates seek deliverance in vague, half-realized science and good feelings. They place a naïve faith in the capacity of practical know-how to yield all those things that *civilized* people — people, that is, complete individually with souls and collectively with a history — need. And of course these reformers may be right. But we must know what makes a people civilized. Is it merely the sum of their "information," their ability to convert effort into cash, their hunger to make more gadgets to perform functions they've yet to question, their bottomless yen for amusement? Or does civilization require something else, something greater and higher — and

something harder? All of us must answer these queries for ourselves. We can but hope that when we do we'll possess the
educated mind and the cultivated heart needed to offer sensible
and wise replies.

John Adams and Thomas Jefferson knew where they stood.
They sought, for themselves and for posterity, the *vita beata*, the
happy life. And they hoped for a stable commonwealth. These
two men knew intimately Aristotle's vital, now neglected distinction between the education that democrats like and the education that can preserve democracy. Good intentions aren't
enough. Nor is uncritical, flag-waving patriotism sufficient to
keep the ship of state afloat and sailing to safe havens. Indeed,
it may be dangerous. Unsheltered and unexcused by the urgen-
cies of war, easy patriotism may become silage for the propa-
gandist and demagogue. We Americans will need heartier fare
if our great experiment is to prove successful through the centuries. If we wish to understand the Founding Fathers from
within, we should heed one simple axiom. *Don't merely read about
them; read what they read — as they read it.* "Classics," wrote
Adams to the sage of Monticello, "in spite of our friend Rush, I
must think indispensable."

■   ■   ■

Talk of the American Founders leads us inexorably to
American qualms about the utility of classics. We like to be useful; nay, we hunger to be useful. Usefulness is a virtue. We don't
care for superfluity, and as a people we are perpetually wary of
those inessential add-ons in our schools like poetry, music, and
art. They seem so unnecessary: not bad perhaps, but nothing we
should give time to until all things needful for the good life —
gadgets, comforts, amusements — are secured. (And somehow

they never are.) These things we can see. More to the point for
some people, they're the things by which one's quality of life is
measured. We also fear wasting our time. Yet, as we have seen,
the Founders as a group had few doubts about the usefulness of
Greek and Latin. For them life was too short and small to contain their utility.

The first and, for the Revolutionary generation, paramount
use was of course civic. Classics pulled citizens out of the innate
parochialism to which all are born, helping those blinded by
their own times — and this is most of us — to see those times
without blinkers, affording a broad view of history and of their
place within it. The history of the Greeks and Romans demonstrated, with unfailing and discomfiting consistency, that we are
not alone, that men and women have faced like predicaments
before. Classical literature showed that the thirst for the New
for the sake of the New is often a mark of both personal and
social immaturity. We are not to be, in one real sense, children
of our time: we are to be children of all time, men for all sea-
sons. Even the moral dicta delivered by the authors of old carried seeds of usefulness for a budding Republic that must
depend upon an upright citizenry for its very survival. The letters of Adams and Jefferson fairly shimmer with the utility of
reading classics; for them this was no merely ornamental skill;
Greek and Latin furnished their minds and formed their political judgment. Classics contained a not-so-subtle spur to grow
up, intellectually and culturally. The Founders took to
heart Cicero's standing, eternal question: "For what is the life of
man, if memory of the past be not interwoven in the life of
later times?"

This spirit floated down slow rivers long after the deaths of
Adams and Jefferson in 1826. Theirs was not the last formida-
bly enlightened generation of presidents. Farther downstream,

Woodrow Wilson asserted that "your enlightenment depends on the company you keep." "We should have scant capital to trade on," he said, "were we to throw away the wisdom we have inherited and seek our fortunes with the slender stock we ourselves have accumulated. This...is the real, the prevalent argument for holding every man we can to the intimate study of the ancient classics," for "what you cannot find a substitute for is the classics as literature; and there can be no first hand contact with that literature if you will not master the grammar and the syntax which convey its subtle power." Wilson's predecessor, William Howard Taft, took a purely practical tack. Aside from the "mental discipline" provided by a classical education, classical studies "are most helpful in the matter of correct English style, in laying sound foundations for grammatical construction, and in furnishing a basis for the study of all modern languages." Grover Cleveland had credited classics with inspiring and forming the clarity and style of the *Federalist Papers* and, as a trustee of Princeton after leaving the White House, he insisted on the university's fidelity to classics. The most muscular defense, though, came from Theodore Roosevelt, a man hot for reform in almost every department but this one. Holding that a democratic nation must provide a chance for elementary education to all its citizens, as well as vocational training to all who need it, he adamantly stood his ground on classics. "Democracy comes short of what it should be just to the extent that it fails to provide for the exceptional individual, no matter how poor his start in life, the highest kind of exceptional training; for democracy as a permanent world force must mean not only the raising of the general level, but also the raising of the standards of excellence to which only exceptional individuals may attain." So "for those who have the chance and desire" to take "a broad and high liberal education...one essential element shall be classical training." Roosevelt lived his creed, maintaining his reading of Greek and Latin amid trust-busting and big game hunting until the end of his life.

But another use of classics, even for these men, was precisely its non-use. Classics is, by a time-honored reckoning, *supra usum* — it's beyond use. Much of its value resides in its superfluity. It sows the seeds of culture. Once more we return to the wisdom of the Renaissance, which posed classical literature as both useful in a full, rounded life and worthy for its own sake. We also return to the difference between education and cultivation; obviously they're complimentary, but they can be distinguished. Today we recognize the value of education, whatever it is we mean by that ungainly, wildly expensive contraption. But the meaning of cultivation has fled the premises. The Founders tried in their time to exemplify both, not just one. And cultivation requires those extras of the higher life, those goals and accomplishments making for urbanity and refinement, breadth and depth. Perhaps one can be "educated" without those extras; without them, one cannot be cultivated. Adams and Jefferson would have understood the claim of the philosopher George Santayana that "Music is essentially useless, as life is: but both have an ideal extension which lends utility to its conditions." "Let us not forget," Emerson once said, "that the adoption of the test 'what is it good for' would abolish the rose and exalt in triumph the cabbage." And man cannot live by cabbage alone.

The idea of *use*, at least as framed by naïve and uninformed — not to say unformed — people is perfectly irrelevant anyway. Knowledge is useful. We know not whither it may tend or what uses it may be put to in the years to come. We cannot know early on what kinds of minds and souls are waiting to develop amongst the young we teach. Not all of them may be fit as lawyers, surgeons, or software salesmen; greatness of other kinds may lie ahead for some — if only they be given the climbing gear early enough so as to help them make their own way. The impact of knowledge is impossible to predict. But this we can know: Ignorance is no asset, and the empty, formless mind is surely a positive liability. Few qualities can be more useful, whatever one's future may hold, than the fortified mind. Parents who cannot see this are shortsighted, misinformed, or vicariously rapacious.

Always must we ask ourselves with each new generation: Do we wish finally to train or to educate? Our reply will do much to determine the kind of world in which we live. We do have choices. We ought to make them with open eyes.

"Education truly conceived is spiritual growth toward intellectual and moral perfection," said Columbia President Nicholas Murray Butler, "and it is not an artificial process to be carried on according to mechanical formulas toward a purely material end." Butler proved himself a prophet back in the second decade of the twentieth century when he spied one nascent trend foretelling worse to come:

> What is now being attempted all over this country is to train youth in a comprehension of a civilization which has historic and easily examined roots, without revealing to them the fact that modern civilization has roots. Phrase making, scattered and unrelated information and vague aspirations for the improvement of other people are, unfortunately, now supposed to be a satisfactory substitute for an understanding of how civilization came to be what it is.... When we turn aside from the study of Greek and Latin...we not only give up the study of the embryology of civilization but we lose the great advantage which follows from intimate association with some of the highest forms of intellectual and aesthetic achievement.

Phillips Academy's Alfred Stearns once said that the true aim of education is to develop the man and woman who are "something bigger and finer than a mere piece of mechanism designed to fit into place in a practical world but [which is] devoid of aspiration and idealism, bereft of vision and imagination, [and] forever denied the privilege of tasting the things of the spirit which alone is life."

Cyril Bailey of Oxford once told an anecdote much to the point. "A former student of mine had gone into business and was in the habit of bringing a Homer or a Virgil in his pocket to the office. His colleagues twitted him; there might be some sense in learning modern languages, but what was the use of all this Greek and Latin?"

He replied to them: "No use, thank God."

"To seek utility everywhere," said Aristotle, "is most unsuitable to lofty and free natures."

Why climb Parnassus?

Why climb any mountain?

■   ■   ■

Yet if we would look for uses of classics, beyond those of shaping ourselves intellectually and aesthetically as individuals — "uses" that alone quite satisfy some of us — we might look to the health of high, and even middle, culture. What about the good of those people who can never receive a full classical education but who, possessing intelligent minds, should know a fair amount of what other intelligent people have known in the past? How can we understand, the argument runs, a term like *Oedipus complex* without having read the Theban plays of Sophocles? How can we know what *Achilles' heel* means, or know who Helen of Troy was without having read Greek mythology?

How can we know the significance of the Battle of Marathon without having read Greek history? Or the meaning of *the die is cast* or the origin of *fiddling while Rome burns* without Roman history? How can we understand the decline of Periclean Athens without having pored over Thucydides and Xenophon? Or that of Rome without having waded through Suetonius and Tacitus? If we would appreciate the greatness of Alexander the Great, surely we must make our way through the chronicles of Arrian. We must read these things in order to be, to use a late term, "culturally literate." Not to know them is not to know who we are or where we came from; it is to be, culturally, like someone whose memory doesn't reach back beyond the day before yesterday. Literature and history both become incomprehensible. How can we read far into modern European or English literature without a solid grounding in classics? Without classics we wouldn't know why Virgil acted as Dante's guide in the *Divine Comedy*, nor would we hear the classical echoes in *Paradise Lost*. Much of Tennyson would be forever *terra incognita*, whatever that means.

Throughout this essay we have highlighted the *argumentum ad formam* more than the *argumentum ad rem*, the case for intellectual formation more than that for content or substance. The former is the runt of the litter nowadays. But the latter case — which I also call the cultural argument — deserves a full hearing as well. And it gets one. This is in fact the case for classics most popularly employed now. The cultural argument is solid but, at least as it tends to be presented now, it's not unassailable. Contrarians wait with rejoinders ready to hand. All this might make some sense, they reply, but it's a matter of efficiency. One doesn't really need to read Sophocles, after all, to know the meaning of *Oedipus complex*. That meaning can be got much more easily and quickly from a dictionary or other reference

book. The same with *Achilles' heel*. The same with all of the
terms and allusions we could muster. Reading classical literature, even in translation, seems an awful lot of trouble to endure
in order to mine the meanings of a few key terms that just happen still to be floating about. All we need to know is where
to go to find them. Of course we might make minor mistakes
if we know only the meanings, not the origins, of those terms.
But we won't be severely handicapped. We can still talk to the
smart people.

It's hard to argue with the practical point here. If all one
wants are bits of information, one can get them within minutes
from a library or off the Internet. No one need learn any languages nor even read any books. It's all free for the taking. Isn't
this what the "Information Age" is all about? Easy access? This
is why I believe that the cultural argument, much as I accept it,
carries unshakable problems in its wake. The case is simply not
strong enough to admit of a sturdy defense for any years-long
curriculum containing subjects as severe and time-consuming
as Greek and Latin. As a conscientious businessman might say
more bluntly, the cost doesn't justify the product.

And then we have *translations*. Granted that we should read
Homer and Hesiod, Virgil and Horace sometime in our lives,
why can't we read them in our own language? What are all
those classical scholars good for if they can't provide us with
accurate and smooth renderings of the works civilized people
should know? We may in fact not want all those "niceties" of
language that Isaac Stuart praised so eloquently. Give us just the
facts. "Much have I traveled in the realms of gold," wrote the
poet John Keats of his classical odysseys, and he, we must
confess, motored largely by translations. Why shouldn't we do
the same?

This is an easier protest to fend off, depending upon one's

reason, formative or cultural, for pushing classics. Although translations should come with a tag of warning, they should not be shunned. They have great value, both intellectual and cultural. T. S. Eliot, a classical literary Humanist, knew that the world of classical scholarship itself cannot survive for long, "unless some knowledge of the civilizations of Greece and Rome, some respect for their achievements, some understanding of their historical relation to our own, and some acquaintance with their literature and their wisdom *in translation* can be cultivated among a very much larger number of people" — among, that is, those who read and those who write. Translations can perform the vital service of opening doors to treasures otherwise closed off to us. And certainly we must concede that much of classical literature is richly amenable to translation. It can and has been argued that one loses comparatively little when setting aside the Ionic dialect of Herodotus for a good English version. We can profit likewise from translations of other historians like Thucydides, Xenophon, Livy, Sallust, Caesar, Suetonius, and Tacitus. To have read them in English is, in some generous senses, practically to have read them. This widely held notion is defensible, though again fair judgment hangs upon what one expects to draw from those translations. Simple narrative translates well enough.

Poetry, though, does not. Indeed poetry has been justly defined as that which cannot be translated. We can get away somewhat with translations when reading epic poetry: the story carries us along and a few striking images remain, pulsating like strobe lights at every mention. Whiffs of the magic come through. But the problem with translations is that those readers unlettered in the original languages can't know what they're missing. Almost anyone who has read, say, the *Odyssey* in both Greek and English finds even the best translation (and there are several splendid ones) grossly inadequate. "It seems to me," American jurist Oliver Wendell Holmes once wrote, "that people who think they are enjoying Euripides, for instance, in the charming translations that we know, probably are getting their pleasure from a modern atmosphere that is precisely what is not in the original." A reader of the original language smells a counterfeit. A translation seems as the shadow of a tree to the tree itself, and the discerning mind will not confuse one for the other. Much of the power and the glory no longer shine within the poem that's been run through the enervating sieve of translation. Something leaks out.

Unfortunately that something is often the very essence that once drove centuries of readers to the poem. We lack that which made it great. We've lost the pearl in the center. The burden of translation is compounded, perhaps beyond the breaking point, with lyric poetry, which is, even in the best hands, not so much translated as guessed and poked at. Sappho and Alcaeus can be incomprehensible in Greek; they're altogether as aliens in English. Reading them in any language but Greek is to spot faint traces of an old erasure. It's like reading the dim etchings of a palimpsest.

■   ■   ■

So we're thrown back to the languages and the key role they play in our cultural and literary life. And we're thrown back upon their content as well as on their disciplinary value. While T. S. Eliot believed in elevating the larger society with the softer, less demanding forms of higher things, he also knew that instruction in Greek and Latin must not only continue unabated, but also that they must resume their perch atop the highest pedestal of scholastic endeavor within the humanities.

They must be acknowledged as the chief humanistic pursuit. "I do not wish to be accused," he said, "of inventing a new heresy to the effect that salvation depends upon getting a first in classics. But the culture of Europe [and, by extension, America] cannot preserve its intellectual vigour unless a high standard of Latin and Greek scholarship is maintained amongst its teachers."

Back in the first half of the twentieth century, Eliot saw myriad efforts to replace the old glues of social and cultural cohesion with new ones, perhaps socialistic or communistic ones. We were to walk with new shoes on new ground. But Eliot wasn't going along. He asserted firmly that "a new unity can only grow on the old roots: the Christian faith, and the classical languages which Europeans inherit in common," roots, he said, which are "inextricably intertwined."

> European literature is a whole, the several members of which cannot flourish, if the same blood-stream does not circulate throughout the whole body. The blood-stream of European literature is Latin and Greek — not as two systems of circulation, but one, for it is through Rome that our parentage in Greece must be traced. What common measure of excellence have we in literature, among our several languages, which is not the classical measure? What mutual intelligibility can we hope to preserve, except in our common heritage of thought and feeling in these two languages, for the understanding of which, no European people is in any position of advantage over any other?

Greek and Latin must be sustained in our schools and colleges, Eliot also said, because their loss can only cause true and rigorous substance to lapse from all pursuits within the humanities, making for a fatal loss of depth in our intellectual life. Intellectuals may still speak in the future, but they won't be qualified; they'll be mere pundits. The "desiccation of the study of philosophy in the universities," he said, citing but one example of the New Ignorance, has come about through "the teaching of philosophy to young men who have no background of *humanistic* education, the teaching of Plato and Aristotle to youths who know no Greek and are completely ignorant of ancient history." A philosopher thinking within the Western tradition who has no Greek, Eliot said, isn't one.

Eliot boldly claimed that not only is the vigorous teaching of Greek and Latin vital to the future of classical scholarship, but also that the very "maintenance of classical education is essential to the maintenance of the continuity of *English* Literature" (my emphasis). Ben Jonson might have written of Shakespeare's possessing "small Latin and less Greek," but that fact showed only one patch in the quilt. For Shakespeare, Eliot said, "lived in a world in which the wisdom of the ancients was respected, and their poetry admired and enjoyed." Upping the ante, Eliot held that classical knowledge is not optional when reading a learned poet like Milton, where "some knowledge of Latin is necessary, not only for understanding what Milton is talking about, but much more for understanding his style and music." Eliot all but claimed the Latinless to be barred from the temple of English muses. "You may write English poetry without knowing any Latin," intoned the most influential English poet of the twentieth century. "I am not sure whether without Latin you can wholly understand it."

Like W. H. Auden after him, Eliot worried for the health of our literary life, which he believed to be disintegrating into discrete groups of the shallow and ephemeral. A healthy literary culture must thrive not on genius — or inspiration — alone. Culture is, in this sense, a web, a network of standards and associations and images, links among minds and spirits, fragile

and easily shattered. For during the previous twenty years, Eliot
said in the early 1940s, "I have observed what seems to me a
deterioration in the *middle literary stratum*, and notably in the
standards and the scholarship which are wanted for literary criticism" (my emphasis). While Eliot, also like Auden, conceded
that the "genius" is ever exempt from these worries — such people always muddle along somehow — the genius doesn't really
handle the tiller. A literary culture cannot be judged properly
by the brightest stars set in its firmament. The greatest writers
don't determine the literary strength of their society. Figures of
the second, third, and fourth ranks do that: the writers, editors,
scholars, critics, professors, and teachers. It is among such people, we'll recall, that Auden noticed the onset of "an appalling
deterioration in precision and conciseness." Thin schooling has
allowed them to lose their formerly strong and sure grasp not
only on information and ideas, but also on language itself.
We're liable now to take the clever, nit-picking dabbler for the
intelligent and well-read man or woman. We've created a world
in which, as C. S. Lewis said, a person feels qualified "to review
books he does not understand, and to be intellectual without
intellect." Eliot blamed this chaotic state of affairs on "the dis-
appearance of any common background of instruction, any common body of literary and historical knowledge, [and] any common acquaintance with the foundations of English literature."
Those foundations, along with Anglo-Saxon and medieval
infusions of French, are largely classical. To be a student of
English literature is — or ought to be — to have sized them up
thoroughly.

A literary culture needs a tradition. And it was Eliot who
wrote that tradition "can't be inherited, and if you want it, you
must obtain it by great labour." As classically educated men,
Eliot, Auden, and Lewis not only deplored the passing of classi-

cal education, they grieved over it. "To lose what I owe to Plato and Aristotle would be like the amputation of a limb," Lewis said. "Hardly any lawful price would seem to me too high for what I have gained by being made to learn Latin and Greek." If any question of the value of classics were to be raised, he said, "you would find me on the extreme right."

That question is before the court again. The gaudy, kitschy contemporary scene has done little to assuage the worries or contradict the prophecies of Eliot, Auden, and Lewis regarding the future of our literary culture. There's been more than a bit of flattening at the top. Who are the Eliots and Audens and Lewises of our time? Who among us now has the sheer weight of learning to match theirs? One day, we may justifiably fear, that "middle stratum" of talent and understanding will no longer rise even to middling. But, in the fashion of the lowly educated and publicly self-regarding, those who compose those ranks won't know it. For they won't know what they don't know. The web will have been broken.

■   ■   ■

Rhapsodies on the benefits of a classical education, whether political, literary, or broadly cultural, ought never to obscure those gifts to the mind and character that the stoutest spirits through Western history have perennially recognized. We need not be intellectual sycophants, slavishly educating ourselves exclusively for the profit of that society in which we move and breathe. Odd people they would be, after all, who would embark on a classical training merely for the sake of the larger culture without a thought for their own mental and emotional enlargement. One embarks on classics for the sake of *self*-culture, first and foremost. Nonetheless, a defense of classical education without a recital of some of those more global gains would be a truncated one. Within much of classical literature we find some of those boons of classics that can be shared amply with those unversed in Greek and Latin, the power residing there shining vibrantly even through translation. We may concentrate on the Greeks for the sake of simplicity.

Greek literature is marked by a peculiar completeness, as even a rough acquaintance with Homer — whoever "Homer" was exactly — demonstrates. Western literature began with him, and he excelled all others. Aristotle said as much. So have many others. "To forget Homer," said poet and critic Andrew Lang with more than a little zeal, "to cease to be concerned or even curious about Homer, is to make a fatal step toward a new barbarism." Novelist Somerset Maugham once averred that "you can't imagine what a thrill it is to read the *Odyssey* in the original. It makes you feel as if you only had to get on tiptoe and stretch out your hand to touch the stars." The *Iliad*, said G. K. Chesterton, "might well be the last word as well as the first word spoken by man about his mortal lot, as seen by merely mortal vision. If the world becomes pagan and perishes, the last man left alive would do well to quote the *Iliad* and die." Emerson said that "every novel is a debtor to Homer." Ford Maddox Ford: "We may presume that anyone who makes any pretence to any shade of appreciation of learning or literature must have at least some knowledge of Homer." E. K. Rand gave a bit of advice to prospective college students: "Buy, beg, borrow, or steal enough of a knowledge of Greek to read Homer in the original." "Just how many years ago Homer lived," he added, "nobody can tell us. That he will live forever is a certainty."

The Greek tragedians from the fifth century BC shared common roots with Homer. No other dramatic tradition seems so amply rounded, so complete. It's as though, while leaving room for infinite elaboration to later generations of poets, playwrights, and novelists, Greek playwrights touched upon every human merit and foible on the stage, setting the human psyche front and center for audiences of all times to enjoy and contemplate. No subject was too grand or noble, nor was any too scandalous or squalid. The entire range of thought and feeling was grist for the poet's mill. We read the *Agamemnon* of Aeschylus and sense a macabre austerity, "his atmosphere charged with mysterious forces, his characters survivals from a heroic age," as Livingstone put it. Then we find Sophocles, "the perfect artist, a master of plot and language, yet a great poet besides," followed by Euripides, a man possessed of "an interest in the life of the common people, his sympathy with the oppressed and suffering, his hatred of wrong, his acute restless brain, skeptic and dreamer." The human heart can want for little more to express its depths. "Let critics of the classics," Livingstone concluded, "produce any other civilization so complete, so fitted to introduce [us] to the activities and adventures of the human mind, so able in every direction to open windows on to life."

If poetry and drama open windows onto the inner life of the Greeks, the chronicles of history they bequeathed to us reveal their link to the rest of the world, as well as their relations among themselves. To this day, in the annals of the West Herodotus remains the "Father of History," the one man who taught all who came after how to marshal one's intelligence and curiosity to record what we discover about the world while being at once engaged and critical. "This is the account of Herodotus of Halicarnassus," he begins his *Histories*, "undertaken so that the achievements of men should not be obliterated by time and the great and marvelous works of both Greeks and barbarians should not be without fame, and not least the reason why they fought one another." Refusing to play the armchair teller of tales, Herodotus took to the road. He was perhaps the world's first multiculturalist. Everything he saw during his long, hot travels took his fancy; he bursts with anecdotes, nuggets of observation designed to convey the fertility of strangeness found beyond familiar shores. Yet he was also a patriot of sorts: "For if anyone, no matter who, were given the opportunity of choosing from amongst all the nations of the world the set of beliefs which he thought best, he would inevitably, after careful consideration of their relative merits, choose those of his own country."

Herodotus wasn't just a historian; he was a psychologist. From him we learn much about the waging of the Persian Wars, but his example also puts us in mind of those "barbarian" peoples who did not possess the capacity for self-scrutiny that so marked the Greeks of the perilous and wondrous fifth century BC. A little later Thucydides almost single-handedly taught us the accurate use of the historical method, the sifting of facts to determine cause and effect. This historian of the fall of Athens reported the progressive disasters — including the Great Plague of 429 — to befall his homeland in the *History of the Peloponnesian War*, and he did so with all the calm dispassion of a sympathetic yet critical stranger. He recounted Pericles eulogizing noble Athenians in the Funeral Oration as men "judging freedom to be happiness, and courage to be freedom." Each city-state earns its history; we reap as we sow. Xenophon carried on the sequel of decline and fall in his *Hellenica*. The Greek historians gave Western civilization its early lessons in the price of liberty and the virtues of public responsibility gladly accepted and discharged.

But philosophy may stand as the greatest single influence of

the classical world upon modern thought. The figures of
Socrates, Plato, Aristotle, and Epicurus, wrote Livingstone, "are
the culmination of the Greek genius, and perhaps its greatest
glory"; they are the "children of the marriage between reason
and life." They range across all fields of philosophical effort,
from morals to metaphysics. "Philosophy has often seemed dull
and dry, but [the Greeks] united logic and feeling, imagination
and analysis, and qualified with radiant vision the dry light of
thought." We saw intimations of their clarity when we dis-
cussed the liberal and humanistic imagination that the West
inherited from Greece and Rome. Those minds lit fires. They
did not squander their time and substance on matters of method
alone: both the ideal and the reality prevailed. The best classical philosophers had a way of reducing questions of human —
and divine — life to their irreducible essences, shearing off
whatever clouded the point on the table. What questions could
be simpler or more profound than *What is the good life? What is
man's purpose on earth? How shall we then live?* Philosophers
craned their necks to the stars. Plato was, Livingstone, said, "at
once poet and philosopher," the farthest-seeing of all thinkers;
Aristotle was, for Thomas Aquinas, *il maestro di color che sanno*,
"the master of those who know." Together they taught us one of
their profoundest lessons, in the words of Plato, τὸ νικᾷν αὐτὸν
αὐτὸν πασῶν νικῶν πρώτη τε καὶ ἀρίστη: To conquer oneself is
the first and best of all victories.

Man, Livingstone wrote, cannot live by "sense and sanity
alone," virtues that characterized the finest modern philosophers all the way up to John Stuart Mill. Even common sense
has its limits. And bare ratiocination, however precise and complex, cannot alone enlighten us. What we need is "a touch of
vision," a sense of wonder and a belief that meaning can be
found within the rough and tumble of life. That sense of

wonder we may achieve, but it's not free. It comes only to those willing to shoulder the task, to bear the burden of rolling the stone up the hill. Greek philosophers, along with their more earnest Roman disciples, sought to make life comprehensible as well as livable. Any reader may be challenged to peruse a decent rendition of Plato's *Republic* or Aristotle's *Nicomachean Ethics* and deny that these men knew and cared about human things, both personal and public — a trait we often seek in vain among the arcane, reticulated pages of contemporary lovers of wisdom.

English essayist William Hazlitt wrote that it is hard to find within people formed intellectually by means other than a classical education "either a real love of excellence, or a belief that any excellence exists superior to their own. Everything is brought down to the vulgar level of their own ideas and pursuits." Surely this overstates the case — but the unnerving truth about the fundamentally uneducated person stands. An education saturating anyone in these great works of the classical past cannot help but enhance the minds and hearts of those enduring it. Our horizons broaden. We not only learn of principles discovered by minds two or three millennia ago, we begin to grasp them. We become bigger, more tolerant, more generous. We grow up. This is an education seeking by its very technique to strike a balance between the high promises of idealism and the unalterable laws of human nature. Airy, idealistic dreams that fail to wake to the morning reality of human nature make for the fantastic chase after the eternally inaccessible, while the claims of human nature that are asserted without the leavening of ideals, those dreams of what we might grow to become out of the clay of what we are, render us scarcely human at all. The cultivated, civilized man and woman know, as Aristotle might have said, that wisdom lies somewhere in the struggle to find the mean. Whatever wisdom is, we're not born with it.

A classical education is more than a discipline of the mind. It's a transformation of mind. A classical education is, as Livingstone called it long ago, "a training in insight and sympathy," a training forever changing one's map of the cosmos; the world becomes a more multi-hued terrain in sharper relief. It has always opened our eyes to worlds both like and unlike our own, affording us manifold images of the Beautiful and the Good. For centuries classical study supplied a lifetime's worth of historical exempla, philosophical axioms, and ideas that shone like gemstones and lent poignancy and *éclat* to our mundane, quotidian lives. It strengthened and ennobled the mind. A classical education still allows us, after years of pain and straining effort, to peek over the wall and see blue mountains rising above the lowlands.

■ ■ ■

The formative case for classics is indeed a relic of pedagogical incorrectness. We can readily see why in the Age of Self-Esteem. Nothing about the experience of having one's Latin participles or Greek accents corrected conduces to one's sense of self-worth and innate brilliance. But we can also see that this approach to forming the mind is "incorrect" only to those people who have read the wrong books and bought all the bad theory that a hundred years of feel-good fanaticizing have dished out. Eliot argued the cultural case primarily: we learn Greek and Latin so as to read them and thus possess within our minds some of the keys to the Western tradition. They are learned for the sake of the treasures they store and sustain. Yet he too acknowledged the idea of formation, both intellectual and cultural. "The significance of [any] type of education," he said, "may lie almost as much in what it omits as in what it includes." We have heard this before. Spinning the idea another way, we might say that a particular course of instruction might indeed be judged according to its utility, but not always in favor of those hot for "useful knowledge": the more "useful" a curriculum, the less valuable it may be for the long-term interests of the learner. That which we get on our own initiative is just as important as that which is taught us in the classroom.

Classical education, properly conducted, works on the principle of Indirection. What we achieve concretely is not as vital to our minds over the long haul as what we're given the power to achieve — on our own. That's what formation is all about. We gain independence. Much there is to be said for any curriculum that doesn't strive to give content so much as it does the tools of skill and judgment that allow us to get that content at our own leisure. Generations of educated men and women, for example, have read and enjoyed Shakespeare without getting him in school. The classroom saw them reading Homer and Horace, counting hexameter feet and agonizing over the force of a Greek particle. They weren't "appreciating"; they were working. They were strengthening their intellectual and aesthetic muscles while learning the glorious minutiae of literary pieces deemed to be those works most worth knowing for a thinking, sentient citizen of the West. They were taking on board knowledge that invited them one day to read Spenser and Shakespeare — or Hawthorne and Melville — on their own with ease. A rich constellation of image and allusion had become theirs. They held within their minds much that has been, for the impoverished appreciators of the world, imprisoned within the headachy, tiny-print realm of footnotes. Ironically, by not reading — and opining over like jesters — a later and softer literature during their early and formative years, they gained over time the capacity to read that same literature better, and with greater enjoyment, for themselves. The reins were theirs. Such learning had also enhanced the likelihood that they would do so. They were not merely educated. They were cultivated.

Here is no small advantage attending any form of education. As C. S. Lewis well understood, strict and traditional schooling, that kind which is "ruthlessly aristocratic, shamelessly highbrow," saves us from the dire hazards of sentimentality and cheap unknowingness. We learn to exercise our sentiments as knowledgeable, not propagandized, people. Classical education is a bulwark against slick stupidity and easy opinions. Far from spiriting us away from the lovely things of the world, it affords greater possibilities of intimacy even with those things we haven't read and been tested upon in school. It opens doors and keeps them open. The trained and cultivated mind is free to enjoy at those times when enjoyment matters most — when we sit quietly by the beach or before the fire with our friends, our drinks, and our thoughts.

■　■　■

A classical education buffers us against the seedier depredations of modern public life. These include intellectual confusion and dishonesty. Multiculturalism — or at least the more rabid manifestations of it — has enslaved the American public schools, and perhaps the American mind, to an unexamined article of faith that all societies — all ways of life, all ways of thinking and feeling, all modes of expression — are equally valuable and worth the narrow beaming of academic study. Education need only catalogue and highlight them for the profit of the prejudiced and mentally pliable. Members of tagged "victimized" groups are made thereby to feel good about themselves; members of tagged "dominant" groups are made to reflect on their retrospective crimes. Here burns yet another insidious form of propaganda. It doesn't train, it harangues; it exploits the ill read and the unsuspecting. Not that all faces of multiculturalism are bad, of course. Knowledge of other societies, cultures, and sub-cultures is positively good and much of it is fascinating — as Herodotus taught us 2,500 years ago. The question is, How will this knowledge be employed? Many of those who stridently, vociferously advocate multicultural education don't put us in mind of Newman's "philosophical habit," that habit most to be desired in those flexing their intellects on the world around them. That cultures are *different* and *victimized* is enough for them; there justification for a thinner, less taxing curriculum ends.

A classical curriculum, though, can act as a healthy corrective to tedious, mindless relativism. It is not so much uni-cultural as *aristo-cultural* — it directs us to models of the best in all fields of human achievement. And we are all "minorities," all of us are "disadvantaged," in the face of superior objects, whether they be words, thoughts, things, or deeds. While many self-proclaimed multiculturalists legitimately desire those salves of "sympathetic insight" claimed by Livingstone to be among the gifts of a literary education, they don't want to raid the bank for them. They demand cut-rate prices. They want their dogmatic proclamations to replace study and contemplation. But the state of mind they wish to engender has neither depth nor staying power. Many of them don't really care for education at all. They prefer political indoctrination. Let us take these partisans seriously as political or social forces, but not as intellectual ones. For even if their political goals be good, multiculturalists ought not to confuse one kind of intellectual training for another. The world might endure worse fates than to be filled with citizens unable to meditate upon those things judged higher and better.

But educated people, of all races and creeds, must develop the ability to recognize those things when they're set before them, regardless of their provenance.

Another excess of modern life — and one not unrelated to well-intentioned, naïve multiculturalism — is intellectual shallowness. This vice besets all of us. Never have so many people earned so many academic degrees and known so little. Yet never have so many thought they know so much. We use big and alien words without having habituated ourselves to their singular atmospheres. Words adopted for the situation — such as the kind employed purely to impress — are not mental furniture we've taken inside to live with but garish deck chairs we rent out for the occasion. We drag them in for convenience when company comes, but they don't belong to us. We repeat the thought-clichés we hear without realizing that we're not thinking our own thoughts but the thoughts of others. Thus perhaps has it always been. "One great danger of the modern world," wrote Livingstone again, "is our susceptibility to the general ideas that float around us, thick as bacilli, in the air, that pass our lips so often, and are so influential in our lives." The antidote to this virus is Socrates' "habit of skepticism," the inclination to ask hard questions and not accept easy answers. What we often find instead, in this comfortably half-educated time, is a virulent strain of unearned cynicism, the rough workings of intelligent minds that haven't yet learned how to think, a trait ironically evident in the idealistic young. But a true education will always act against this unearned cynicism, this dour take on the world unchecked by reason and sympathy. It will help to free us from the snares assailing our fellows who live their lives "at the mercy of phrases."

• • •

"A stream of tendency cannot be dammed by argument," said American classicist Paul Shorey almost a century ago. We cannot plead our way back to classics. The countervailing gusts are too great. Just decades after the christening of the elective system, Shorey saw that American colleges and universities, with the best of democratic intentions, had created the easy "bargain-counter, sample room, *à la carte*" path to the college degree. Knowledge was beginning to lose its very shape. The natural sciences could withstand the onslaught. Precision is essential to scientific practice; inaccurate science cannot survive. But the humanities, he saw, can march by more lenient orders. They can be softened — and then they can be faked. No one need prove he knows anything once the specter of Appreciation enters the groves of academe. And Shorey saw it creeping into the classical schoolroom with calls not only for "useful knowledge," but also with fervent entreaties to allow Greek and Latin to stand down and have teachers teach only "cultural" — that is, non-linguistic — sides of the classical world. Current attacks on classics, he said, were "inspired by the revolt against discipline and hard work." As with so many before, he knew that this road, if followed, would lead us to perdition. Last Rites for the humanities could be intoned forthwith.

Yet Shorey also looked to the future with hope in saying that there will always be the saving Remnant who, facing the frigid winds that blow, will "recognize that a real education must be based on a serious, consecutive, progressive study of something definite, teachable, and hard." Knowledge must have traceable contours. A true and high education cannot be browsed and bought as at a bazaar. Some earnest and serious people will always seek to discipline their intelligence, "suffusing thought with feeling, informing feeling with thought."

Classics and the hard, natural sciences, thought by some to

be natural enemies, are, in one key sense, not enemies at all. They are really complementary. They both demand exacting effort and measurable results; they require long apprenticeships. They are inflexible. And even their obvious differences show a certain harmony. Science, Shorey said, gives "utility, discipline, and a kind of culture" while classics yields "culture, discipline, and a kind of utility." That middle element is critical. It ensures that the hidden treasure of real knowledge may eventually be found by the diligent. Classics and science can and should stand tall against the soft and fickle seductions of non-knowledge. Together they could make formidable allies.

By losing their grip on the requisites of discipline, the humanities stand to lose all of their lasting value. And, sailing as always as the flagship of the line, classical learning needs to be protected from the pick-locking vandalism of reformers. "Information, knowledge, culture, originality, eloquence, genius may exist without a classical training," Shorey declared, but "the cultural *sense* and a sound feeling for the relativity of meaning rarely, if ever" (my emphasis). Nor can modern studies in the new humanities save us. Modern literature can be counted on to convey to the student neither discipline nor culture, being but "the ephemeral productivity of the hour." Anyone not reading on his own the good novels of his day, or those of the day before yesterday, has no business pretending to a humanistic education anyway. Regardless of his protestations, he doesn't really want such an education; he simply wants an elaborated, literary experience of his own time — in itself no bad thing — festooned with the trappings of learning. But like a fine wine, the best literature needs time to sit and ferment before being judged as commendable for use in nurturing the young mind. Chaucer and Shakespeare might well have crossed that line, but Homer and Virgil have crossed it most certainly.

And Chaucer and Shakespeare knew it.

John Stuart Mill's father taught his son to speak ancient Greek before he could speak English. A stroll through Mill's *Autobiography* can make us despair of ever knowing anything when we see what an intelligent twelve-year-old can do when given wise and proper guidance. Mill never forgot the lessons of hard learning and he raised the flag for classical education all his life, sometimes to points of extravagant, indefensible exaggeration. But his was not an original case. Time told the tale and proved him right. "Mill may have overestimated the powers of acquisition of the human mind," Shorey said, "but he was far nearer right than we are, who bestow degrees on students who have merely deigned to listen to a few chatty lectures" — or, we may add, surf a few websites and write a spate of dull, rancid, immature, incomprehensible essays. These are not the durable artifacts of education.

■   ■   ■

Scott-King, a character from one of Evelyn Waugh's late social satires, *Scott-King's Modern Europe*, is a classics master teaching at an English school called Granchester. World War II has recently ended, and the world is changing once more. And the school, the head master believes, must change with it. A new world waits for the dawn. Modern subjects must overtake that crusty old classical curriculum. But Scott-King, having just returned from a summer's frolic in that modern world, is serenely recalcitrant.

> "You know," [the head master] said, "we are starting this year with fifteen fewer classical specialists than we had last term?"
> "I thought that would be about the number."

"As you know, I'm an old Greats man myself. I deplore it as much as you do. But what are we to do? Parents are not interested in producing the 'complete man' any more. They want to qualify their boys for jobs in the modern world. You can hardly blame them, can you?"

"Oh, yes," said Scott-King, "I can and do."

"I always say you are a much more important man here than I am. One couldn't conceive of Granchester without Scott-King. But has it ever occurred to you that a time may come when there will be no more classical boys at all?"

"Oh, yes. Often."

"What I was going to suggest was — I wonder if you will consider taking some other subject as well as the classics? History, for example, preferably economic history."

"No, head master."

"But, you know, there may be something of a crisis ahead."

"Yes, head master."

"Then what do you intend to do?"

"If you approve, head master, I will stay as I am here as long as any boy wants to read the classics. I think it would be very wicked indeed to do anything to fit a boy for the modern world."

"It's a short-sighted view, Scott-King."

"There, head master, with all respect, I differ from you profoundly. I think it the most long-sighted view it is possible to take."

■   ■   ■

Teach we must. Children have to learn something. But where do other pursuits of the mind fit into the classical schema? Perhaps not all people can devote their school years to the humanities: Who would fly the airplanes, build the bridges, and program the computers? Naturally we must say that those taken with an ardor for scientific and technological knowledge and achievement must be allowed to go their own way. Indeed they should be invited to do so. The world needs them. Yet the irresistible *either/or* does not impose itself right away, or at least it doesn't have to. Much depends on how soon classical studies are to begin in one's life. We should open the classical path to all able students — and as early as we possibly can.

The greatest mistake we Americans make in our schools is wasting our pupils' time and mental energy. We start too much too late. Today those who would enter the well-trimmed gardens of classics usually begin their journey with the languages — almost always Latin — in high school. Is this too late? Literally, and quite obviously, No. Many who have gone on to become formidable classical scholars began their classics in high school; some have begun in college; a few have begun even later. Their mature scholastic accomplishments can be breathtakingly grand. And some defenders of the current regime have posed the example of this talented regiment as proof that timing counts for little. We have time. Whenever talent and desire deign to come together, they say, anything is possible.

But what, we might ask, is probable?

We're wont to say that *it's never too late to start* any endeavor we care about. Often this is true. But is it always? Surely the goals we hope to achieve must align with the effort we expend. Do we wish to be amateurs or professionals, to dabble or to master? Perhaps we ought to ask ourselves if it's never too late for a pianist or violinist aspiring to the concert stage to take up the instrument. However *possible* some things may be, is it realistic to expect a Horowitz to take up his piano scales at the age of eighteen? Reality intervenes eventually. Life offers a wealth of possibilities. But it offers fewer as we get older and choices become more complicated. Every door opened is another two or three — or ten — doors closed. Each path taken breaks off into yet another. The uncomfortable fact is that some things must begin early if they are to flower fully. They must enjoy the morning sun. Within the high, rarefied realm of classics, one may certainly begin honing later in life the skills and judgment needed to become a pure scholar out to expand the bounds of knowledge. Thus also might one become a doctor or engineer or writer.

Yet would that late-blooming classicist be, in the sense Humanists over the last five hundred years would have recognized, *cultivated* by his learning? The ability to perform technical feats, after all, does not necessarily make for the civilized man or woman. And, as we have seen, it is the formative, humanizing balms of classics that cultivated, classically educated people have, right up to the youths of our grandparents, urgently pressed. Classicists tend, in my limited experience, to be among the most intelligent, accurately minded people to be found in any college or university — a distinction they share with physicists — though, as a group, they no longer travel the Humanist's road. Their temperament is largely scientific, as befits the philological or historical enterprise. But regardless of their depth of understanding in one closely circumscribed patch of knowledge, one often finds within them signs of neither wide reading nor deep insight. They know more about, say, linguistics or the excavations at Pylos than Jefferson did, but one can't imagine their bringing anything like Jefferson's intellectual candlepower to a conversation.

But then who could? Maybe no one — except perhaps someone with Jefferson's mental furniture and training. And that's the point. Their knowledge is not at fault. It's their method of, if not motive for, getting it. However exceptional they may be as scholars, they were not taught during their seminal years in the way Vittorino da Feltre, Erasmus, or Arnold would have taught them. And sometimes it shows. Most are not, in the highest and best sense of the word, Humanists. They may have knowledge in abundance. But has that knowledge cultivated them? Were they here to do so, Jefferson and Adams could answer that question competently after no more than five minutes' acquaintance with them.

So when should we begin to impart those balms of Greek and Latin? I have no special qualifications to speak on dense matters of pedagogy, and so I have scant right to pronounce upon prescriptions. But a few things I will venture to say, mainly because they've been said, and more cogently, by my betters. Let's begin here: Any lower school aspiring to help the intelligent children to be their best, to allow the smart to rise and reach heights undreamt of, will give full credit to those children for possessing minds capable of great things. Children are to be sympathized with and respected, not coddled, nor are they to be humored. Their roads aren't always to be made smooth.

Teaching in that school will start slowly, but with an eye to building solid, steadfast foundations, not procuring fast results; children should be treated like plants needing ceaseless tending. Classical instruction should begin as early as possible. There's no reason why Latin should begin much after arithmetic — say, at the ripe ages of eight or nine. T. S. Eliot held that "to postpone the introduction to Latin to the age at which a boy [or any child] appears to be more gifted for languages than [he is] for other studies is to postpone it too long." This would not have to be the Latin many now remember from high school. *Amo, amas, amat* does not need to be quite as dry an exercise as perhaps it must be for a fifteen-year-old, who has some time to make up.

The pace will be slower, but just as sure. Teachers will pounce upon the advantages each age group presents. Children up to the age of ten are keen to memorize, and their brains are still flexible enough to store much. For these children "Latin class" will mean little more than memorizing and being quizzed upon word lists and declension and conjugation endings. Pupils will read and write simple sentences as soon as possible.

Good teachers will firmly resist pupil — and, even more, parental — complaints against the use of drill as "deadening" or "uncreative." Neither group likely knows what it's talking about and must not be patronized but ignored. The aim at the early stages will be to allow prudent repetition to burn the words and forms of the language into pupils' minds until apprehension becomes easier, more natural. Students are being accustomed to something, in more than one sense, foreign. They're developing new muscles. This will take time and pain.

Of course we also must declare, directly and without hedging, that a course of study in classics is not vocational. It hasn't been for two or three hundred years. If one's principal concern be for the salability of Greek and Latin, for its exchange rate in the marketplace, then by all means he would be better advised to pursue a technical training in some field of interest suiting his aptitude. He has already decided what he — or his child — should get out of school. Let him not be disappointed. As a foundation for a cultural education, classics probably isn't for him anyway, and it should not be forced upon him. But let us beware. We should be solicitous of all promising young men and women possessing the talented, curious minds able to embrace classical study and reap those lifelong benefits people of discernment have always known it to lend. We cannot now know the gifts these culturally competent people might one day bestow as citizens upon a parched, shallow world. They will serve all of us.

There is a time for play and a time for work. School can be an enriching, enjoyable place, and a place some students may look forward to attending every day. Those are fortunate children with fortunate parents. But children's approval should not be our first concern. Like a healing doctor, we know this will hurt; we might as well say so. School should be a *serious* place. Dullards must not set the pace. Students should be encouraged to develop a sense of their smallness alongside the world's riches. Humility remains a decent aim for the well-educated mind. Let us not try to do too much. Those subjects that can be got outside school doors — things like fashion design, computer training, and photography — should be. Dissipation of effort can lead to despair; the world outside will catch up with the young soon enough. School ought to be a training ground for the intellect, not a clearinghouse for "skills": and if it's to be the latter, we should admit it. Whatever we decide to teach young people who will one day step forward to run the world — and why should we teach *anything* other than languages, mathematics, and geography before the age of thirteen? — let's remember, as the Humanists taught, that we reap as we sow. These are human beings equipped both with minds and souls. Bend their twigs we must. Just so they grow hale and well.

■   ■   ■

The word *Humanism* has studded these pages like rivets ranged along the hull of a ship. This is, as we saw earlier, a risky word to use today. Any word lacking a firm anchoring threatens to float adrift, lost to the haphazard mercy of random currents. I have strained, though, not to let too much slack in the line linking my case to this old and august idea. I have used the term both tightly and loosely: tightly, as I've tried to hold a mooring to the understanding of Humanism lighting out from the Renaissance, from the school of Vittorino da Feltre and the learned works of Erasmus; loosely, as it no longer means quite the same thing. It's branched off into untraceable nooks — some of which are lions' dens. Humanism, as I have used it here, is not a philosophy. Still less is it a religion for the irreligious. It has neither the steel tenets of the one nor the stony dogmas of the other. Humanism sails other waters, by other charts.

Humanism is a temper of mind and an elevation of heart. It's not a philosophy of life so much as it's an approach to living. It's a state of mind more than the substance of mind. It's a disposition that both forms and informs. It's the house we build on the hard rocks of philosophical and spiritual foundations. Humanism, Eliot observed, "can have no positive theories about philosophy or theology. All it can ask, in the most tolerant spirit, is: Is this particular philosophy or religion civilized or is it not?" The work of Humanism, properly seen, is not "to refute anything. Its business is to *persuade*, according to its unformulable axioms of culture and good sense." Humanism at its best "makes for breadth, tolerance, equilibrium, and sanity. It operates against fanaticism" of all kinds. One can be a Christian Humanist. One can also be an atheistic or agnostic Humanist. We need subscribe to no such definite or indefinite creed to gain entry into the club.

Yet a club of sorts it makes. Humanism may not decide entirely the destiny of our individual souls, but it may determine the destiny of our civilization. It may not mold completely our quality of life, though it may come to have everything to do with the quality of our inner life. It can sculpt our souls. It can open those gates to wider experience that most people have kept shut out of ignorance or fear. And here we bump against one unyielding precept — alongside that of judicious and enlightened selection — evolved from Humanism. Man may not be the colossus some secular spirits would have him be, armed with the strength and wisdom of the gods, but he has partaken of ambrosia. He has squinted through the veil and seen just enough of divinity to measure himself by it. The Humanist knows both the strengths and the frailties of man. He strives. But he knows the bounds of his striving.

We come back to where we started. The inner takes precedence over the outer. For the inner is eternal. Our task in this life is to form — and re-form — ourselves by the best standards and patterns prior generations have found and refined. Only then might we take on the burden of reforming others. The charity of Humanism starts with the self, though it isn't necessarily and of its nature selfish. The Humanist knows that one must scale mountains before feeling the elations of triumph, that one must fight battles before tasting the fruits of victory. He must cultivate within himself the *habitual vision of greatness* and the *conscious ideal of human perfection*. Nothing is given. All is earned. And the earning begins with the climbing. Man may not be able to transcend the gods, but he can, over time and with struggle, transcend himself.

Little wonder that classical education — the splendid rigors of Greek and Latin — fits so well, so exquisitely, with the ancient mission of Humanism that long ago sent man on a quest to conquer himself. The mission and the curriculum walked abreast. Humanists knew that nothing worth having would come without hard labor. The vision of greatness and the ideal of perfection, though, were not quite enough. Visions and ideals need a path, a way, a roadmap people can use so as to arrive at those better, more permanent things that the wise were always seeing dimly whenever they strained their eyes. So man turned a mirror on himself, looked soberly, and — one day — began to write accounts of the discoveries made on the grandest odyssey of them all: the journey to the core of the human mind and soul. The grateful among us read them.

■   ■   ■

"Latin and Greek are not dead languages," J. W. Mackail once said. "They have merely ceased to be mortal." Parnassus — that resplendent symbol of inspiration, eloquence, refined polish, and grace — has lodged within the Western mind a majestic image of the Beautiful and the Unattainable. Its steep, forbidding peaks, its cloud-girt summits, stood out against the sky, throne of Apollo, abode to the Muses, and source of inspiration for untold pilgrims seeking artistic perfection and the peace that comes at the end of arduous achievement. They came to the sacred shrines of Delphi, nestled at the foot of the mountain, to pay homage and offer sacrifice. Mount Parnassus brooded over them as they prayed; they could measure themselves against the vast, immense shadow it cast upon all below. Those suppliants knew and felt the power of the Greek proverb that "The gods sell all good things — for toil." Parnassus reminds us, even now, that we must struggle and sacrifice, even to become fully human. Few reach the crest. But it's the climbing that counts.

Greek and Latin have claimed their rightful plinth within the hallowed precincts of our cultural pantheon. They too deserve the homage due to the undying. The classical tongues still provide corridors leading into the holier sanctums of our higher culture. For over two thousand years they have stood as twin gates before the foot of Parnassus. They have lent us the tongues of immortals. And they have kept the long, twilit memories of the Western world alive. Amnesia cripples. But elected amnesia destroys. We ought to heed the warning laid at the close of the *Pervigilium Veneris*: we must not, as a civilization, "lose our Muse through being voiceless," so that Apollo "regards us not." We should not lapse into the proverbial sepulchral quiet of Amyclae, only to "perish by silence." The favor of Apollo is no mean thing to lose or relinquish.

Felix qui potuit rerum cognoscere causas. Happy the man who can understand the causes of things. The Virgilian dictum sat at the heart of the Renaissance belief that civilized men and women must know their origins, that they must tap depths, that they must climb mountains and follow rivers to their sources. Happy the man also who can utter and enshrine those causes and origins with fitting words. He plays the guardian. We must be Arcadians, not Utopians. The tablets must be kept. Much there is to preserve, and we must shoulder the burden of preserving and safeguarding. We become both civilized and cultivated through the high act of preservation. We raise ourselves above the commonplace, breathing fresher air than that breathed by those chained to the four walls of their little worlds.

Ingenuas didicisse fideliter artes emollit mores nec sinit esse feros, Ovid wrote from exile. To have learnt conscientiously the noble arts civilizes one's way of life, lifting it above savagery. For centuries classical education set about the task of teaching the noble arts of the mind and heart, and it can do so again. Those arts are not dead. They're merely hibernating. A clever and ingenious world must find within itself once more the humility to learn — and to teach — those noble arts if any semblance of civilization, any shard of inner greatness, is to survive the havoc wrought by generations of aphasia and well-meaning neglect. We can regain our memory and tell its tales to those waiting to hear. The best education, the highest and most bracing education, does not scorn the ground; without the ground we cannot

spot the horizon. Yet it doesn't disdain the stars. It shows us
how to be fully human — and to exercise all the powers proper
to a human being. It bids us, as Pope once inscribed, "to trace
the Muses upward to their spring."

Bibliography

Ascham, Roger. *The Scholemaster*. Edited by R. J. Schoeck. Ontario: J. M. Dent & Sons Ltd, 1966.

Auden, W. H. *Forewords and Afterwords*. New York: Vintage, 1989.

————. *A Certain World*. London: Faber and Faber, 1971.

————. *Nones*. New York: Random House, 1950.

Auerbach, Erich. *Literary Language and its Public in Late Latin Antiquity and in the Middle Ages*. Translated by Ralph Manheim. Princeton: Princeton University Press, 1965.

Babbitt, Irving. *Literature and the American College*. Washington, D.C.: National Humanities Institute, 1986.

Barzun, Jacques. *Begin Here*. Chicago: University of Chicago Press, 1991.

————. *The Culture We Deserve*. Middletown, Conn.: Wesleyan University Press, 1989.

————. *Classic, Romantic, and Modern*. Chicago: University of Chicago Press, 1961.

Beman, Lamar T. *Selected Articles on the Study of Latin and Greek*. New York: H. W. Wilson, 1921.

Bennett, Charles E. and George P. Bristol. *The Teaching of Latin and Greek in the Secondary School*. New York: Longmans, Green, and Co., 1903.

Bolgar, R. R. *The Classical Inheritance and Its Beneficiaries*. London: Cambridge University Press, 1954.

Bonner, Stanley F. *Education in Ancient Rome*. Berkeley and Los Angeles: University of California Press, 1977.

Bowra, C. M. *A Classical Education*. London: Oxford University Press, 1947.

Boyd, William. *The History of Western Education*. New York: Barnes & Noble, 1966.

Brink, C. O. *English Classical Scholarship*. London: Clarke/Oxford University Press, 1985.

Brinsley, John. *Ludus Literarius or The Grammar Schoole*. Edited by E. T. Campagnac. Liverpool and London: Constable & Co., 1917.

————. *A Consolation for Our Grammar Schools*. Edited by Thomas Clark Pollock. New York: Scholars' Facsimiles & Reprints, 1943.

Burnet, John. *Essays & Addresses*. London: Chato & Windus, 1929.

Butler, Nicholas Murray. *The Meaning of Education*. New York: Charles Scribner's Sons, 1915.

Butler, Samuel. *The Life and Letters of Samuel Butler*. 2 vols. London: Jonathan Cape, 1924.

Cappon, Lester J. (ed.). *The Adams-Jefferson Letters*. 2 vols. Chapel Hill: University of North Carolina Press, 1959.

Clarke, M. L. *Classical Education in Britain, 1500-1900*. London: Cambridge University Press. 1959.

————. *Higher Education in the Ancient World*. London, 1971.

Costello, William T. *The Scholastic Curriculum at Early Seventeenth-Century Cambridge*. Cambridge: Harvard University Press, 1958.

Curtis, M. H. *Oxford and Cambridge in Transition, 1558-1642*. London: Oxford University Press, 1959.

Dawson, Christopher. *The Crisis in Western Education*. Steubenville, Ohio: Franciscan University Press, 1989.

De Burgh, W. G. *The Legacy of the Ancient World*. London: MacDonald and Evans, 1923.

Eliot, T. S. *Christianity and Culture*. New York: Harcourt Brace Jovanovich, 1977.

————. *Selected Prose*. Edited by John Hayward. London: Faber and

Faber/Penguin, 1955.

————. *The Classics and the Man of Letters*. London: Oxford University Press, 1943.

————. *The Sacred Wood*. London: Routledge, 1989.

————. *Selected Essays*. London: Faber and Faber, 1951.

Elyot, Sir Thomas. *The Governor*. Edited by S. E. Lehmberg. London: J. M. Dent & Sons Ltd, 1966.

Emerson, Ralph Waldo. *Emerson on Education*. Edited by Howard Mumford Jones. New York: Teachers College Press, 1966.

Farrar, F. W. *Essays on a Liberal Education*. London: Macmillan and Co., 1867.

Findlay, J. J. *Arnold of Rugby*. London: Cambridge University Press, 1925.

Giamatti, A. Bartlett. *A Free and Ordered Space: The Real World of the University*. New York: Norton, 1988.

Gildersleeve, Basil Lanneau. *Essays and Studies*. Baltimore: N. Murray, 1890.

————. *The Selected Classical Papers of Basil Lanneau Gildersleeve*. Edited by Ward W. Briggs Jr. Atlanta: American Philological Association/Scholars Press, 1992.

Gordon, G. S. (ed.). *English Literature and the Classics*. Oxford: Clarendon, 1912.

Gummere, Richard M. *The American Colonial Mind & the Classical Tradition*. Cambridge: Harvard University Press, 1963.

Gwynn, Aubrey. *Roman Education from Cicero to Quintilian*. London: Oxford University Press, 1926.

Haskins, Charles Homer. *The Rise of the Universities*. Ithaca and London: Cornell University Press, 1957.

Hirsch, E. D., Jr. *Cultural Literacy*. New York: Houghton Mifflin, 1987.

Hutchins, Robert. *The Conflict in Education in a Democratic Society*. New York: Harper & Brothers, 1953.

Jaeger, Werner. Paideia: *The Ideals of Greek Culture*. Translated by Gilbert Highet, vols. I, II, and III. London: Oxford University Press, 1943.

Jebb, R. C. *Essays and Addresses*. London: Cambridge University Press, 1907.

Jefferson, Thomas. *Crusade Against Ignorance*. Edited by Gordon C. Lee. New York: Teachers College Press, 1961.

Jenkyns, Richard. *The Victorians and Ancient Greece*. Cambridge: Harvard University Press, 1980.

Kelsey, Francis W. *Latin and Greek in American Education*. New York: Macmillan, 1927.

Kennedy, George A. *The Art of Persuasion in Greece*. Princeton: Princeton University Press, 1963.

————. *The Art of Rhetoric in the Roman World, 300 B.C.–A.D. 300*. Princeton: Princeton University Press, 1972.

Kristeller, Paul Oskar. *Renaissance Thought and the Arts*. Princeton: Princeton University Press, 1980.

Laurie, S. S. *Lectures on Language and Linguistic Method in the School*. Edinburgh: Olover & Boyd, 1899.

Lewis, C. S. *Rehabilitations and Other Essays*. London: Oxford University Press, 1939.

————. *The Abolition of Man*. London: Macmillan, 1947.

————. *Surprised by Joy*. New York: Harcourt Brace, 1956.

————. *Selected Literary Essays*. Edited by Walter Hooper. London: Cambridge University Press, 1969.

————. *On Stories and Other Essays on Literature*. Edited by Walter Hooper. New York: Harcourt Brace Jovanovich, 1982.

————. *Present Concerns*. Edited by Walter Hooper. London: Fount, 1986.

Livingstone, Sir Richard. *Defence of Classical Education*. London: Macmillan, 1916.

————. *The Legacy of Greece*. London: Oxford University Press, 1922.

————. *Education for a World Adrift*. London: Cambridge University Press, 1943.

————. *Education and the Spirit of the Age*. London: Oxford/Clarendon, 1952.

————. *The Rainbow Bridge and Other Essays on Education*. London: Pall Mall Press, 1959.

Mackail, J. W. *Classical Studies*. New York: Macmillan, 1926.

Marrou, H. I. *The History of Education in Antiquity*. Translated by George Lamb. New York: Sheed and Ward, 1956.

Martin, Everett Dean. *The Meaning of a Liberal Education*. New York: Norton & Company, 1926.

Mill, John Stuart. *John Stuart Mill on Education*. Edited by Francis W. Garforth. New York: Teachers College Press, 1971.

Milton, John. *Complete Poetry and Selected Prose of John Milton*. New York: The Modern Library, 1942.

Murray, Gilbert. *The Religion of the Man of Letters*. Boston and New York: Houghton Mifflin, 1918.

Nettleship, Henry. *Lectures and Essays*. London: Oxford University Press/Clarendon, 1895.

Newman, John Henry. *The Idea of a University*. Notre Dame: University of Notre Dame Press, 1982.

Newsome, David. *Godliness & Good Learning*. London: Cassell, 1961.

Nock, Albert Jay. *The Theory of Education in the United States*. Chicago: Henry Regnery Company, 1932.

————. *Memoirs of a Superfluous Man*. London & New York: Harper & Brothers, 1943.

————. *The State of the Union: Essays in Social Criticism*. Edited by Charles H. Hamilton. Indianapolis: Liberty Press, 1991.

Ogilvie, R. M. *Latin and Greek: A History of the Influence of Classics on English Life from 1600 to 1918*. London: Routledge & Kegan Paul, 1964.

Rees, B. R. *Classics*. London: Routledge & Kegan Paul. 1970.

Reinhold, Meyer. *Classica Americana: The Greek and Roman Heritage in the United States*. Detroit: Wayne State University Press, 1984.

Richard, Carl J. *The Founders and the Classics*. Cambridge: Harvard University Press, 1994.

Sandys, Sir John Edwin. *A History of Classical Scholarship*. Vols. II and III. London: Cambridge University Press, 1908.

Shorey, Paul. *The Assault on Humanism*. Boston: Atlantic Monthly Press, 1917.

Stanley, Arthur Penrhyn. *The Life and Correspondence of Thomas Arnold, D. D.* Boston: Fields, Osgood, & Co., 1870.

Strauss, Leo. *An Introduction to Political Philosophy: Ten Essays by Leo Strauss*. Edited by Hilail Gildin. Detroit: Wayne State University Press, 1989.

Stray, Christopher. *Classics Transformed: Schools, Universities, and Society in England, 1830–1960*. Oxford: Clarendon/Oxford, 1998.

Stuart, Isaac W. *On the Classical Tongues and the Advantages of Their Study*. College of South Carolina, 1836.

Tarn, W. W. *Hellenistic Civilization*. Cleveland and New York: The World Publishing Company, 1961.

Taylor, Samuel H. *Method of Classical Study*. Boston: Brown and Taggard, 1861.

Thomson, J. A. K. *The Classical Background of English Literature*.

London: Allen and Unwin Ltd., 1948.

Thoreau, Henry David. *Walden.* New York: Grosset & Dunlap, 1910.

Van Doren, Mark. *Liberal Education.* Boston: Beacon Press, 1959.

Watson, Foster. *The English Grammar Schools to 1660.* London: Frank Cass & Co. Ltd., 1968.

Waugh, Evelyn. *Scott-King's Modern Europe.* Boston: Little, Brown, 1949.

————. *A Little Learning.* Boston: Little, Brown, 1964.

West, Andrew F. (ed.). *Value of the Classics.* Princeton: Princeton University Press, 1917.

Whitehead, Alfred North. *The Aims of Education and Other Essays.* New York: Macmillan/The Free Press, 1929.

Weiss, Roberto. *The Spread of Italian Humanism.* London: Hutchinson & Co Ltd, 1964.

Woodward, William Harrison. *Vittorino Da Feltre and Other Humanist Educators.* London: Cambridge University Press, 1912.

————. *Studies in Education during the Age of the Renaissance, 1400–1600.* New York: Russell & Russell, 1965.

————. *Desiderius Erasmus Concerning the Aim and Method of Education.* London: Cambridge University Press, 1904.

Index